# JESTING APOSTLE:

## THE LIFE OF BERNARD SHAW

*Also by Stephen Winsten*

Jesting Apostle

# JESTING APOSTLE

*The Life of Bernard Shaw*

*by*

STEPHEN WINSTEN

**With 33 Illustrations**

LONDON

HUTCHINSON

*Hutchinson & Co. (Publishers) Ltd.*
*178–202 Great Portland Street, London, W.1*

*London   Melbourne   Sydney   Auckland*
*Bombay  Johannesburg  New York  Toronto*

*First published 1956*

To

JONATHAN AND JANE

"Life, happy or unhappy, successful or unsuccessful,
is extraordinarily interesting."
from *Days with Bernard Shaw*

# LIST OF ILLUSTRATIONS

# ACKNOWLEDGEMENTS

I must express my special obligations and thanks to Professors E. H. Gombrich, A. W. Lawrence and G. P. Wells; to Lord Dunsany, Sir Osbert Sitwell and Sir John Rothenstein; to Mr. Leonard Woolf, Mr. Robert Speaight, Dr. Leonard Colebrook, F.R.S., Mr. Adrian Conan Doyle, Lady Wood, Dr. Giles Romanes, Mrs. Marjorie Wells, Mr. Digby Besant, Mrs. H. Romanes, Emrys Hughes, M.P., A. Fenner Brockway, M.P., Mr. Michael Rothenstein, Mr. D. R. Wigram, Dr. Anderson, Raymond Barker, Nix and Co., The Society of Authors for the Public Trustee and to Messrs. Gollancz, Longmans, Green and Co., and John Murray.

It was only through the inspiration and indefatigable aid of my wife that the work, in spite of ten years' effort, was completed at all. We both found as we went through the vast array of original material that a new vision of G.B.S. had to be created, for in spite of the many books published on his life and work, his childhood, youth and early years in London were still uncharted territory and they were fundamental to the understanding of the older man. This period particularly interested me, for I had already written much, perhaps too much, about his old age and things that puzzled me became crystal-clear after the revelations of the first thirty years. Of course, all the documentary evidence would have given us only a distorted picture if we had not the day-to-day conversations with Bernard Shaw himself, conversations which grew more intimate with the years. We soon learnt to separate the truth from the fiction and though the truth as told here may appear duller than the figure G.B.S. projected of himself, it may prove of interest after the bubble reputation of the fictitious figure has burst.

There is no attempt in this book to evaluate the plays although we had discussed all of them with the author himself and had heard the rendering of them from his own lips. Limitation of space alone prevented our giving what might well have been a novel conception of his dramatic inspiration. Perhaps that will come on a future occasion, but we had to satisfy ourselves this time with one character only, the person behind the creations.

The letters from Leo Tolstoi, Sir Osbert Sitwell, Sir William Rothenstein, Virginia Woolf, Sir Arthur Conan Doyle, T. E.

Lawrence, Dean Inge, H. G. Wells, Sir Almroth Wright, Dr. Annie Besant, Sir Henry Wood, Sir Horace Plunkett and many from Bernard Shaw have never been published before; and the conversations with Rabindranath Tagore, Stalin, Mahatma Gandhi, Albert Einstein, William Morris, Beatrice and Sidney Webb, Granville Barker, and Oscar Wilde are given as reported to me by G.B.S. himself. The extracts from his speeches are from his own scripts and the story of his early days in London from his unpublished records.

S. W.

*Oxford.*
1946–1956.

# Chapter One

WHEN, on the twenty-sixth of July 1856, a third child was born, a boy this time, Mrs. Carr Shaw determined not to have any more children. She had her bed transferred to another room, gave over her children to a woman whom she flattered with the title of 'nurse', and did all that was possible to forget that she was a mother and a wife. She had had enough of married life. Her husband laughed at this whim as he had laughed at all his misfortunes. Twenty years older than his wife, at forty-five he had become a pitiable old tippler. His wife had grown weary of his stale old stories about his relatives and the numerous hints thrown in that he had married beneath him. As a husband he was a pathetic creature: he had no inheritance, no profession, no manual skill, no qualification of any kind except that he could talk. The fact that he was a Protestant with English connections in Catholic Ireland and that he could say that he was related to a baronet served to bolster up his snobbery, even though the baronet, Sir Robert Shaw, disowned him.

The infant boy was christened George Bernard by his paternal uncle, the Reverend William George Carroll, Rector of St. Bride's, Dublin; and as the infant's godfather was too intoxicated to turn up, the sexton was ordered to make the vows instead, just as he might have been ordered by the Rector to put more coal on the fire. Mrs. Carr Shaw had no use for the ceremony because she could not see why a religious sanction should be given to a product of one of her husband's drinking excesses.

She had unfortunately been brought up with ruthless severity by her great aunt, a lady who had set her heart on making her charge a paragon of all the lady-like virtues and accomplishments, fit to marry the highest in the land. The niece, however, had her own thoughts, for she regarded her training as the worst form of slavery, and her great aunt as a tyrant from whom she must escape as soon as possible. This freedom was only to be obtained by marriage, the sole occupation permitted to a respectable young lady. At twenty years of age she yielded to the least likely of all her suitors because he seemed a harmless man who could turn everything into laughter. Everything with him was dubbed 'a pack of lies' and this fitted in admirably with her own attitude to her rigid training. Naturally she had not the least knowledge of what marriage entailed; and as to money matters, she took for granted that food, clothing and shelter came as a matter of course to good people.

George Carr Shaw started his married life with the best of intentions. He had no illusions whatever about the happiness that was associated with marriage. Like everything else he expected it to turn out a 'pack of lies'. He had no use for happiness or for beauty but he did fear the loneliness of old age. The honeymoon was spent in Liverpool with distant relatives, and after a few days the bridegroom had almost forgotten the presence of his wife. She knew him as a keen teetotaller, for in their courting days he held forth most eloquently on the evils of drink whenever they encountered a tipsy man. But even then her suspicions were aroused, for after a solemn exhortation he would collapse into anti-climax and declare that all teetotallers were 'a pack of liars'. Now, after marriage, his restraint grew too much for him and one night he arrived home so drunk that his wife had to undress him and put him to bed. Opening the wardrobe to put away his clothes, she found it full of empty bottles. Her first reaction to this shock was to run away and to find employment anywhere, to go under another name and remove herself as far away as possible from this beast of a man. On the way to the docks, however, she was molested by roughs and thought it safer to return to her husband, insisting that they must return to Dublin immediately. To show that he was sorry, he promised to stop drinking for ever. To prove his concern for her he sold his pension of sixty pounds a year, his sole means of support, and with the proceeds embarked on a business completely new to him, the corn trade. He assured her in all solemnity that this would make them rich in a very short while and that they would then be able to live in a big house.

He started up his new business at Rutland Avenue, Dolphin's Barn; customers came to him from everywhere because he was genial and never insisted on payment. For the first time Mrs. Carr Shaw was faced with real financial hardship and this she regarded as even more degrading than marriage: she watched the heaping up of humiliation and she had to make do with servants of doubtful reputation because they were the cheapest to be had. But as she had chosen against the advice of her great aunt, she cherished her defiance, whatever sorrow it brought upon her. In this way she developed a marvellous capacity for solitude and self-sufficiency. Children arrived and the agony of their arrival made her even more determined to conceal her distress and to bear it on her own.

The three children, except for an occasional indulgence, spent their days with 'nurse' in the dark forbidding underground kitchen, eating with her when she happened to feel hungry herself. When the be-draggled 'nurse' went visiting the more homely slum across the river, she took the children with her: Agnes and George were trundled along in a high rickety perambulator, while Lucy, the eldest, walked beside it. Whenever the nurse wanted to add to her five pounds a year by picking up an English soldier from the barracks, she would leave the children outside a public house, giving them an opportunity to see the sights and to hear the shouting and the quarrelling, the laughter and the weeping.

When Lucy and Agnes were old enough, their father amused himself by telling them bits of family history: that their mother's grandfather was a pawnbroker, a 'man who lived like a fly on the muck that the poor could scrape together', while his own father was a solicitor, a man of means, and a near relative was a baronet. He would end this history with paroxysms of laughter. He did not add that this pawnbroker grandfather was the only one who took the least interest in their welfare, and that he, more than any of the Shaws, assumed the life of a gentleman.

Lucy, the eldest, was born hating her father. She had no trust in him and was convinced that the whole world was laughing at him because of his behaviour. On the other hand, Agnes, pretty little red-haired Agnes, adored her father and devoured his stories of the wonder-ful life that was his before marriage, and when he ended his stories with 'it's all a pack of lies', laughing as he uttered the now familiar words, she too laughed, for this appealed to her imagination. Mrs. Carr Shaw did not interfere since this made him happy, and even acquiesced in his drinking because the alternative was abject misery for him. What haunted her was the certainty that little George, their only son, would be a repetition, perhaps with all the weaknesses and excesses of the father magnified tenfold.

George Carr Shaw resigned himself to being a poor man and found much to laugh about: the very thought of a man of his birth taking to business was a laughing matter to him. It was, of course, a condescen-sion on his part, for he always remained above money considerations and told everybody that the corn business was a gentleman's hobby. When a customer came to pay his debts George Carr Shaw was so overwhelmed that he plied him with drink and both celebrated the honesty of the debtor until there was little of the money left.

Meanwhile, Mrs. Carr Shaw was searching for a way out of her squalid life, giving no hint of this resolve. Lucy was always urging her mother to leave home, for from the age of three she had shown a tendency to domineer. She was always spreading mischievous tales about her father and when they proved of no avail she would try other methods, for example, playing on self-pity, pleading that she had poor clothes as compared with her neighbours, and Mrs. Carr Shaw was sufficiently impressed by her plaint to take her off to her grandfather, Walter Gurly, hoping to persuade him to take the children, for she would gladly have handed over all three to anyone willing to adopt them.

The two younger children, Agnes and Bob, as Mr. Carr Shaw preferred to call his son, were left in his care and at once there was a transformation. He took his parenthood so seriously that he completely neglected the business, insisting on taking them for long walks along the evil-smelling riverside streets, and to amuse the older child he would pretend to throw the boy into the river. Once he actually lost his balance and both fell in. Fortunately he was an excellent swimmer and when he emerged with Bob, he rebuked Agnes for shrieking when there was no cause for it. After this Mr. Carr Shaw thought it better to take the children to the Mill and to originate amusements for them there. He would pretend to be reading from the Bible, improvising exciting and bloodthirsty stories and inventing intriguing tortures for the villains. The children naturally associated these stories with the Book: when they wanted a story they would point to it and there was nothing he enjoyed more than taxing his creative genius to the full. There was a glorious sense of freedom without her and Lucy. Regularly he would report progress to his wife, knowing all the time that she was not in the least anxious about them; he wrote because writing gave him yet another opportunity for using his gift in making mock of everything. But on the eleventh of August, 1857, she received the following letter:

"Poor Bob had a narrow escape on Tuesday morning. He was sitting on the kitchen table in charge of Nurse, who merely, she says, stooped down to pick up something off the floor, when he suddenly fell back and his head went slap through a pane of glass and against the iron bar outside. Miraculous to say he was not even scratched. Had he fallen with his face against the glass, he would have been ruined. I was in the dressing room at the time, and when I heard the crash I ran down and found Nurse so paralysed with terror that she could hardly lift the poor fellow up. I do not know how the poor fellow escaped but it does not appear to have given him a *pane* in the head."

A man who derived fun from such an incident belonged to a

world which she had ceased to understand, for her world was grim and she had forgotten how to laugh. She could not pretend to feel what she did not feel and lying was to her a sin against the Holy Ghost, and exaggeration and mockery were as evil as lying. Her husband, on the other hand, had only to move his lips and words would run away from him in an excess of laughter. The poor little fellow being 'ruined', growing up with some horrid deformity or becoming a half-wit would have been in a line with their other misfortunes: everything about their life, it seemed to her, was doomed to failure and misfortune. She could only blame herself for all this.

After reading her husband's letter to Lucy, she said: "Bob has had a tumble. I expect your father wants us to return." There was nothing for her but to go back to the home where she felt so alien. It was a hell which sent out circles and circles of despair. Dublin did not attract her; it stood for poverty and loneliness; to her it consisted of nothing but six large military barracks, five prisons and a park turned into a military dump. Those who were able fled from Dublin as from a plague: over a million had crossed the Atlantic Ocean. She was in the habit of treating Lucy to her adult confidences; she would say to her, 'All marriage is Dead Sea fruit,' and Lucy, plump, fair Lucy, would repeat these incomprehensible words as though to memorize them.

Bob learnt to read without effort, picking up words as a magnet picks up iron filings, greatly helped by his father's cunning habit of rhyming. Mr. Carr Shaw called it word-matching and thought that he, himself, had invented this trick, although Thomas Moore's verses were on everybody's lips. He would bring home certain points in spelling by such rhymes as:

> I heard
> You're the third
> To spell bird
> Like word.
> How absurd!

To Mr. Carr Shaw all spelling was absurd. One of these rhymes, uttered with much hilarity and *repeated ad nauseam* was:

> Adam was strong but ugly in look;
> Eve was pretty but a very bad cook.
> Poor Adam,
> Poor Eve,
> The Garden of Eden they had to leave.

One afternoon in the quays, when father and son were sheltering in the portico from the rain, Bob surprised the crowd by reading a poster aloud. Mr. Carr Shaw beamed with pleasure and celebrated the achievement by sharing his drink with the little fellow. When Bob reached the questioning stage his father, under the pressure of the child's "what? what? what?", improvised answers on the spur of the moment that proved most satisfying. Lucy hated her brother's continuous interrogation and she whipped him with cruel words, causing their father to laugh at her precocious tongue.

The time soon came for Bob to go to school and he was so over-come with nervousness that when his teacher, a lean, timid old lady, asked him whether he could read, he replied at once, "No," and when he was shown a book, he seemed unable to distinguish one letter from another. But this could not be kept up for long, for when any of his class mates made an error in his reading, Bob could not refrain from correcting him. He made himself popular by repeating lines in the playground, boasting that they were composed by his own father:

> Harry Parry was a giant who
> Just grew and grew, just grew and grew;
> He had to stand like a long barge-pole
> With his head sticking out of the chimney-hole.
> And when he walked he had to carry
> The house with him, did Harry Parry.

or:

> If I had a horse, I'd ride it
> But if I had an ass I'd chide it;
> As it wont let me ride it,
> As it wont let me ride it,
> I'd chide it, I'd chide it.

As he went up from class to class, he gained a certain notoriety for his impertinence and audacity in openly correcting the teachers during their lessons, blurting out anything that came into his head with the idea of making himself appear master-of-all. It was obvious to him, for example, that the teachers knew nothing at all about the Bible since the passages they read aloud did not tally with those he had heard his father read. In fact, most of the information his school-teachers proffered was at variance with that given by his own father, whom he preferred to believe, and so a sneer formed itself on the boy's face which irritated the teachers. It was always facing them when they talked. After a while they discovered that the best way of keeping him quiet was to set him writing stories of his own. These were never read by them, and when Bob discovered this fact he amused himself by writing the wildest things, often making fun of his teachers. It was almost as good as sitting on the doorstep, surrounded by the boys of the neighbourhood and telling them stories in the light of the moon; then, hunger alone dispersed them, driving him down into the basement to eat badly-cooked potatoes, mostly diseased, and to drink tea which had been left to draw on the hob until it was pure tannin. Often there was nothing to be found in the kitchen and then he would sit at the table until he fell asleep with his head on his arms. One thing he longed for above everything else: it was to possess a revolver with which to shoot, to shoot his teachers, to shoot all those who laughed at his father so that eventually he and his father would be left alone together, telling stories all the rest of their days.

A change of control in the school turned the easy-going life into one of rigid discipline. He was no longer permitted to write stories; it was mass teaching with a vengeance. Correct pronunciation was inculcated by collective reading and the Sermon on the Mount was thrust down by threat and punishment. Instead of going to school the boy took refuge in the Mill where Mr. Carr Shaw, after expatiating to his son on the supreme necessity of going to school, ended his discourse with, 'School is the most damnable purveyor of lies ever invented.'

Since no one interfered with his truancy, he tried absenting himself from church on Sundays, for he could not subject himself to the torture of sitting immobile and speechless in a dark, chilly church when he knew that the world outside was filled with light. No one at home made the least effort to induce him to go to church. Lucy alone gave him the promise of a horrible hell, but this threat seemed too far away to frighten him. His parents were incapable of beating him into any shape under any sort of provocation. One thing alone seemed of consequence to the father and that was that his son must never forget the class he sprang from.

His mother, however, did not mind what the boy did. She heard the children arguing, and how they argued; she heard Bob laughing while Lucy was crying, she saw Agnes brooding the whole day long, pale and timid, never uttering a word, and her one desire was to find a means of saving the girls from the misery she was suffering. When, therefore, she heard of a music master who was supposed to work miracles with people of no talent, it stirred hope in her that he might make something of her life. She asked his advice and for the first time told of her desperate plight and opened her heart to a stranger. This man not only understood but offered to teach her if she gave in return occasional help as he had a bad housekeeper who repulsed many pupils. She kept knowledge of all this from her family.

George John Vandeleur Lee was about her own age, lame in one foot but of great health and vitality. A genius of a conductor, a master in bringing out talent, he converted Dublin from a dead city into a centre of musical activity. He was an original in character, generous hearted, defiant of convention and never afraid to express his heterodox views. His house stood out as the only one in Dublin where, night and day, summer and winter, all the windows were wide open. He had his own ideas of health and seemed to have an intuitive knowledge of healing. His house had become the social centre of the town, attracting students and music lovers, who gathered round him as disciples of his particularly successful technique. Into this circle Mrs. Carr Shaw came and every contact with this musician helped to restore her courage and to bring back her vitality. Her life had become strangely real, yet, so well had she learnt to hide her feelings, not one of her family seemed to notice it.

During one of Bob's explorations into other people's orchards he was disturbed by the sound of voices. With pocket full of apples, eating a raw carrot which he had dug up with his fingers, he felt trapped. He hid behind a tree, expecting strangers to descend on him, but to his surprise he saw his mother walking beside a lame man whom he had never seen before and what was more surprising, it was his mother who was talking excitedly while the beardless man was listening intently. He could hardly believe his eyes and ears, and though he wanted to reveal himself, he refrained because they walked by oblivious of everything. So his mother had a secret life of her own, just as he had; she too went truanting from home.

One day this lame man came to their home at 3 Upper Synge Street, and from that moment everything changed. He came again and again and other people came, and his mother sang and laughed and it was his father who now seemed lost in his own home. People came from every corner of Dublin, Catholics and Protestants, rich and poor, to rehearse under the inspiration of this strange man. Vandeleur Lee called his mother Bessie and she called him Lee and worshipped him unashamedly; to her he was right in everything he did. His technique of voice production became an article of Faith with her. He, himself, called it the Method and was flattered by her complete devotion to it.

It was not only music which was brought with such force and joy into the house, but he actually talked to them of a way of life: fresh air was not an evil but a necessity, brown bread was healthier than the

Lee surrounded by his disciples. Mother (Mrs. Carr Shaw)
on extreme left, Father on extreme right

33 Synge Street, Dublin
Birthplace of G. B. S.

George Bernard Shaw
with
M. Edward McNulty (*standing*)

Torca Cottage, Dalkey, presented by Vandaleur Lee to
Mrs. Carr Shaw. "I am a product of Dalkey's outlook"

white bread which they had been accustomed to think genteel, and he even taught them how to wash without soap, since soap was dear, by splashing cold water every day all over the body and especially into the eyes. He was outspoken about sleeping, condemning the double bed and advising married people to sleep in separate beds. He had no use for heavy ornate furniture and presented them with their first bamboo chair.

Lucy resented the presence of this stranger who claimed so much of her mother's attention but when he called her 'Princess' she unbent and permitted herself to be trained by his system, for she had a lovely voice. Agnes could not overcome her timidity and sat apart from it all. As for Bob, Lee decided quickly that the boy was an outrageous liar, a braggart and a barbarian. The boy preferred his life in the street, his street battling with other streets and he always running away at the least hint of danger.

Mr. Carr Shaw himself was so bewildered by these happenings that they seemed to him quite unreal and he expected Lee and all that Lee had conjured up to vanish like a dream. It was only when his wife sang 'My Heart Ever Faithful' that he had to admit conquest. His drinking lapses grew less frequent and there was never the least friction between Lee and him.

One day Vandeleur Lee heard Bob reading aloud to his sister Agnes and was impressed by the amount of meaning the lad put into the words, the music of his speech and the rapt attention of the girl. He decided to take him in hand but Bob refused to be taught singing. Lee tried it through reading, giving him the Bible to read aloud to him. On one such occasion Lee was shocked by the sudden angry outburst of the boy: "My father told me lies! I cant find any of the stories he told me were in the Book!"

"All fathers have to lie to their children," Lee answered, "or their children would never believe them." This statement shot through Bob's brain to reach the risible part of it for he laughed as he had never laughed before. Lee had discovered the way to Bob's mind.

The mesmeric conductor was soon to prove more of a benefactor to the Carr Shaw family. On the death of his own brother with whom he had shared a house he decided to move to a more spacious house. This could not be achieved while the tyrannical housekeeper was still with him. Mrs. Carr Shaw came forward with a brilliant suggestion that they should set up house together and that the housekeeper could go to her Great Aunt Emily, the tyrant of her childhood and thus tyrant would be matched with tyrant. The plan succeeded, and the Lee-Shaw household was established at 1 Hatch Street, a substantial corner house

in the opulent part of Dublin. Here they could have orchestral rehearsals instead of mere piano accompaniments, here too they could
entertain greater crowds on social occasions. It was a very great day
when the Lord Lieutenant himself attended a concert at the Antient
Concert Rooms in Brunswick Street, early in 1866, with Mrs. Carr
Shaw singing solo parts. She sang so beautifully, her mezzo-soprano
voice trained to perfection by Lee, that the important visitor thanked
her personally before the crowded and enthusiastic audience. After the
concert she could not contain her pleasure and overflowed even to the
point of showing affection to her three children. Bob shrank from her
touch because he suspected that she was intoxicated.

"Your mother will sing one day in London before the Queen,"
Lee assured the children.

Feeling that she had at last proved her worth, Mrs. Carr Shaw
called on her sister-in-law, a lady who had always shown extreme
contempt for her. On being announced, Mrs. Carr Shaw heard her
sister-in-law exclaim, "Oh, that bitch!" She never forgot this incident
and never forgave the whole Shaw family. She had no wish to see any
of them again.

Lee's reputation grew rapidly, the wealthiest and most talented
sought lessons from him and some of his pupils had to be handed over
to his factotum, Mrs. Carr Shaw. She had mastered the Method and
proved a most successful teacher. She was now invited to sing ballads
in drawing-rooms and it was thus that she came to know Oscar Wilde's
mother, who ran a *salon* in Dublin. She was even approached by a
Roman Catholic priest and at his invitation permitted herself to enter
the Roman Catholic Chapel to sing a Mass by Mozart.

It was extraordinary that at a time when morals were bound by
shackles of steel, devout Catholic and proud Protestant accepted this
*ménage à trois* as natural and above suspicion. Lee and Bessie seemed
to rise into a world where they were not judged by ordinary standards
and were considered beyond reproach.

In 1866, when Bob was ten years old, his mother took him for a
walk to Dalkey, a beautiful spot on the coast, not very far from
Dublin. It was the first occasion when mother and son walked together;
on no account would she permit the picking of flowers, for to her it was
like murder. They stopped at last at Torca Cottage, situated high on
the hill with a majestic view of sea and sky, and both looked long at the
endless pictures Nature had painted so magically. As they turned to go
his mother asked him what he thought of the place, and the only word
that he could think of was "heaven". To his surprise and infinite delight
she told him quietly that this house had been given to them by Lee as

a summer residence. The boy showed his gratitude by grasping his mother's hand and kissing it again and again. He felt a curious jolt in him as he did this, as though he had just been brought to life, for everything became clear and beautiful and joyous.

"We owe this happiness to Lee," his mother explained.

After this there was only one obstacle to complete happiness and that was school. Bob loathed it all the more since it stole sunshine from him, and the many precious hours which could be spent at Torca Cottage. Here, at Dalkey, there were numerous illustrated and well-printed books which Lee passed on to him. Bob spent hours reading and copying the illustrations when he was not roaming the cliffs and the hills.

He was not aware that a struggle was now going on for the control of his soul for though Mr. Carr Shaw had ceased to have any say in family matters he was working diplomatically through relatives, and induced his brother-in-law, the Rev. William George Carroll, Rector of St Bride's, Dublin, to take Bob in hand with a view to his entering Trinity College and then eventually the Church. The Rector was only too happy to do this for in his heart he wanted to counteract the influence of Vandeleur Lee, whom he called 'The Jew'. The boy, however, made very little progress, for he was prejudiced against anything connected with the Church, where, as he said, "Every separate stone, every pane of glass must have sowed a separate evil passion in my young heart."

Lee was unaware, or pretended to be unaware, of Mr. Carr Shaw's activities and watched with interest Bob's intelligent response to reading and drawing. The little fellow certainly had a mind of his own. He was now called 'Sonny' and 'Bob' fell into disuse because the boy strongly objected to it. He also objected to being called 'Ginger', 'Bullocksoup' or 'Copperhead'.

Lee had formed a friendship with an artist named Mr. Peach, who had decorated the Antient Concert Rooms for a special occasion, and when the question of Sonny's training came up, Peach suggested the Catholic School, where he was the drawing-master. Sonny was therefore sent to this school, the Central Model Boys' School in Marlborough Street, where he had to bring five shillings periodically as payment for the teaching. Lee was given to understand that it was better from the art point of view than any of the more genteel schools and had the added advantage of complete equality. To Sonny's horror, however, when he became accustomed to the vast establishment, with its heavy unscaleable iron railings shutting out the world, he discovered that most of the other boys were the sons of tradespeople and retail shopkeepers. Though his own father had a little village shop attached to the Mill at Dolphin's Barn, Sonny thought of himself as the son of a gentleman and therefore of a different caste from all the others.

Mr. Peach reported to Lee that George Bernard Carr Shaw, in spite of every encouragement, showed no enthusiasm for anything. Lee begged his artist friend to be patient and to persist in his efforts because the boy was now in his thirteenth year and they did not know what to do with him. Peach tried a different approach. He took Sonny to the Dublin Art Gallery and introduced him to the old masters, talked to him about great men, and also took him on his painting expeditions. The boy's response was to make adverse criticisms of his teachers. To please Lee, Peach kept the boy at his side during the play interval and walked up and down with him in the quadrangle reserved for the staff. This only served to increase Sonny's conceit, and Peach eventually came to the conclusion that the boy's derogatory attitude was entirely due to the fact that he was a master at a Catholic School and told Lee that the boy was a snob and not a learner.

Mr. Carr Shaw was glad that his son showed the independence of mind of a Protestant and the dignity of his class by refusing to learn at such a school and sent him next to an educational institution under the auspices of the Incorporated Society for promoting Protestant Schools in Ireland. This school had a high-sounding name but was worse than the other. It was situated in Aungier Street and was called the Dublin English Scientific and Commercial Day School. It set out to prepare young gentlemen for the new world of science and trade, but all Sonny learnt there was an original method of torturing the teachers. He formed a secret society sworn to give topsy-turvy answers to questions asked by teachers and to play pranks with the text by putting in 'not' where the affirmative was called for and to compete always for the bottom place in the class. One of the masters was so infuriated with this 'devil incarnate' that he smacked him brutally on the ear; Sonny left school never to return.

It was obvious that his school record was not likely to get him into a suitable profession. Manual work was not even considered and his handwriting was so feeble, actually sloping in the wrong direction, that it would never qualify him for a clerical post. The boy himself was unconcerned so long as he could while away the days at the Dublin Art Gallery, listen to the rehearsals at home or disappear into the hills. Lee argued with him about the necessity of contributing to the family income but with no avail and this appeal to his personal pride just made him laugh. His parents never argued with him; Mrs. Carr Shaw had never expected anything from her son, being convinced from the beginning that he would shape into the image of his father, but Mr. Carr Shaw knew that if the worst came to the worst, influence could push Sonny into a post.

In the spring of 1871, armed with an introduction from one of his uncles, R. F. Shaw, of the Land Valuation Office, he was installed as junior clerk in a highly exclusive estate office. From now Sonny became known as George Bernard Carr Shaw and everybody called him George. He was treated by his colleagues with the utmost contempt, for they could boast of their college education. In reality George was the errand boy of the office, also having to file the incoming letters and take impressions of the outgoing letters in a copying press before posting them. It was 'George do this' and 'George, don't do that' and more than once he heard himself described as a 'guttersnipe'. This he attributed to the fact that he had once attended a Catholic School. He could not get over this humiliation and he harboured a grudge against Lee.

He wanted very much to win favour with these graduates, watched their behaviour and imitated them as far as he could; he worked assiduously at his hand-writing and achieved the copperplate expected of him. Spelling was his bugbear, his tendency was to be phonetic; and he suffered all the more keenly because the others used this weakness to prove his lack of culture. When he left work at the end of the day, he returned to his home with a critical eye and felt uneasy in the busy anarchic atmosphere. The office was an anchorage from the deadly day-dreaming of Agnes, the gloomy prognostications of Lucy and the imbecile chuckling of his father. Although he was not allowed to give an opinion, he listened attentively to the conversation of his colleagues. If he dared to contradict them, as he often felt tempted to do, the whole pack would have been on him. Almost inaudibly, excerpts from his wide repertory of Opera, the familiar language of his home, came to his aid and once or twice he fell into singing aloud and was pleased to find that he had an appreciative audience. No word of encouragement was offered, but their silence was expressive enough. Then he found himself talking, at first unheeded by the others but very soon gaining their ear. They took it upon themselves to explain what he wanted to say as though he had not the means to express himself adequately and he invariably felt unhappy because his thoughts had been misrepresented. His colleagues were to him a composite image, with one face, one speech and the same laughter. He talked to 'them' and 'they' talked to him. In one of their conversations the question of art cropped up. This time he held forth for quite a long time and strangely enough there was no interruption. Suddenly he stopped dead and raising his head, he laughed to himself. They frowned and asked him to explain his strange laughter. "It's all a pack of lies, that's what art is," George heard himself saying.

Religion was one of the favourite topics in the office and again George could not restrain himself from voicing his own convictions. He heard them say that a world without God would be 'a homeless chaos' and George countered this by announcing that he had given up saying prayers and attending church and now felt a greater sense of moral responsibility because the blame for what he did was on him and not on God.

"If you go on arguing about things you know nothing about and saying these wild things," they told him, "you will be digging your grave with that sharp tongue of yours."

After his confession about the state of his soul, he felt thoroughly miserable for he had admitted, openly, that he was different from everyone else. Yet he could hold two opposing views at the same time, for while he told them that he had given up saying prayers, he knew that he had never ceased to say them, but they were improvisations which he enjoyed making. He did not say them to any specific deity but they came to him all the same.

The more they argued at the office, the more he felt the need for working out a consistent philosophy. He argued within himself throughout the day and throughout the night, but when expressed aloud, his ideas did not convince the others, nor himself. At last, the senior partner of the firm, Mr. Charles Uniacke Townshend, put a stop to all argument by prohibiting any further references to religion or politics in the office. The staff had to sign a statement to that effect and when George put his signature to the document, he felt as though he had signed his own death warrant. He chafed under this restriction and submitted only because of the independence that the £18 a year gave him.

Lee was the only one in the house who sensed George's spiritual agony, but, as was his wont, he asked no questions and waited for the lad's confidence. To encourage him, Lee told the young man the story of his own life: he too had come from a genteel background, and his people were no less poor than George's and they had to let a room in the house to a young violinist whose playing drove his own relations crazy. To Lee the sound of the violin was magical and he became a sympathetic listener; and from a listener, he became an apt pupil who wanted to become a soloist. Lee joined musical societies, managed to get into an orchestra, and mastered one musical instrument after another. Later he shared a home with his brother who was a great help because for years Lee earned practically nothing. Then, to become a teacher of singing, he studied the anatomy of the throat and picked up knowledge about sound from reading Tyndall; later he studied under an Italian opera singer, Badeali, and learnt how to preserve the voice throughout life. In this way he developed his own Method, which brought opposition from the more academic and orthodox music teachers. In fact they all tried to drive him out of the profession but he persisted and finally accomplished everything he had set out to do. This disregard for orthodoxy he extended to every field of learning, taking nothing for granted and invariably learning that the generally accepted view was wrong.

Lee knew perfectly well by now that George was of the kind who needed someone on whom he could lean and as his father could no longer act as the prop, the youth was turning to Lee who stood for everything contrary to the father's traditions. An incident happened which strengthened Lee's position in the eyes of George: Mrs. Carr Shaw had fallen ill and no one knew what it was, in fact they despaired of her life. Lee was away at the time and Mr. Carr Shaw had sent for his brother-in-law, a naval doctor. Lee returned meanwhile, at once took the case in hand and when the doctor eventually came, he could only say magnanimously, "My work has been done for me," for he found Mrs. Carr Shaw walking about and active.

# Chapter Two

A GENIUS could not be confined for all time within a Carr Shaw household and Dublin had nothing more to offer Lee who felt that his work had been completed there. He thought it best to leave while he was still young enough to start afresh. He would have gone much earlier but he felt under an obligation to Mrs. Carr Shaw, very much as a gardener to a garden. He was sorry, in a way, for the Dublin people who still flocked to his concerts and operas, but he knew that if he did not go then he would never go, sentimental attachment had a way of playing hell with resolution. He did not know how the void would be filled after he had gone, but he had done his best to prepare Mrs. Carr Shaw to continue his work in Dublin. Above everything else he would miss Torca Cottage at Dalkey where he hoped to return one day, with enough money to enjoy a leisured old age.

It did occur to him that he might take George to London, but after watching the lad he concluded that London was not the place for him. Lee had often pondered on his own presence in the Carr Shaw family and blamed himself for creating values for them which were alien to their nature. The lad would be happier left in the estate office to which he was obviously well fitted; Lucy should have married, instead of being unsettled by her mother's notion that she was a *prima donna*; and Agnes too might have been active and useful, instead of losing herself in a romantic dream of him. George's exaggerated Irish accent would mark him as an outsider in the London circles where Lee would mix. Lee was going to be a voice specialist with an establishment in Park Lane, a stone's throw from Buckingham Palace.

After Lee's going, life with the Carr Shaws drifted back to poverty and dullness. Without the presence of Lee the Method lost significance, Lucy's cynicism pervaded the house instead, and her father's silent paroxysms of laughter took on a ghostly quality. George now kept away from the house as much as possible.

Lee was not a good correspondent, but George wrote on behalf of them all and punctuated his descriptions with numerous and humorous illustrations. He advised Lee about London, for he knew all about the Metropolis from reading Charles Dickens, nor did he hesitate to tell Lee how to deal with the English but made no mention of things at home. So Lee did not hear that Agnes was fast going into a decline because she was pining for the only man she had ever cared for.

24

They were taking the advice of a doctor, the Rabelaisian brother of Mrs. Carr Shaw, who paid visits between journeys. This Dr. Walter Gurly believed in whisky as the cure-all and himself loved it so much that he could not understand how Agnes could refuse it. Uncle Walter, as he was generally called, was a most exhilarating person, robust and full-blooded. Unlike Lee, he stood for dissipation as the supreme human quality: a short life and a merry one. The best-educated member of the Gurly family, he gained the double distinction at his public school of being able to consume more drink and getting venereal disease earlier than any other pupil. By coaching and by cramming, he had managed to scrape through his examinations and so was in a position to deal with the sick and to certify them when they were dead. The scoffer and the rake had a way of appealing to George's sense of the comic. Now that religion and politics were taboo at his office, the young man's conversations with the other apprentices became extremely colourful, if scarcely idealistic. In defence of her brother, Mrs. Carr Shaw answered defiantly: "Better to be yourself than to please everybody else but yourself. It takes all sorts to make a world."

When, at last, a letter from Lee arrived, informing them that Queen Victoria as well as Mr. Gladstone had expressed interest in the Method, for both had acknowledged Lee's circular letter through their secretaries, and that peers and bishops, generals and Members of Parliament had shown equal enthusiasm, Mrs. Carr Shaw visualized all the aristocracy desiring to learn singing. This decided her. She gathered her two daughters and set out at once for the golden pavements of London, leaving her husband and son to fend for themselves. With the money left to her by her grandfather, the pawnbroker country-gentleman, she arrived in the capital of England and found Lee installed in a handsome house in the famous Park Lane, while she could only take a small villa at 13 Victoria Grove, Fulham Road. She had no doubt whatever that Lee could use his great influence with Royalty to turn Lucy into a *prima donna*. Lucy, on the other hand, scoffed at her mother's ambition for her; she was lazy and ill-tempered, but this made no difference to her mother's vision of her daughter sweeping London off its feet. Every effort was made by Mrs. Carr Shaw to renew the Dublin footing with Lee, but he now wanted to live his own life and was unwilling to become the butt of Lucy's rudeness. He invited Mrs. Carr Shaw to assist him in his teaching and paid her generously for taking part in the musical At Homes; he also gave her the part of Donna Anna in a performance of *Don Giovanni*, but he insisted on a purely formal relationship, only sometimes visiting

13 Victoria Grove. Lucy deliberately stopped the association and then they saw nothing more of Lee.

Mrs. Carr Shaw now had a hard struggle to earn anything, and it was fortunate that she had the legacy as well as her husband's regular contribution of one pound a week to fall back upon. She needed all the money she could get because Lucy refused to work and Agnes was too ill and had to be sent to the Isle of Wight for special treatment. Dr. Walter Gurly also sent her sums occasionally, which she invariably returned, feeling humiliated by his generosity.

George chuckled cynically in Dublin, for he felt that he had been left to carry the father whom he could neither love, nor hate, nor discard. The furniture in Hatch Street was sold and father and son moved to humble lodgings at 61 Harcourt Street. Here he became conscious of a curious fact, that, throughout all these early years he had lived in a house where music was as natural as air, where everyone else, except his father, could play the piano, he himself could do what only an infant could do, pick out a tune with one finger. He found himself hungering for the music which he had taken for granted, believing until then that it would always exist for him. In desperation he stood staring at the old piano which he could not bring himself to sell and determined to master it. He bought a technical handbook containing a diagram of the keyboard, and without any mercy for other people in the house, insisted on teaching himself to play the overture to *Don Giovanni*. The result was particularly unsatisfying to himself and cruel to the other lodgers. However, after months of unwearying practice he reached a workable technique of his own, knowing it to be wrong in every respect. A new person had come into his life, a person of his own age, a bank clerk who had literary ambitions. Matthew Edward McNulty and he formed a pact of friendship to read French works and English poetry and then to discuss these critically. They were not merely to converse but to write their thoughts and then submit these writings to one another. George added accountancy to his studies so that he could keep up with his friend. This went on for a little while only because McNulty was transferred to Newry by the Bank of Ireland, but they arranged to correspond daily, this time discussing everything and everybody, politics, books, religion, people they met, all in the strictest confidence, each letter to be torn up as soon as answered so that no trace of the correspondence should be left. This was a precaution George insisted upon because friends were so likely to turn into enemies. This interchange was most useful in the lonely evenings for the letters not only guided George's reading but drew out whatever capacity he had for writing. These letters were embellished with drawings, verses, playlets, problems in arithmetic, accountancy, Latin and French quotations. George discovered that the best way to elicit information was by contradicting, as this caused the other person to produce his own evidence and the assumptions on which his conclusions were based. McNulty had to warn him frequently against covering up his lack of knowledge by a pretentious literary style, and strongly advised him to keep to the vernacular as far as possible. George often grumbled about the extreme monotony of his work in the office and his friend assured him that it was the best possible work for one who was interested in other matters, because as office work did not take up much mental energy, the brain was free to concentrate on major interests. At least, that was how he, himself, found it.

This advice made George more amenable to office life, and his quiet efficiency won the confidence of his employer. Now and again there would be the inevitable outburst when George would blurt out some bitter retort. One of these stunned his colleagues into an enraged silence: "Children should hate their parents, not love them."

When Mr. Charles Uniacke Townshend, his employer, called George to his office, he trembled in fear that he might be dismissed; this would have meant complete annihilation, for with the pound they were sending regularly to Mrs. Carr Shaw they were entirely dependent on his earnings. It was not as he feared. A vacancy had occurred unexpectedly, no less than the position of head cashier, and Mr. Townshend invited George Bernard Carr Shaw to fill the gap, pending the engagement of a cashier of maturer age. The employer was impressed by the calm way George took on this responsibility and his salary was doubled. The young cashier found no difficulty whatever in the work assigned to him: he was now responsible for the collection of rents, the paying of interests and insurances, in fact he had become a miniature banker and handled much money. To the amusement of his colleagues, he came in an immaculate black coat and he did his utmost to act the responsible cashier, insisting on being addressed as Mr. Shaw. Mr. Carr Shaw boasted on all sides of the phenomenal success of his son and asserted that now Lee had left, the boy was finding his legs.

This professional elevation inspired him to gallantry and he was seen walking out with a lady. His love-making consisted of talk and more talk, while she listened and laughed. She thought him the maddest young man on earth but did not mind walking with him because cashiers in land agencies did not grow on bushes. The torrent of talk was ceaseless and as far as material needs were concerned he might have lived on air. Her laughter grew more mechanical as time went on and then she stopped laughing and stopped listening. He suspected ulterior motives, that she had mercenary aims, and when he heard that she had a sister to provide for, at once concluded that she wanted to marry him to her sister and so rid herself of an encumbrance. This was his first attempt to court a female and he decided never to repeat the experiment.

He wrote long letters to his mother and to Agnes; now that they were away he felt closer to them. He informed them that since his papa had fallen down on the doorstep in a fit, he drank much less and laughed much more. In fact Papa Shaw was much happier away from his wife and daughters and had begun visiting all the Shaws again and was in great form as a profound wit. "No father showed to best advantage before his wife and children," George stated conclusively.

Mr. Carr Shaw wrote his own weekly letter and to entertain them, gave a vivid description of George falling "underneath a horse and coming out of the accident a little hoarse", ending up with "since George has become a cashier, there is more cash here and more cash there".

Lodging in the same house was a man who complained of George's attempts at playing the piano. Mr. Carr Shaw learnt from his cronies that this man was the son of Mr. Alexander Bell, an author and Professor of Elocution at George's old school. George went straight away to apologize for the vile noise he had been making and explained that he hungered for music and as he had no one to teach him, he had to teach himself. Mr. Chichester Bell was a music-lover himself and offered his tutelage. Later George discovered that Chichester Bell was a qualified physician but had thrown over medicine in favour of chemistry and physics which he had studied under Helmholtz in Germany. This was George's first contact with a scientist.

Bell lent him books by Tyndall and Trousseau and taught him Italian, but the young man was no good at learning languages. Chichester Bell was an enthusiast for Wagner and George rushed round the Dublin shops to buy anything by this composer. He managed to buy a vocal score of *Lohengrin* and after singing the first two bars became a disciple of Wagner.

This association with Chichester Bell came at a decisive moment in George's development. His sudden elevation in the office had puffed up his conceit and his only confidant, Edward McNulty, was far too gentle and tolerant to prick it, but Bell was a mature, experienced man and did not hesitate to point out George's lack of knowledge and despised his superficial wit and nihilistic cynicism.

George's position in the office brought him much knowledge of legal and economic matters: part of his work consisted of collecting rents and he was appalled by the power of the landlord and came to the conclusion that all rent was theft. When he expressed this opinion to Chichester Bell, he was surprised to find that the latter was not in the least shocked, but expressed an opinion much more extreme than his own: that all profit was theft. From this moment, every time George made a payment or accepted rent, he hoped that it would be the last. Another point that was brought home to him by his work, was the falsity of the assumption that inequality of work demanded inequality of pay. He would have accepted the most responsible post for far less than that of a junior clerk, for there was ample compensation in the increased responsibility.

It was not until 1875 that George began to feel that his opinion mattered to the world. He was now in his twentieth year and as he read the newspapers, he felt that his knowledge was wider and deeper than any journalist's. He edited a little paper of his own with a circulation of one, that is, McNulty. He made up his own news about events happening in far away China and he wrote pompous leading articles advising this ruler and that ruler, especially in financial matters. He considered himself, as both a legal and financial expert, above the usual tub-thumping and whitewashing politicians. The more he studied events the greater grew his contempt for democracy.

The noted revivalists, Moody and Sankey, visited Dublin and George pretended to himself that it was psychological curiosity that compelled him to join the huge crowds that gathered every day to hear them. To Moody and Sankey, Dublin was a city of iniquity with the Catholics rolling, blind drunk, singing obscene songs throughout the streets, girls seduced by the English soldiery and all needing redemption through the word of God. George, the avowed atheist, heard of their reputation as spell-binders and was also attracted by the mass singing in which he heartily joined in. There were converts by the thousands, and these not only confessed their sins, real or imaginary, but made it their mission to impel those less willing, those less enlightened, to become one with God. Two men approached George and asked him why he preferred sin to redemption and they received a long argument which conveyed that goodness and evil were so intertwined that even they could not distinguish one from the other. "If I must believe in something, then it would be in Satan and not in your God." The upshot of this experience was a long letter to the Editor of *Public Opinion* under the modest signature of 'S'.

This was not his first attempt to break into print. Four years before, he had sent a long description of a street fight, in which a physical coward almost slaughters a renowned pugilist and had given a most vivid account of every move by the combatants. It was only at the end of this article that the reader discovered that it was all imaginary. This effort was returned to him by the paper to which he had sent it, the *Vaudeville Magazine*, with the following note:

"You should have registered your letter; such a combination of wit and satire ought not to have been conveyed at the ordinary rate of postage. As it was, your arguments were so weighty that we had to pay twopence extra for them."

This reply discouraged George from any further association with the Press until he had forgotten the insult. The great stir that Moody and Sankey created in Dublin made him feel alone in his opinions and it was therefore imperative for him to give them utterance. He loved the idea of being in a minority of one, entirely forgetting, for the moment, his written promise to his employer not to get involved in religious or political discussions.

The letter was not written in white heat. It was framed and re-framed until he felt that every word was a thrust.

April 3rd, 1875.

Sir,

In reply to your correspondent 'J.R.D.' as to the effect of the 'wave of Evangelism', I beg to offer the following observations on the late 'revival' in Dublin, of which I was a witness. As the enormous audiences drawn to the evangelistic services have been referred to as proof of their efficacy, I will enumerate some of the motives which induced many persons to go. It will then be seen that they were not of a religious, but of a secular, not to say profane character.

Predominant was the curiosity excited by the great reputation of the evangelists and the stories widely circulated of the summary annihilation by epilepsy and otherwise of sceptics who had openly proclaimed their doubts of Mr. Moody's divine mission.

Another motive exhibits a peculiar side of human nature. The services took place in the Exhibition Building, the entry to which was connected in the public mind with the expenditure of a certain sum of money. But Messrs. Moody and Sankey opened the building 'for nothing' and the novelty, combined with the curiosity, made the attraction irresistible.

I mention these influences, particularly as I believe they have hitherto been almost ignored. The audiences were, as a rule, respectable, and as Mr. Moody's orations were characterized by an excess of vehement assertion and a total absence of logic, respectable audiences were precisely those who were least likely to derive any benefit from them.

It is to the rough, to the outcast of the streets, that the 'awakenings' should be addressed, and those members of the aristocracy who by their presence tend to raise the meetings above the sphere of such outcasts are merely diverting the evangelistic vein into channels where it is wasted, its place being already supplied; and as, in the dull routine of hard work, I think it would be well for clergymen who are nothing if not conspicuous, to render themselves so, in this instance, by their absence. The unreasoning mind of the people is too apt to connect a white tie with a dreary church service, capped by a sermon of platitudes, and it is more likely to appreciate 'the gift of the gab', the possession of which by Mr. Moody nobody will deny, than that of the Apostolic Succession which he lacks.

Respecting the effect of the revival on individuals I may mention that it has a tendency to make them highly objectionable members of society, and induces their unconverted friends to desire a speedy reaction, which either soon takes place or the revived one relapses slowly into his previous benighted condition as the effect fades, and although many young men have been snatched from careers of dissipation by Mr. Moody's exhortations, it remains doubtful whether the change is not merely in the nature of excitement rather than in the moral nature of the individual. Hoping that these remarks may elucidate further opinions on the subject,

I remain, Sir, Yours etc.;

S.

This long psychological analysis amounted to his father's formula: 'It's all a pack of lies.' The respectable person George had in mind, that is the person who derived no benefit, was himself: and the individual whom the revival made highly objectionable was his own father. Poor Papa had discovered that he was a miserable sinner and tortured himself into greater misery by contemplating all his sins, only to relapse again into his previous happy condition.

The initial 'S' might have stood for Shelley; there was the same defiance of authority, the same challenge to popular opinion, the same contempt for divine power. George preferred Shelley's appeal to Mr. Moody, and Mozart's to Mr. Sankey's. He declared himself a sceptic and defied the threat of summary annihilation by epilepsy. The fact that he survived to write this letter to the Press was ample proof to him that Mr. Moody was wrong.

Considering the circumstances, it was a courageous, if not fully convincing, letter. It would have been more courageous had he given his full name to it, for it was not modesty which caused him to withhold his name but the fear of his employer who was a patron of the revivalist meetings. It was not possible to remain anonymous long in Dublin although the Journal refused to divulge the name of the wicked writer of the letter. The result was a request that his employer wanted to see him. The letter was shown to him and he was asked whether he was the author of it. He denied it, but his cowardly answer rankled in his mind, for he knew that Shelley would not have escaped the consequence in that way. He had missed a magnificent opportunity "to defy Power which seems omnipotent". He felt like a plant that managed to remain upright after its roots had been cut from underneath; it seemed to him that the world was so arranged that those who were by nature gentle were forced to be defiant, while the defiant ones were pressed back into meekness through fear. He was losing his self-respect for the sake of respectability. He had set himself to attain the stature of a Michelangelo or a Shelley and yet authority could reduce him to acquiescence.

George's income was now £84 per annum and every penny was necessary because Agnes was desperately ill at Ventnor. He heard from Lucy that all that was possible had been done for her, but when he read the description of her treatment he laughed sardonically. It was all contrary to Lee's teaching: the windows were kept fully shut to prevent a draught, the heavy curtains shielded the invalid from sunshine and the food was all wrong. Lee could have saved her as he had once saved her mother; but Mrs. Carr Shaw had put Lee right out of her mind. Agnes died in 1876, the very moment when George decided to throw up his post as cashier and go to London.

An anonymous nonentity, twenty years of age, beardless when younger men flaunted magnificent beards, without vocation, without introduction, possessing one suit of clothes, one pair of boots, one hat and his speech all wrong, this poor bewildered emigrant crossed the Irish Channel. On his arrival at Victoria Grove, his mother neither rebuked him for throwing over a good post, nor wished to know what he was going to do with himself. She accepted him with resignation and gave him to understand that she was finding it impossible to get new pupils or retain those she had. He made her teach him the Method and how to play the piano and Lucy accompany him in duets.

*p right :* Mrs. Charlotte Shaw: first year of her marriage to G. B. S.

*low right :* 1898. The Isle of Wight

*p left :* George Bernard Shaw: first year of marriage

*Below left :* Charlotte Shaw at 10 Adelphi Terrace

its application, nor so uniformly successful in its results, as to warrant a universal adoption of it.

At some future stages of your career, I may again address you on the great subject of yourself. Till then, be assured that I will continue to feel for you the romantic affection of a parent, tempered by the rational interest of an experimental philosopher.

The end of his first MS. : January 1878

With his sister Lucy after the
death of Agnes, 1876

Care of D: Gurly
Leyton Essex 14th July
1884

Gentlemen
Will you oblige me by reading a MS novel of mine, for which I am desirous to find a publisher? It is of the usual length, and deals with modern society

After the 1st prox: my address will be 37 Fitzroy Street W.

I am, Gentlemen
your obedient servant
G B Shaw

Mess? Smith, Elder & Co.
15 Waterloo Place
S W.

His novels refused by every publisher

Lucy refused to see any good in her brother; she taunted him and he held back obvious retorts because of her devastating tongue. He had expected her to have become a Patti by now but her answer was: "I've given up long ago pretending I was a Patti. I'm much more of a *patisserie* than a Patti. You wont be able to pretend in London as you did in Dublin that you are a genius." She despised genius worship and she declared that if ever she stooped to marry it would be to the most commonplace man. However, she dismissed marriage as 'Dead Sea fruit'.

George wrote his first London letter to McNulty to make it perfectly clear why he had left Dublin:

"I did not burn my boats for the sake of a flame. My prospects in Dublin were stupendous. The employer's daughter would have been mine for the asking and partnership in the firm assured. The only obstacle to the fortune was that I cared neither for the post nor for the daughter, not insuperable, I admit. I was full of politics and religion and these were, as you know, forbidden. Here am I, in London, without the credentials of a peasant immigrant and I still bear traces of the Shaw snobbery which considers manual work contemptible, and on no account will I enter an office again. You are the only person in the world to whom I am a person with an identity and a soul. That is why I cling to you. Strangely enough I am not in the least depressed, but elated, if anything, because it had to be.

I have a notion hazy that mother thinks me crazy and Lucy thinks me lazy."

3rd June 1876.

He found London a vast wilderness of faces, not one of which showed the least interest, the slightest curiosity, or the faintest response to his existence. He might have been a ghost or he might not have been there at all. Perhaps a little boy, an English Bob might have peered up with amusement at this tall, reedy, pale-faced, red-haired figure glaring into the chaotic world with fierce blue eyes.

One day his mother cursorily mentioned that she was teaching the daughter of Lawson, the artist, and that he lived at Cheyne Walk on the Thames Embankment. This was what he needed and his mother arranged an introduction. But when he arrived at the house the very next Sunday when the Lawsons had their At Home, he grew very nervous, pacing up and down before plucking up courage to pull the bell. He had come armed with all the social technique culled

C

from a book on etiquette, but this only added to his self-consciousness which made him talk unceasingly in a strident voice, the one jarring note in a harmonious atmosphere of old masters and modern books. He was certain afterwards that they must have thought him discordant, crudely self-assertive and insufferable. He thought of never showing himself to the Lawsons again, but his native common sense, eagerness to study art with the renewed ambition of becoming a Master like Michelangelo or Rembrandt, sent him once more to Cheyne Walk. This time he did what the others did, listening patiently and not trying, as had been his custom in Dublin, to out-talk the others. The Lawsons were extremely cordial and he thought that he was exceptionally favoured by them. This encouraged him to ask how one took up the study of art in London.

Mr. Lawson was at once interested and asked to see his work.

"I have no work to show," George confessed, "but it is the only work in the world that I want to do."

Lawson warned him that for every artist who makes a reputation there are hundreds who die broken-hearted and even those who achieve fame are not entirely happy.

George's retort astonished the Lawsons: "The same also applies to marriage and yet people still marry."

It seemed to George that they had gone out of their way to discourage him. The three cardinal sins, according to Chichester Bell, were Discouragement, Deceit and Despair and the greatest of these was Discouragement. It was difficult enough to be young and adrift in an alien land, and a little encouragement would have gone a long way. He walked the dingy, depressing streets of Fulham, arguing with himself, his head a chaos of bold resolution battling with timid prudence. One day his eye caught a poster announcing that Charles Bradlaugh would be giving an address at the Hall of Science in Old Street.

To attend this meeting meant a walk of many miles because he had no money for an omnibus and would not ask his mother when his legs could do the work. It was an adventure into regions unknown to him. Lost in crowds he found courage because as he mattered to no one, he mattered only to himself. Utterly exhausted he reached the unprepossessing hall and listened in awed silence to a spell-binder, who, though an avowed atheist, used every form of hypnosis and magic to work on his audience as Moody had done in Dublin for religion. It needed courage to strike a questioning note in this assembly of worshippers and though George dubbed himself an atheist, the same itch to contradict made him stand up with a question:

"Does Mr. Bradlaugh regard science as the grossest of superstitions and likely to create much suffering?"

The speaker asked for the questioner's name and the young man
answered distinctly, "George Bernard Shaw." Charles Bradlaugh
repeated the question and asked whether he had caught the name
correctly. For the first time in his life the young man heard his name
announced in public. To emphasize his reply, the speaker informed his
audience that his two daughters were taking lessons in biology, and this
he would not have permitted if it had any association with superstition
or suffering. George Bernard Shaw again rose, but the speaker ignored
him and continued with the declaration that the two greatest forces for
good in the world were science and birth control.

He attended their next meeting to hear Annie Besant and was
convinced that she was greatness personified. She was upholding the
teachings of the Reverend Mr. Malthus who advocated the voluntary
limitation of the family and she denounced the miserable subterfuges
women had to resort to when they found that they were pregnant.
"Because birth control was not an open and honoured thing the
knowledge of it had to be conveyed by gossip, and sexual intercourse
was made the occasion of great anxiety instead of a pleasure."

Shaw now took every opportunity of calling himself an atheist and
was disgusted that those people who held the same opinions as Bradlaugh, Besant and he, persisted in calling themselves agnostics. Both
Bradlaugh and Annie Besant were subsequently arrested for publishing
a pamphlet, the Knowlton Pamphlet, which upheld the teaching of
Malthus, and George Bernard Shaw attended the trial before the Lord
Chief Justice, and to his horror heard the two atheist 'saints' sentenced
to six months imprisonment. At once Shaw offered to help in the
distribution of the banned book, but all the others were puzzled, still
regarding him as an Irish Catholic because of the strange question he
had asked at the Bradlaugh meeting.

He was so enraged by the miscarriage of justice that he called
himself an anarchist because authority was the main obstacle to progress, the authority of school which was confused with education, the
authority of the Church which was confused with religion and the
authority of medicine which was confused with healing and now it was
the authority of law which was confused with justice.

He forgot the reason for crossing the Irish Channel, forgot that he
wanted to be a Michelangelo, for there were meetings everywhere and
he was fully occupied going from one to the other; the air was charged
with articulate thought and he felt he must be in with everything.
There was a meeting which drew him early in case it was crowded

out and his long walk from Fulham to Soho proved in vain. It was a talk on Socialism by a Russian Prince, Prince Kropotkin. George Bernard Shaw was the first to arrive and almost the last, for there were only five people in the bare basement, where the address was given. This time George Bernard Shaw was subdued for he was impressed by the quiet, gentle manner of the speaker, his profound knowledge and his strange *naïveté*, for Prince Kropotkin believed in the innate goodness of humankind, a belief he, himself, could never accept. Everyone seemed to think it imperative to convert everyone else to his own way of thinking. It was obvious to George Bernard Shaw that the English were a metaphysical people, glorying in soot and whitewash controversies. The Secularists, for example, argued frivolously about the magical elements in the Bible and because they could prove scientifically that this or that was impossible, they dismissed all religious belief as humbug; while the Christian Endeavour Apostles played on the fact that Charles Darwin was a regular churchgoer and held, therefore, that his scientific theories did not reflect in any way on the Bible or on religious belief.

At another meeting he was amused to hear a justification of unemployment and poverty: if goods were to sell in a competitive market, labour must be cheap, and there must be a pool of unemployment, for otherwise labour would demand higher wages. The workers must therefore accept destitution and unemployment to further the commercial interest of the country, which, in its turn, was motivated by one thing only, the ultimate good of the workers. Do away with poverty and you do away with prosperity. Shaw could not put his finger on the fallacy, for he loathed poverty and hated the acquiescent poor. He noticed that it was taken for granted everywhere and by everyone, that progress was continuous and that Great Britain was growing wealthier and wealthier.

"Why is it," he asked himself, "that when the pleasant side of a picture is shown to me, I cannot help seeing the unpleasant side?"

The Lawsons sent him an invitation to a meeting to be addressed by William Morris, whose name was new to him. It was crowded with a completely different audience. The speaker was the most handsome man he had ever seen and he was physically drawn to him; he was not a spell-binder like Bradlaugh or Annie Besant, for he was hesitant, always groping for the right word, contemplative, thinking aloud and holding forth on the mighty subject of Art.

"People say to me often enough: if you want to make your art succeed and flourish, you must make it the fashion: a phrase which

I confess annoys me; for they mean by it that I should spend one day over my work to two days in trying to convince rich and supposed influential people, that they care very much for what they do not care at all. . . . . You will determine to bear no longer that short-sighted reckless brutality of squalor that so disgraces our intricate civilization."

George Bernard Shaw saw at once that this wise speaker had laid his finger on the problem confronting humanity: the brutality of squalor, for he realized that ugliness was brutal and that squalor was equally brutal. Shaw would have gone up to William Morris to thank him for these enlightened words but here he was too aware of being an unemployable to have the right to approach this man. He returned to Fulham determined to find an independent existence for himself.

There seemed only one thing left for him to do immediately and that was to go to Lee at Park Lane before his clothes became too shabby to be seen in that neighbourhood. His shoes were already pathetically worn but as he was the only one who knew the state of the soles, these did not worry him as much as the shiny state of his suit and the frayed sleeves. Lee was glad to see him but was disturbed to hear that George had thrown over a lucrative post and was now drifting aimlessly in London, depending for his bread and butter on his mother. As he had many contacts with music publishers he gave George Bernard Shaw an introduction to a music shop near Baker Street. It was not what the young man wanted, but he could not refuse Lee's persuasive plea, especially as he wanted to come to Park Lane again, and so he found himself behind the counter selling music scores. He proved an excellent salesman, polite, knowledgeable and meticulously honest.

Lee was pleased with his success and brought him additional jobs to do: a publisher who had some old blocks asked Vandeleur Lee if he knew of a person who would be able to put verses to these. Shaw worked at these verses as though he had been commissioned to paint the Sistine Chapel. The publisher, however, thought he knew better, and without consulting the poet, altered them beyond recognition as he needed them purely for distribution for school-prize books and 'anything was good enough for children'.

Lee also introduced him to a man who needed a medical essay for use in an agitation against patent medicines. The man found the young man's essay most gratifying, for the author of it had spent weeks at the library amassing facts, until he felt he could have written a book on the subject, and naturally it was not merely patent medicines that he denounced but the whole medical profession in general. He received five golden sovereigns for it and the promise of an introduction to a friend who was agitating against the condition of slaughter-houses. On the strength of this promise Shaw settled into an intensive study of the whole question and from that moment stopped eating flesh of animals: "The one thing in my life which combined practice and precept."

Vandeleur Lee was a friend indeed for he gave over the post of music critic on a paper called the *Hornet* to his young friend. Unfortunately, this inexperienced critic made the mistake of giving his own views when all he was required to do was to pander to popular opinion. However, it gave him an opportunity to hear Wagner himself conduct his own music and to praise him as the greatest living composer.

With the money so earned, Shaw spent many an evening at the house of a gentleman whose profession it was to coach candidates for legal and civil service examinations. He made rapid progress and was assured a place in the junior division if he took the examination, but he could not overcome his antipathy towards being examined and so did not sit for it.

Among the people who sought to be trained by Lee was a strange man in high checks and loud voice who seemed to know more about music than Lee, more about books than Shaw and more about art than Lawson. This man was Dr. Aveling, Professor of Anatomy at the London Hospital but it seemed that he had no faith in the healing power of his colleagues and preferred the revolutionary method of the mesmeric Lee. He would say, "I always go to artists when I'm ill." This man liked George Bernard Shaw and took him to see Henry Irving and Ellen Terry in *Hamlet*. Both were deeply moved, Aveling by Ellen Terry's beauty and tenderness and Shaw by Henry Irving's power. After the theatre Aveling insisted on treating him to a lavish meal, but George Bernard Shaw spoilt the evening for him by eating sparsely and turning down anything that smacked of animal flesh.

When Aveling learnt that Shaw worked behind a counter he persuaded him to throw it up immediately and promised to get him more suitable work.

# Chapter Three

GEORGE R. SIMS, a journalist, started a paper called *One And All* and Aveling, being a friend of the Editor, suggested Shaw as a possible contributor. An invitation arrived at Victoria Grove like a bolt from the blue, and at once Shaw mapped out a series of essays to range over completely new territory: "On Being Thought Mad", "On Being an Alien", "On Being Uneducated", "On Christian Names", "On Wanting to be Someone Else".

As he sat down to write, the chaotic ideas seemed to coagulate into a heavy depressing lump that pressed on his brain. He was certain that when he had something to give to the world it would come easily and happily, it would trip on to the paper as it must have done with Shakespeare and Shelley. He had no doubt that writing was to them as natural as the taste of water in one's mouth. Yet the feel of paper excited him: he wanted to write.

Lucy had an hypnotic effect on his brain; he felt that she was stampeding his thoughts with her rebukes. He could laugh at the weaknesses of his father but Lucy mocked him all the time, justifiably, no doubt, but it was devastating. He wanted to feel that one day he would do something magnificent but she made him feel that nothing he would ever do would be of consequence. She was probably right but what was the use of being right if it disabled one!

By sheer effort of will he completed the article on Christian names and advised parents to stop the infliction of historic names on commonplace children. This article was accepted and the first person to congratulate him was his cousin, Cashel Hoey, the popular novelist. She was one of those people who knew everybody worth knowing, that is, all those who had achieved success: Tennyson, George Meredith, John Morley, G. F. Watts . . . and she promised to give Shaw introductions to one and all. Nothing happened, and when he visited her he had to sit and listen from the moment he entered to the moment he was shown out of the door.

There was one other house which he could visit besides Lee's at Park Lane, the Lawsons' at Cheyne Walk, Cashel Hoey's at Campden Hill, and that was at the furthest end of London on the east side. His uncle, Dr. Walter Gurly, had started a practice at Leyton, a respectable suburb near Epping Forest, and when Shaw heard this he decided to walk right across London. It was to be an all-night walk and there was no need to tell his mother because she would not notice his absence. He looked forward to matching himself against the loneliness of night.

As he left Fulham behind and walked along the river he thought of how little he knew about his mother, about Lucy, about himself even. These people, passing him by, hastily, leisurely, silently, what large tracts of the ego remained unexplored. He found himself laughing at that stupid contraption, the body, with which he had to represent himself, and in which he had to do his thinking. No one had even attempted to tell him why he had been born, nor why he must go on. If it was merely to reproduce his own kind then there was no reason whatever for his existence. He could not accept the new-fangled notion that the object of life was survival and the strong survived at the expense of the weak, for he believed that the man who lived most intensely was he who permitted himself to be used up for a great purpose. By now he had arrived in the heart of London, in the narrow streets, lined on both sides by dark and secretive counting houses, here and there lonely shadowy figures disappearing in the gloom, or lying in the sheltering porch. He was tempted to sing aloud and dare the walls to throw back the sound, but instead he hurried on and was soon walking through the squalid slums. And was consciousness of purpose a fulfilment of man's existence? Can the great purpose ever be achieved if these are the people through whom the purpose must work? Children being dragged along so late at night, their eyes looking large and haunted, recalled how he, himself, was once dragged into the Dublin slums. The elimination of poverty, this, he was convinced, must be his main concern: it must be exterminated root and branch. But how? Surely others had come to the same conclusion with this evil thing staring everybody in the face? Then why had nothing been done? Why were there so many poor? He must find an answer to the question.

Right in the heart of this slum, within a minute of the road he was walking through, Charles Bradlaugh, the personification of the noble mind to Shaw, lived in two tiny rooms in 29 Turner Street, Commercial Road, because he was fighting against the threat of bankruptcy, due to liabilities incurred in consequence of his battle for political and religious liberty. Shaw wanted to call on his hero but it was enough that he saw the windows behind which great speeches were composed. He felt that it was an honour to be denounced as a 'monster of wickedness and a wanton blasphemer', and to have one's speeches judged as 'drivelling words run mad'.

Braced by the sharp winds blowing over bleak fields, for he was now in the outskirts of London, he arrived at last at his uncle's cottage at dawn and gave a thunderous knock to the tune of *Lohengrin*. It was enough to awaken the whole village of Leyton. His uncle put half his body out of the window, and on seeing his 'stick of a nephew' was intensely relieved because he had feared it might be a patient. He came down to open the door, dressed in a mixture of day and night attire, immediately brought out a bottle of whisky and was pleased that his nephew refused it, and while he drank stared at his nephew's pale face, felt his chin with his hand and thought the hairless face unnatural. Forthrightly as always he told his nephew that he must be impotent, that he should eat quantities of meat, drink beer as often as possible and enjoy himself a little more.

As Shaw had no intention of having a family the information did not worry him. Family relationships seemed to him so utterly ridiculous that he meant one day to denounce them. He was driven back home in the buggy with the injunction that he must not come to Leyton until he had an occupation.

After this, Shaw was interviewed by employers and each time he prayed that he would be turned down. He had a genius for saying the thing which would most upset the prospective employer; at a shipping office, when it appeared that Shaw was the very man for the post, he was asked his religion and the reply came, 'atheist'.

He could now truthfully say that he had trodden down the pavements of London in search of work and that no one wanted him.

He decided to give himself six months of intensive writing and on no account to permit himself to be pushed into a job. This time he would work away from home, so many hours a day, with no temptation to play duets with Lucy and no interruptions by domestic ties. The British Museum became his haven.

The other people working in the British Museum Library did not know that this white-faced young man was engaged in a stupendous undertaking, no less than a moral guide to humanity. Had they known they would not have been in the least curious, for many of them were occupied with equally extravagant ideas and were seeking support from the past to prove that their ideas were not entirely original. The young man was not guided by such stars, he depended entirely on his inspiration. He was now in his twenty-second year and felt therefore in a position to teach the world what he himself had not learnt. He would divide the book into ten parts: the first would address itself to a female of five, the next to a male of the same age, and so on till twenty. That was as far as he could go with humanity, as every man over twenty, in his eyes, was a scoundrel.

He admitted to himself that he knew practically nothing about children, having never been a child himself; and suspected that a child's reaction to advice was to do the opposite, but that would not deter him from telling the truth. It was time that adults treated children seriously and gave them a realistic account of the world they had to live in.

As he wrote he realized his literary mission was to be a mental scavenger, for as the years went on the world became cluttered up with obsolete ideas, delusions and lies and no eliminative process had been invented for ideas as that which functioned in the human body. In a rapidly changing world there was no room for mental garbage.

Lucy and he had reacted in totally opposite ways to their anarchic upbringing. Lucy yearned for the conventional life and idealized everything commonplace but Shaw wished to change the life about him into his own pattern. When at last he wrote the last words to his first Guide, he felt a glorious exaltation, for the wit and the profusion of ideas warmed his heart and made him hum with happiness:

> "At some future stages of your career I may again address you on the great subject of yourself. Till then be assured that I will continue to feel for you the affection of a parent tempered by the rational interest of an experimental philosopher."

He called this Guide "A Practical System of Moral Education for Females" and was pleasantly surprised to find how wide a field he had covered. He omitted nothing. What amazed him was the way he grew increasingly cynical as the writing went on and he was shocked by the candour of his views. This Guide was the mental equivalent of the revolver he had longed to have when a boy; now he was a mental highwayman with a more deadly weapon.

After this he took it as his right to assume an authority in conversation, an equality in terms, which only success could have made becoming. The rude retort and the authoritative pronouncement came pat from his lips. He was thought stark, staring mad by Cashel Hoey, and the Lawsons were made very uncomfortable by the remarks he blurted out at their At Homes.

He denounced Cashel Hoey to her face as a 'mercenary hack' and informed her that he had not the jaws to crunch her three-volume novels. She stared at him aghast and decided that he needed work to restore his sanity and she suggested that he apply to her friend, Arnold White, who would find him a post in connection with a new-fangled invention which was to revolutionize communication between people far apart. The Edison Telephone Company of London needed 'young men of patience, intelligence and good address' to persuade house-holders to permit the Company to put poles on their roofs to carry lines. Unemployment was increasing in a diabolical way and even the banks were failing, and so it was of no use for Shaw to expect to make money from writing since books were not being bought.

Arnold White was not impressed by Shaw but he sent him to the district where they expected most difficulties. Fortunately for Shaw, his friendship with Chichester Bell had given him sufficient knowledge of physics to impress the shopkeepers and householders in the East End of London that he was the power behind the invention. He was deeply interested in the way people responded to new ideas; everywhere he met with obstinate opposition and overcame it with humour, ridicule and bullying, convinced that things were only believed when they were made incredible enough. The pole symbolized the triumph of the incredible over the commonplace.

His method of approach was never direct: it was futile to knock at a door and ask the occupant to put up a pole. He would first inspire an expression of utter incredulity by telling him that within a short while people would be able to converse thousands of miles apart as they now converse on their doorsteps; he quoted Tyndall and Helmholtz and said that all that was needed to prove to them that what he foretold was as simple as talking was to put up a pole. As a Dubliner he knew the value of snobbery and so he approached the clergyman, the doctor and the schoolmaster, and once they agreed the others fell into step. One of the people he approached happened to be a scientist who knew the works of Darwin, Tyndall and Helmholtz by heart and with him Shaw forgot his professional mission and proceeded to smash these scientists into smithereens. He ridiculed and exposed every inference of science and justified every superstition. Within a short while Shaw was without work and without the will to settle down to a definite task, for there was a sense of guilt when he picked up a pen to write. Entirely without inspiration, he avoided the British Museum and the National Gallery for they seemed to stand there uncaring whether he went in or not.

At Lee's place he met James Lecky, an enthusiast for phonetics and shorthand, punctuation and language reform. Lecky's extreme and revolutionary ideas in these things made him a missionary seeking everywhere for converts. Shaw's youth attracted him and it seemed from the way this young man held on to him that he had made a disciple after his own heart. Shaw confided to him that he was without work and that if he did not find something to do, he would become a laughing-stock like his father, without the consolation of drink to make life endurable. "You need interests," Lecky advised him, and he introduced him to Richard Deck, a poverty-stricken old man, French by birth, with a room in Kentish Town, holding large schemes for regenerating the world. Shaw spent many an evening in Kentish Town and it was through Richard Deck that his Irish accent approximated to the best London speech. Deck also took him in hand about his appearance, stopping him from plastering his hair flat on his head and teaching him to bank it up so that he looked less like a woman. Besides these he fed him with ideas with the intention of turning this young man into an orator able to give voice to the Lecky-Deck philosophy.

In this way George Bernard Shaw learnt that there was a philosopher named Proudhon who had written a book called *What is Property?*, to which he made the answer 'Theft'. It was a book Shaw himself might have written. They both read Proudhon together, laughing at his wit and his paradoxes, at his prods at popular opinion, his abuse of everything and everybody; the more Shaw read Proudhon, the more he was struck by the similarity of opinion, for the words by Proudhon, "Whoever lays his hands on me to govern me is a usurper and a tyrant and I declare him to be my enemy," was like a cry from his own heart.

On a November evening in 1879, both Lecky and Shaw attended one of the weekly meetings of the Zetetical Society, held in the rooms of the Women's Protective and Provident League, in Great Queen Street, Long Acre, London. The subject for debate was 'The State and the Family'. He was there to make his maiden effort and had therefore prepared his speech in writing. He had been told that there would be complete freedom of discussion about political, religious and sexual matters and that women took an important part in the debates. The problem for him was how to get what he wanted to say across the void which had a way of deflecting thought and making it sound unbearably pretentious and foolish. He had often tried to work out the secret of Lee's magnetism and how it was that some people had the power of creating awe. He practised often and hard before a mirror, trying this and that posture, the easy smiling presence against the heavy imposing figure, the hand on the lapel as against the hand in the pocket, the soft persuasive voice against the sonorous, the indifference to jeering and the pause for applause. In his imagination he held his audience spell-bound, playing on their minds as a violinist on his instrument.

His turn came and his hand shook so violently that he could not read his speech and he was certain that what he was saying sounded ill-considered and foolish. The laughter his speech provoked was no doubt due to his Irish intonation and his peculiar mannerisms, for he had forgotten his consonants and studied gestures, his paradoxes and syllogisms, his pauses and quotations and the words seemed to come from outside him. In his nervousness he sat down abruptly. Lecky pretended not to notice his shaking limbs and congratulated him on his maiden effort. Shaw vowed to himself he would join the society, go every week and speak at every debate until he had become a fine debater and a fluent speaker.

At the third meeting George Bernard Shaw was proposed as chairman and from this vantage point his attention was struck by a man younger than himself, rather below middle height, with small hands and feet and a profile that suggested an improvement on Napoleon the Third. Shaw was particularly impressed by the fine forehead under remarkably thick dark hair, and was fascinated by the eyes which were constantly changing in expression, one moment looking at the world with great sadness and the next with pleasure, giving the impression that the statements he uttered were a matter of the lips only, while his mind was absorbed with deeper things. This young man made no effort to make himself heard or understood: he used notes, read them, ticked them off one by one, threw them on the floor and was as calm and cool throughout his performance as a mechanical instrument. He obviously knew all there was to know about the subject discussed and played on facts and figures like a person practising scales. Here was the complete Philistine who, most likely, had never heard of Beethoven and did not care a hoot for Wagner, who talked about human beings as though they were ciphers: so many unemployed, so many married and so many with a score of children. No passion entered his speech and yet he succeeded in doing what an orator could never have done. Shaw watched his performance with awe and the awe turned into worship and the worship into affection. He decided that he must win the friendship, force the friendship if necessary, of Sidney Webb, for this was his name.

Shaw's great opportunity came when the Society paid to Art the tribute of setting aside an evening to it. Here at last he was perfectly at home: he declared that his schooling had been a complete failure and that the aesthetic education he had received out of school was his salvation although it was never likely to bring him a penny. Sidney Webb followed him with the suggestion that as a result of the mechanical revolution people would eventually have to spend three or four hours a day in routine work and the rest of the time could be given over to artistic pursuits. But he had to point out that there were already many thousand artists in the country, most of them starving, and that therefore Mr. George Bernard Shaw was unwise in encouraging others to take up art. French bohemianism never did appeal to him but what was wanted was a solid respectable life based on shorter hours of work, better pay and education for all. This clash of opinion strangely enough brought Webb and Shaw together. It was to Shaw's credit that he realized that he had lived too intensely on his imagination and was in danger of becoming a creature of wind and therefore he needed Webb as an anchor. Webb found him amusing and gained much from his association with Shaw.

Shaw became the Richard Deck with Webb, taking him in hand and teaching him elocution, but this did not suit Webb who maintained that he found that men became humbugs when they learnt elocution. However, he did get Webb to walk for exercise, for until Shaw had come upon his scene it had never occurred to this industrious civil servant that such a thing was necessary; there was much to do and little time to do it in, and he considered that even food and sleep were impositions. Compared with the extraordinary singlemindedness of Sidney Webb, Shaw felt his own life to be a hotch-potch of cross-purposes; whenever he was doing one thing, he felt that he should be doing another. Webb did not show the least curiosity as to how Shaw spent his days.

Inspired by Sidney Webb's practical approach to all problems he set himself the task of finding out whether the Arts were exhausted. This study resolved itself into a kind of literary accountancy which he worked out in a long paper entitled 'Exhausted Arts'. After a survey which occupied weeks of his time he concluded that it was impossible to look with complacency on the successive blocking of all the arts by the great artists . . . 'In music, art and literature, a mighty harvest has left the soil sterile.' Shaw's response to this state of affairs was: 'The arts are exhausted. Long live the arts.'

He felt called upon to take up his pen and address the new world ushered in by Ruskin, William Morris and Wagner.

He condemned himself to fill five pages of a quarto sheet a day, dull or inspired. There was so much of the clerk in him that if his five pages ended in the middle of a sentence he did not finish it until the next day. On the other hand, if he missed a day he made up for it by doing a double task on the morrow. Often days, weeks went by without seeing a soul. In his imagination he told himself stories and had wonderful conversations where he split himself into many personalities. The gulf between the life within and the life without was so immense that the feat of engineering required to bridge it was beyond his power. What overwhelmed him was that communication was so poor that it was only when they conversed within himself that there was laughter and understanding. If progress were dependent on verbal expression then the human being was going backwards rather than forwards. A few choice spirits, poets and philosophers, tried hard to push the world forward but the world reeled back again in spite of all their efforts and crushed them.

It was as well that he lived on the assumption that life was a jest, for something happened to test his power of laughter to the full. He had saved up a sum of money to buy a suit to his own design, having given much thought to the ideal wear for the adult male, a suit made of a material that one could have washed at home and which permitted the body to breathe. He was rather proud of his legs and ankles and he decided on knickerbockers to match a handsome belted jacket. On his way to the tailor, he met Dr. Aveling who had shown much interest in his 'progress'. They talked about Darwin whom Aveling had met and the greatness of this biologist and his largeheartedness and Shaw's opposition to the ideas generally associated with Darwin softened. When Aveling made the request for a small sum to tide him over a difficult period, Shaw gave all he had; he had waited so long for a new suit and it would not matter as much as all that if he would have to wait a few more weeks. Weeks went by and months but there was no sign of the money, for Aveling had obviously overlooked this trivial matter; but to Shaw it was a catastrophe because he could no longer be seen in the suit he was wearing, he could only go out at night and then only walk in the shadows lest the fierce lights of the gas-lamps showed up his tattered and discoloured clothes.

Yet Aveling was the only man who came to visit Shaw while he confined himself to his room. They talked about God and science and human destiny, but never about such mundane things as money. Shaw sat admiring Aveling's clothes, which were smart and colourful. Above all, it was Aveling's modesty that appealed to him for he never tried to score off the other; he took it for granted that Shaw knew more than himself and there was never a hint of sarcasm or sneering.

George Bernard Shaw put down this strange experience with Aveling as Stage Two of his life: the first was when he began to have moral scruples, but this second stage was much more involved because it had to take into account that no man was scrupulous all round. He had according to his faculties and interests certain points of honour, whilst in matters that did not interest him he was often careless and even wicked. Having come to this conclusion from bitter experience he declared that we must finally adapt our institutions because if the opposite were attempted, that is trying to force human nature in a mould of existing abuses, superstitions and corrupt interests, explosive forces would be produced which would ultimately bring down humanity. This was already happening for it was difficult to find a really happy face anywhere.

At the end of two years he had completed three novels and was only stopped by an attack of small-pox which disabled him.

1879 *Immaturity*
1880 *The Irrational Knot*
1881 *Love Among the Artists*

The novels were neatly written in his own hand and there was only one copy of each. He enclosed a letter to the Publishers which read as follows:

> Care of Dr. Gurly
> Leyton Essex 14th July
>
> Gentlemen
>     Will you oblige me by reading a MS novel of mine, for which I am desirous to find a publisher? It is of the usual length, and deals with modern society.
>     After the 1st prox. my address will be 37 Fitzroy Street W.
>
> I am, Gentlemen
> Your obedient servant
> G. B. Shaw.

While convalescing at his uncle's place at Leyton he earned a few pounds by counting the votes at an election, and with this money he was at last able to buy a new suit.

## Chapter Four

ANOTHER person who entered George Bernard Shaw's life was an Eton master, J. L. Joynes, a product of Eton and King's College, Cambridge, and a character if there ever was one.

Joynes was asking himself the same questions as Shaw and was answering them very much in the same way. They met because of their conversion to vegetarianism and both recognized their identity of interests immediately, and conversed as though they had been brought up together. Joynes dismissed the Eton background as Shaw rejected the Irish background: their private lives had developed outside these surroundings. In the company of Joynes, Shaw developed a wit which deeply impressed his friend who tended to take life solemnly; too often the wit had a flavour of frivolity but Joynes had no doubt whatever as to Shaw's sincerity. After meeting Shaw he returned to Eton and kept his friend, Henry Salt, also an Eton master, laughing at the latest quips of this brilliant discovery.

Shaw's notion of a Public School was derived from the stories his Uncle Walter had told him and he wondered how a man like Joynes could stay on in such a den of corruption. Joynes never made the least effort to justify the ways of the school or schools in general: secretly he counted the days when he would be able to walk out of the place, never to return. He could not and would not do what Shaw did, that is sponge on his parent, and he differed from Shaw, wanting to identify himself entirely with the poor, for he felt that he had no right to comfort while there was poverty and misery in the world. Shaw thought such a policy unwise because compassion degraded both giver and recipient. As both discussed the universe, it was as though they held the future of civilization in the palm of their hands and they had no doubt whatever that their views would triumph. Both agreed that the difference between a wage-slave and a man of independent means was so great that they could well be counted as belonging to a different species. Strangely enough it was Shaw who behaved as the man of independent means with the cultured tastes of one, while Joynes regarded himself as a wage-slave. Joynes was of a delicate constitution but Shaw was convinced that it was he and not Joynes who would die young. He had long periods of complete exhaustion, followed by very painful headaches and was always surprised to find himself alive after each attack.

While Shaw continued with his unremunerative writing he and his mother could not go on occupying a whole house because the money coming in was diminishing rapidly and they were behind in rent. They had to humiliate themselves by moving into a second-floor flat in Fitzroy Street and from there soon after into an even cheaper place into rooms over a small shop at 36 Osnaburgh Street, a decaying street. Lucy refused to enter this house and preferred travelling with a touring company, playing insignificant parts in Gilbert and Sullivan Operas and staying in cheap boarding-houses. This tour included Dublin, but when there she had to meet her father if only to discuss finances. Mr. Carr Shaw was shocked to learn that she had actually descended into professional acting and asked whether it was true that George was emulating Nebuchadnezzar by feeding on cattle fodder? Lucy assured him that her mad brother was more hopeless than the Biblical King. She found her father a changed man, very old, sincerely teetotal and not too talkative.

One day, after a long walk through Hyde Park, in an ecstasy of contemplation Shaw arrived home to find his mother lying unconscious on the floor. His first thought was to call Lee, but he was not certain how his mother would take Lee whom she now considered a charlatan. He remembered Lee's method of healing by applying cold poultices on the forehead, took his mother in hand and watched the colour slowly return to her face. She was full of apology for this faint.

He sat down at the table which was littered with papers and books, some of these overflowing on to the floor. At that moment he was reading Walt Whitman's *Leaves of Grass*, Edward Carpenter's *Towards Democracy* and Prince Kropotkin's *Mutual Aid*, and he derived a strange physical strength from the magic of their presence. By him were copies of the *Reformer* in which Annie Besant and Bradlaugh had a curious custom of printing full-length reports of the legal trials in which they were almost continuously involved. There was also a copy of the *Essex Standard* sent to Shaw by Dr. Gurly in which the two atheist leaders were dubbed as 'that bestial man and woman, who go about earning a livelihood by corrupting the young of England'.

He needed all the strength he could muster to buttress his stoicism for he was now faced with a new possibility: that of his mother's death. He knew that he could never live alone, although, within his mother's *ménage*, he seemed to live a completely independent existence. This did not mean that he did not take an interest in all that was happening, he wanted to know the economics of the home, the people that his mother and Lucy met and made a point of meeting his mother's pupils and occasionally visiting them at their homes. But suddenly to be thrown completely on his own resources was a situation he could not envisage. He could not help comparing their life with that of another Dublin family recently come to London. Lady Wilde had now settled in London and had continued her *salons* with her son Oscar, who had just come down from Oxford, as the bait for artistic and literary society. She herself had a lovely speaking voice and always gave an air of romance and sorrow, while her son was rich in quip and paradox. Mrs. Carr Shaw and George Bernard were both invited and it was at these *salons* that Mrs. Carr Shaw's pupils were given their first opportunities to sing in public.

George Bernard Shaw was not at home among these brilliant people and much preferred the company of rebels and so-called disreputable people and the meetings in Hyde Park where ideas gathered as quickly and thickly as paper in the gutter.

He did his utmost in his own eccentric manner to be extra courteous to his mother's pupils because every penny was now necessary as the legacy had dwindled, and he boasted to his mother that he was of great financial value to her because the presence of a young eligible man was the chief draw for her pupils. It was one of these, a young nurse from an Essex hospital, sent by Dr. Gurly to his sister for singing lessons, who seemed to Shaw a likely companion to take the place of his mother. Alice Lockett was as pretty as a dairymaid and had a charming voice and yet seemed a commonsensible body to him. He set himself the task of wooing her and preparing her to accept his original views. Though at first she was flattered by his attentions, he bewildered her by his exaggerated gallantry and ultimately repulsed her.

On the night of September 5th, 1882, Shaw walked casually into a meeting of the Memorial Hall, Farringdon Street, and listened to a lecture on Land Nationalization by the author, Henry George. Henry George was an ideal orator, for he combined passion and logic, personal experience and theory, sympathy with the poor and an understanding of the underlying causes of poverty. He was an American who lived in San Francisco, had seen that place grow from a mere camp into an enormously wealthy city and the incredible fact was that the richer the city became, the greater the poverty of the people. In other words, the advance of civilization was always accompanied by an appalling reduction in the standard of living; everywhere, progress brought on poverty. Science was rapidly revolutionizing the processes of production but no one had yet worked out how this vast increase of wealth could be put to the service of humanity.

George Bernard Shaw left the meeting, working out the problem of poverty: he realized that equality of opportunity could never be, because endowments, physical, mental and spiritual, differed widely, but equality of income must happen if the world was to be made bearable. From now on both Shaw and Joynes became enthusiastic disciples of Henry George and both applied themselves to an intensive study of economics, and imperceptibly passed from Henry George to Karl Marx. They ultimately settled upon the theory that with increasing population the marginal workers became valueless and these were glad of any opportunity of earning their keep; that is, as a result, the capitalist could always get as much labour as he wanted for bare subsistence wages. As improvements in the processes of production made more and more workers valueless, the wages for those who were fortunate enough to find employment tended to stay at subsistence level. Therefore, the Henry George solution of land nationalization was not enough, for if all the land were nationalized and capital was still privately appropriated, the Georgite would, in the words of Shaw, remain, 'the chaplain of a Pirate ship'. If inequality was to be totally eliminated, it was necessary to go much further and dispose entirely of the marginal workers by maintaining full employment. Shaw was not foolish enough to direct his indignation at the machinery itself, for if society were properly organized machinery could well become a liberating force, increasing the standard of life all round.

Karl Marx's terrible power of invective, hatred and irony deeply impressed George Bernard Shaw; the picture drawn of a villainous system of society gripped his imagination, as though the lid of hell had been lifted and he was permitted to look down into it. His solution to poverty became simplicity itself: the socialization of the means of production, distribution and exchange. Thereupon, he and Joynes left the Land Reform Union and attended the meetings of the Social Democratic Federation. Dr. Aveling was already a very active member of the latter society with a seat on the executive and he was living with the youngest daughter of Karl Marx, Eleanor Marx-Aveling. Eleanor was a brilliant intellect, a fine linguist and an author and translator of many books and plays. She and Aveling had collaborated in the writing of some of these and seemed to everyone a perfect example of companionship-marriage.

The most prominent member of this Federation was H. M. Hyndman, a cultured financier, who in appearance was like the deity in Raphael's Vision of Ezekiel. He was a brilliant controversialist and like his master, Karl Marx, an equally brilliant hater, taking a dislike immediately to Aveling and then to Shaw. This imposing person in the movement looked as if he had been born in a frock coat and top hat, though he preferred working with proletarians rather than with people of his own class, Shaw, however, suspected his sincerity and would not believe a word he uttered. Joynes, on the other hand, thought of Hyndman as a God substitute and was devoted to him.

This new-found devotion to Social Science gave a new direction to George Bernard Shaw's novel writing. In a short while he had two more novels going the rounds of English and American publishers, the result being the same as with the other three. He had gone out of his way to make his fourth novel, *Cashel Byron's Profession*, popular, exciting and with a love interest, a pugilistic interest and a happy ending, but though he had been so accommodating, the publishers would not have it. When Mrs. Robert Louis Stevenson read *Cashel Byron* she shut the book with a bang and flung it away because he made the hero exclaim, 'I hate my mother'. All heroes in the eighteen-eighties had to love their mothers and in due course the rest of their relatives.

The fifth novel bore the mark of his socialist faith: it dealt with a socialist who inherited a fortune, married and found that the company of a beautiful wife prevented him from giving himself entirely to the cause. He left her and masqueraded as a labourer. This novel gave Shaw a grand opportunity of creating a new character, expressing the new ideas and feelings which had come into the world. Sidney Trefusis, the Socialist, would one day, he hoped, become a household name like Oliver Twist or Hamlet.

The allowance from Ireland had stopped coming and it looked as though both would starve. To save the situation Shaw asked Joynes to do something for him. Joynes had now thrown over his Eton post but the Eton and Cambridge credentials gave him immediate entrance to the very best circles: George Meredith, G. F. Watts, William Morris, Tennyson and William Archer were glad to associate with him. Whenever and wherever he could he praised his Irish friend, 'a genius if there ever was one'. This genius he recognized in Shaw's talk rather than in his writing. After looking through Shaw's novels he felt that if he could persuade Shaw to transfer his brilliant talk into his work, his fame would be established. Why could he not write as he talked? He put it down to the intervention of Literature, trying to write like the Immortals instead of being himself! Joynes advised him to damn style and to get on with what he had to say. He begged of him to cease trying to be professional.

When Sidney Webb discovered that Shaw was a continuous failure as a writer he advised him to give up writing, but Shaw laughed and replied that he had never been interested in literature for its own sake and that all he wanted to do with his pen was to convert socialists to Socialism, Christians to Christianity, Freethinkers to thinking freely.

George Bernard Shaw was now in demand as an orator. He loved to hear his voice filling the hall, so that all could hear without effort: he enjoyed mightily the musical cadence of his speech, the vivid periods and the anti-climax that brought the house down. He knew that he was a success as a speaker because the laughs came when he intended them to come, the opposition when he meant to provoke it, the applause when the prepared retort came pat. Every organization wanted this brainy young man as an aunt sally but he was never overthrown. The verdict generally was: 'It was all rot but very brilliant.'

H. M. Hyndman, on hearing Shaw speak in Hyde Park, was downright angry with him because of 'his sheer buffoonery', and declared that Shaw took a personal delight in playing the malignant imp in the movement. "What Shaw's real opinions are at any particular moment nobody can say but himself, and ninety-nine times out of a hundred he does not tell you."

Mrs. Carr Shaw had actually obtained a post as singing mistress at a school in Clapham, and as Shaw never accepted a penny for his speaking and never earned a penny from his novels they were entirely dependent on her earnings. She still retained one or two private pupils. One of these was a wealthy widow with a house in London and one by the sea. She became a great friend of both mother and son, showering presents on them and opening her home at all hours of the day to the son. It was not unusual for Shaw to leave her place at the early hours of the morning, and their loud conversation and laughter disturbed the neighbours. Mrs. Jenny Patterson was a vivacious lady, loud spoken and temperamental and much older than he; his failure and fragility brought out an aspect of femininity to which he was unaccustomed, pity mingled with passion, adoration for his wit mingled with ardour to which he could not fully respond. He knew that it was his duty to keep away but his knowledge of women was so cursory and his curiosity so intense that in spite of his remorse he continued a relationship of which he was afterwards ashamed and which almost drove her mad. Mrs. Carr Shaw knew what was happening to her pupil but she felt that it was not for her to interfere in matters of romance, knowing that all that kind of thing ended in nothing, and she would, on no account, trump up a moral case against her son.

When, however, it came to her knowledge that her son had been speaking at street corners and in the parks, she was deeply insulted. Well, all the men she had known had let her down, then why expect her son to be any different? She had always wondered what form his defection would take, for he did not drink and he did not steal.

Joynes was the first visitor to Fitzroy Square and Mrs. Carr Shaw took to him at once because she heard that he was the son of a musical mother and that he had been a schoolmaster and a son of a housemaster at Eton. Both agreed that the greatest thing in life was goodness. She thought him the most courteous and sympathetic gentleman she had ever met. When, mischievously, her son announced that Joynes was a Socialist, in her eyes the most repugnant thing on earth, she took it to be her son's silly way of teasing her. It was difficult to take him seriously. It was from Joynes that she first heard her son described as a genius. It was obvious that the young gentleman had not yet seen through her son's blarney.

"Geniuses grow on every bush in Ireland," she warned him. "One has only to stretch a hand to be stung by a totally incapable person in the guise of a genius."

Sidney Webb was the other visitor to be introduced to her. She stared at the little man "eating greedily, talking speedily, and looking weedily", as she later described him.

"You must think me very dull," Sidney Webb said to her before he left, "I thrive on dullness."

She noticed that her son was anxious to please this man and argued very little with him, obviously overawed by this man who had a ready answer for everything. She also noticed the number of words that ended in 'ism' and how they talked of the great statesmen as if they were uninformed.

"We must see that the people who matter are made aware of the facts," Sidney Webb repeated again and again as if this were an article of faith.

Joynes invited George Bernard Shaw to his father's home at Eton to introduce him to his family. There Shaw met Henry Salt and his wife Kate. Salt was five years older than Bernard Shaw and already sported a sumptuous beard. Born in India, springing from a military family, brought up conventionally, educated at Eton and King's College, Cambridge, he had become a crank of cranks, in other words: a humanitarian, a socialist and a vegetarian. To him the opposite of the word 'crank' was 'cad'.

Shaw had to admit that Eton produced a higher proportion of eccentric characters than the ordinary school. He had formerly considered it the bulwark of Toryism but he now ventured to prophesy that Eton would produce the first Socialist Prime Minister. He learnt from Salt that he was going to burn his boats and settle down to a simple life on the land. Shaw could not help remarking that the burning of boats had become an incipient disease among world-betterers. Every other man he had come across had given up a safe and lucrative post to go into the wilderness. "I started the fashion years ago," he told them, "I escaped respectability by the skin of my teeth."

Kate Salt was a woman of ethereal beauty: she had dark raven hair with large eyes and a Dante-like profile and made him feel ashamed of his petty adventures with his other female acquaintances. He had never seen anyone like her and after hearing her play Beethoven, he constituted himself her 'Sunday husband', a term he invented to denote the most idealistic relationship with women. He teased her about leaving the luxuries of Eton for an insanitary cottage in the wilds of Surrey but he threatened to swoop down upon them like an eagle and stay like a dove.

Until he had met Kate Salt, Shaw knew nothing of the existence of a group of boat-burners called the Guild of the New Life, to which she belonged. Its object was to create a way of life based on unselfishness, love and wisdom and they did their utmost to put into practice immediately what they considered right. Among the members were Havelock Ellis, Edward Pease, H. H. Champion, Percival Chubb and Edward Carpenter. Shaw attended their meetings and although they dwelt, in his opinion, too much in the idealistic spheres, they were of a high intellectual calibre and he knew that they were influential and could be of great help to him.

This guild was not a political organization for members believed that what they stood for could be put into practice without having to convert everybody first of all. They meant to obtain their emancipation from 'selfishness, rivalry and ignorance' by working on the land. Shaw was convinced that these splendid people would soon break up into quarrelsome unemployables, for syllogisms would never grow potatoes, and ideals never wash pots and pans. But he could not resist them and wore the sandals made by Edward Carpenter, once a Fellow of Trinity Hall, Cambridge, as a sign that though he was not entirely of them, he trod the same ground.

George Bernard Shaw learnt from these people of the existence of Urnings, the name given to the Intermediate sex who were neither completely male nor completely female and could reach intimacy without the intervention of sex, not that they thought sex sinful or degrading. It described his own position because he felt much more female than male.

Still seeking an organization to which he could give himself wholeheartedly he came across a leaflet entitled *Why are the Many Poor?* and this was published by the Fabian Society which met in a street once familiar to him, Osnaburgh Street. He found at their meetings a group of highly intellectual people and only one artisan amongst them. This artisan had written the leaflet and had not a hint of a solution to the problem of poverty. But the name of the society attracted him with its classical association.

The Guild of the New Life had split into two and this was the section that devoted itself to the political aspect of the problems that confronted the country. In Shaw's opinion there was every need for an organization to counteract the influence of exasperated sentimentalists and theorists to whose leadership a mob of desperate sufferers was abandoned. His other socialist friends were wont to present civilization as a popular melodrama with grasping obese devils on one side and saintly starving workers on the other. Shaw did not see things like that although he appreciated the value of such a presentation if the people were to be won over. He had learnt from the writing of five novels that the majority of people had, at the back of their minds, the infantile belief that goodness must inevitably triumph over evil and all would be well. In his own view, evil, vulgarity and deception won all along the line and a saint could succeed only if he posed as a satanic monster.

He could not work up any enthusiasm for the poor, whom he regarded as stupid rather than Christlike. The fact that these stupid people were exploited by the Capitalists made them no heroes in his sight. He found that ill-used people like the workers were much worse than the well-used people, those with education and leisure; and he refused to tolerate poverty as a social institution. For this reason he sought the sanctuary of well-used people and joined the Fabian Society, at the same time keeping in touch with the other Socialist organizations.

Engels, the great friend of Marx, and patron of the Avelings, naturally poured scorn on this new organization. He laughed at the idea that this ambitious group could not possibly entrust the social revolution to the rough proletariat alone and were kind enough to set themselves at its head.

George Bernard Shaw was now developing a beard which took on a Mephistophelian guise. He liked to think of himself as unique and indefinable and the most striking personification of the progressive movement. He was an unemployable who worked harder than anyone, a penniless person who enjoyed the delights that only wealth could afford, a genius with nothing to his name. He did not feel in the least out of place with these young high-spirited people who came to the

Fabian meetings held in each other's drawing-rooms. They played high jinks with the current ideas, quarrelled vehemently and settled their quarrels by writing Tracts. This Socialist society was individualism run wild, for it believed, as far as it had any beliefs, that in economics the need was for organization and more organization; but in individual life, the need was for freedom and more freedom. All agreed about one thing and that was that Shaw was the most brilliant individual they had ever met and so he was invited to write a Tract. His final observation almost gave them a sense of unity for it united them against him: "That we had rather face a civil war than another century of suffering as the present one had been." What the civil war would have achieved outside confusion and bloodshed, he did not say. He was wise enough to realize that another person was needed to consolidate the society into something purposive and he persuaded Sidney Webb to join.

Salt and Joynes feared that Shaw had turned respectable, a calamity no self-respecting person could endure. When Shaw pleaded that one must be practical, they took him at his word and found him work. A friend of theirs, William Archer, literary critic on the *Pall Mall Gazette*, theatre critic on the *World* and the translator of Ibsen, was a graduate of Edinburgh University and editors generally felt that he could write about every subject he had not read at the University. Joynes approached this man and interested him in Shaw. William Archer took him in hand, sent him books to review for the *Pall Mall Gazette* and, miracle of miracles, Shaw was paid for this. He handed over the whole amount to his mother and invariably sent the papers to his father who was now convinced that his son had achieved greatness.

Mr. Carr Shaw was living in a room in a respectable suburb of Dublin and he could boast to his landlady about Shaw junior. However, within a short while the old man was gathered to his fathers in Mount Jerome Cemetery. When Mrs. Carr Shaw heard of her husband's death she was not interested for she had regarded her marriage as a mistake and she preferred to forget about it. As a result of his death, a small sum of money came in most usefully to George Bernard for with this he could buy the Jaeger suit which he had helped the founder of this firm to design and which he could only now afford. This cost him about six pounds but he thought of it as an investment because he hoped it would last him forty years at least.

His method of criticism was to select a book on a subject he knew little about and before reading it glance through other books on the same subject at the British Museum Reading Room. When he felt that he knew all there was to know about the subject, he glided lightly through the book to be reviewed, picking out paragraphs which would give the effect of an article written by an omniscient critic. The reader became more interested in the critic than in the book itself, for Shaw ranged over autobiography, sociology and current falsehoods, whatever the subject. He wished that a way had been found of expressing contradictory thoughts in the same breath, for in every article he sent out it would have been possible for him to have given the other angle. Fortunately for the critic, however, newspapers were ephemeral and the article of today became ancient history on the morrow. Whatever he did had to be morally justified and placed on the highest pedestal possible, and so he claimed that journalism was the contemporary art form.

The authorities did not make it easy for the Socialists to hold open-air meetings; while Salvationists, Freethinkers and Christian Evidence speakers were left alone, the police had orders to stop Socialist propaganda. In Dod Street, in the dock area, each of the Socialists took it in turn to risk imprisonment in the fight for free speech. October 11th was fixed for George Bernard Shaw's turn and it was well for him that by then the police had been instructed not to interfere, for the repercussions might have been serious since his mother had applied for a new post as singing mistress at the North London Collegiate School and a son in prison might have prejudiced her chances.

Mrs. Carr Shaw obtained this post. The minute states:

"I propose to appoint Mrs. Carr Shaw, a widow, who has specially devoted herself to voice production. She is an intimate friend of Mrs. Bryant's and has been for some time teaching in the Clapham High School.

December 7th. 1885."

The North London Collegiate School was founded by Frances Mary Buss to provide for girls a liberal education up to the standard of the best boys' schools. Miss Buss, the daughter of an artist, was a person with a mission and looked out for teachers of character, enthusiasm, and integrity. She was deeply impressed by the forthrightness of this elderly lady. Mrs. Carr Shaw threw herself into the work with so much vigour that the school gained a reputation for its choir singing and invitations to train other school choirs came pouring in. Thus, with several schools and private pupils she was fully occupied.

George Bernard Shaw also obtained an additional post, that of Art critic to the *World*. Edmund Yates, the editor of this fashionable weekly, had offered this post to William Archer, who passed it on to George Bernard Shaw whose need was greater than his own. Archer never ceased to help him, appreciating the sparkling wit, the tremendous gift as conversationalist of the Irishman and above all his conscientiousness in carrying out every duty assigned to him.

Archer invited his protégé to collaborate in a play which was sure to bring in sufficient money to liberate them both from the drudgery of journalism. Shaw was to supply the conversational matter and the humour while Archer, with his comprehensive knowledge of the stage, supplied the plot which was a compound of all the box-office attractions. Here at last was the heaven-sent opportunity for Shaw: to achieve immediate success in a new medium, a medium which he tended to despise up to now. Archer warned Shaw that what was wanted was not a so-called artistic success appealing only to the intellectual few, and the last thing he wanted was an exciting debate on the stage. Shaw pleaded that the play must return to its original religious function or perish but Archer wanted a box-office return and was amused by Shaw's insistence on the religious motive in drama when it was their anti-clerical views that bound them so closely.

Shaw looked at Archer's plot and immediately hatched his own, perversely distorting it into a realistic exposure of slum landlordism. The result shocked Archer, for though he too hated slums and shams, he knew that this play would do them no good.

Shaw had another abortive manuscript in his chest but now the position was different for he could describe himself as a critic, and that was an honourable position and gave an air of responsibility to his ideas and ideas with him were the most exciting things on earth. Though he enjoyed writing that little conversation piece for Archer, he did not think that the writing of plays was the work for him.

He was more conscious than ever of the part fantasy was beginning to play in contemporary life and that a truer conception of history would be a sequence of illusions, one illusion being replaced by another, while life itself went on in dull uneventful routine. Capitalism, for example, was not an orgy of human villainy but a Utopia that dazzled capable and public-spirited men from Adam Smith and Cobden and Bright. The upholders of Capitalism were mostly dreamers and visionaries.

The same with the theatre: he recognized that there was method in the frivolity, sentimentality and voluptuousness, since it reconciled people to insupportable conditions by making them think that the true life was lived on the stage and that life lived on that plane was exciting and led to supreme happiness. This illusion was a cunning device to

absolve them from the effort of facing their own situations. Karl Marx
and Ibsen, who took it upon themselves to disturb this fantasy existence,
caused spiritual agony and were hated for it. When Shaw watched his
own illusions he came upon an abyss of superstition as dark and forbidding as that of the so-called unemancipated; but in his case the
follies were buttressed by reason and the more shallow and chaotic
his feelings, the more subtle, the more brilliant, the more eloquent was
the superstructure.

Socialism could become popular only when it substituted new
fantasies for the follies of the old, and the reason for his success as a
propagandist was that he was one of those new fantasies. Although
Shaw felt more at home among the Fabians and in their drawing-
rooms, he enjoyed the fun of revolutionary ardour; wherever there
was a possibility of a conflagration he was there: a fight for free speech,
a forbidden demonstration, a deputation, a poster parade to sell a
socialist paper, a dockers' meeting, the tall, reedy, red-bearded figure
could be seen, deliberately conspicuous. He never flattered the workers,
nor conveyed that revolution would solve everything, and seemed to
endow everything with laughter. Those comrades who suspected his
motives for being in the movement had to admit that he worked as
hard as any of them in the menial tasks involved: he was ready to
address envelopes in a dark, candle-lit room, he was ready to help in
sticking forbidden posters on the walls in the early hours of the morning
and he never hesitated to sell pamphlets. He would even 'oblige with a
song and a little bit on the piano'.

There were men who consistently opposed him. They found it
difficult to explain their opposition: it was more of a physical antipathy
than anything else. The movement naturally contained all sorts and
he knew all along that all the propaganda in the world would not
convert these eager fanatics into sensible people; he had no faith that
universal education would achieve the purpose because he had never
got over his contempt for schooling, and at moments he thought that
these very comrades would prove an obstacle to progress, but his
passion for world-bettering was such that he held on fast to the little
hope the movement afforded. He enjoyed the sordid side of the business
and the play of motives: every aspect of human nature fascinated him.
"It is good for me to be worked to the last inch while I last," he wrote.

He knew that beyond the destructive philosophy and the cunning
analysis he had the simple faith that could not be denied, the base of
the pyramid of his life: that life itself was good. However much he
contemplated, however much he condemned the past and overthrew
the present, the structure of the soul remained the same. The things

that truly delighted him were simple things: he dressed simply, ate simply and his room was a cell.

He liked going to the Salts because they were equally simple folk and they could gossip endlessly without inhibition or pretence, for though his circle of acquaintances was very large now, there were few he could talk to without affectation. Tilford was his second home and he escaped there whenever he could. He could not join in their ecstasies over Thoreau, though he knew perfectly well that he owed his income to the fact that William Archer shared their enthusiasm and even called his house "Walden". His sense of mischief was so ingrained that nothing was holy: no intimacy above betrayal, no loves above mockery.

After staying with the Salts he sent an article on his visit and signed it 'S', reminiscent of his first letter, way back in Dublin. It appeared in the *Pall Mall Gazette*. It told of

"the uneven, ankle-twisting roads, the ditches with their dogs, rank weeds and swarms of poisonous flies, groups of feeble-minded children torturing something; dull, toil-broken, prematurely old agricultural labourers, savage tramps, manure heaps with their terrible odours, the chain of milestones from cemetery to cemetery . . ."

It was a frightening description written to entertain the lofty urban reader, but it did not deter him from leaving the salubrious Tottenham Court Road area to go again and again to the hazards of Tilford. Nor did these 'hazards' prevent William Morris, Eleanor Marx-Aveling, Prince Kropotkin, Swinburne, George Meredith, Hyndman and Edward Carpenter from frequent excursions to this village. He was certainly a reckless mischief-maker and knew himself to be such.

"Whenever there was a quarrel I betrayed everybody's confidence by analyzing it and stating it in the most exaggerated terms. Result: both sides agreed it was all my fault. I was denounced on all hands but forgiven as a privileged Irish lunatic."

Strangely enough, in spite of this reputation, people found themselves confiding in him: women told him of their miserable lives at home, men of their infidelities, young people gave him a present of their aspirations and old people passed on their wisdom and experience. He listened, appropriated them and passed them on as his own. He became the sorting-house of every extravagant suggestion and he could be relied upon to make the wildest ideas appear reasonable and the simplest ideas appear fantastic. He had a ready ear for amateurs who were despised and boycotted by the professionals in the worlds of science, medicine and art. The fact that he had to make himself comprehensible to the masses was a humiliation to him, however much he pretended to enjoy it; he felt that the mob received his ideas just as "a cannibal accepted the teaching of St. John or an Oxford undergraduate the philosophy of Plato or the poetry of Euripides".

None of his friends thought of him as settling down to reviewing books and art criticism: they all expected bigger things of him, but he always let them down. He based his real reputation on his failures: his failure as an artist, his failure as a novelist and his failure as a dramatist. His dream was to achieve a failure that would shake the world. He was under an inner compulsion to be a failure.

Another failure was to come. The Cause was in dire need of a rollicking marching song and Shaw tried his hand at providing one. The Anthem of the Socialists was the Red Flag and he shocked the movement by calling this lugubrious lament the 'funeral march of a fried eel'. Nor was he happier with 'England Arise' because it put the clock back; were not all the Empire builders proclaiming that the sun never set on their possessions? Once he followed the Salvation Army band for a long way with the hope that the words would come to him, while marching to the sound of his beloved brass band, but nothing came to him but a few 'obscene images'. William Morris, Joynes and Edward Carpenter were more successful in adding to the socialist hymnal which became popular in Socialist Sunday Schools and the Socialist Churches. It was said that on one occasion, when Shaw was delivering a 'sermon' at one of these churches, a devout Anglican wandered in and did not notice the difference: the lean preacher in the Norfolk suit aroused no suspicion because he raged against the 'sins of society' like the tubbiest bishop.

In this transition period, the world-betterers found it difficult to throw over the nomenclature of convention: vegetarian dishes were named steaks, Sunday meetings were called, by the Socialists, Socialist Churches, and the Rationalists attended Ethical Churches.

One of the books Shaw brought down with him to Tilford and which aroused his uncritical enthusiasm was Samuel Butler's *Luck and Cunning*. It was the first book reviewed by him which impelled him to meet the author. On the whole he feared meeting authors but in this case he was willing to take the risk because this book gave him at last a scientific prop for his faith.

Now he understood why he had an irrational antipathy to Darwinism from the very beginning. He had already been shown the fallacy of Marxism by a Unitarian minister, Philip Wicksteed, who wrote an article in *To-Day* criticizing Marx; and now it was Samuel Butler's turn to make Shaw conscious of the distinction between Darwin's *Evolution* and *Creative Evolution*.

When Samuel Butler invited Shaw to Clifford's Inn, he brought Salt with him, because, as he said, "All men who meet me for the first time take an instant dislike to me."

Henry Salt noticed that Shaw showed a profound reverence for Butler, although the two creative evolutionists could find no point of agreement. Butler was enthusiastic about Handel and despised Wagner, he liked bawdy jokes and scoffed at vegetarianism. It was only too obvious to Salt and Shaw that Samuel Butler nursed a private grievance against society which had never been transmuted into a political philosophy.

After this meeting, Salt and Shaw discussed the purpose of creation. Both agreed that civilizations did not grow with superb aimlessness, developing, declining and then leaving nought but emptiness: there was a purpose behind everything and Man was the instrument through which the Purpose was being fulfilled. Shaw's concept of God differed from the generally accepted one, for according to him, God was neither Omniscient nor Omnipotent and had to feel His way by trial and error. God was not all-merciful since each error involved endless suffering and therefore there was no room for pity because the Life Force, Shaw's pet name for God, needed sacrifices in order to learn. Salt and Kate thought this conception the most inhuman they had yet encountered. It was human sacrifice gone mad.

# Chapter Five

GEORGE BERNARD SHAW was now complaining that "my hours that make my days, my days that make my years, follow one another into the maw of Socialism; and I am left ageing and out of breath without a moment of rest for my tired soul".

There were two contemporaries from whom he longed to have approval as they belonged to a world, a spiritual world, which he hoped one day to inhabit. Tolstoy's peasant smock appealed to him, and so did William Morris's aesthetic blue shirt. In his opinion they were the opinion-makers of the day. Had these magnificent word-spinners exploited the art of lying they would, no doubt, have been honoured by those in authority, but instead, they did not hesitate to speak the truth.

Quite unexpectedly an invitation arrived from Hammersmith for George Bernard Shaw to dine with William Morris. This arose in a roundabout way: on a previous occasion, Shaw had thrown out a suggestion to Joynes, completely unpremeditated, of course, that as editor of *To-Day* he might do much worse than to run one of his much-rejected novels as a serial. Joynes selected for this *An Unsocial Socialist*, and was only too glad to follow it up with *Cashel Byron's Profession*. The success of these serials encouraged Annie Besant to publish *The Irrational Knot* and *Love Among the Artists* in her paper *Our Corner*. From now, whenever Shaw addressed meetings, the Chairman invariably introduced him as the 'famous author, greater in the opinion of many than Rhoda Broughton or Robert Louis Stevenson'. Never had an author, with no published book to his name, been so enthusiastically acclaimed. William Morris was one of the readers and he was sufficiently impressed to invite him to dinner at his London home.

This was not the kind of invitation whch Shaw entertained because, as a vegetarian, he rarely found anything edible. But to be in the presence of William Morris was not an opportunity to be missed. When he arrived in the Jaeger suit he wore for the occasion Mrs. Morris made no effort to disguise her disapproval of him for she half suspected that her husband had invited this young man as a suitable match for her daughter May, and this she would never permit. She loathed Shaw from the moment he entered and refused to be drawn into conversation with him, and when she heard that he did not eat meat or fish she refused to stay in the room. William Morris felt called upon to treat his visitor with a gentleness which disarmed the author of *An Unsocial Socialist*. He told Shaw that he would gladly give up every luxury both in furniture and diet and live in a white-washed room and feed on bread, cheese and apples.

They did not discuss literature or art, for these were subjects William Morris left for very intimate friends, but instead the host referred to the German elections, where he feared that Bismarck's iron fist would prevent the Socialists increase the number of seats, however much they gained in numbers, and then he boasted of the large audience, almost forty, that listened to him at Walham Green, a district Shaw knew only too well as he had lived nearby on his arrival in England. Morris complained that he was listened to with no enthusiasm by the puzzled crowd.

Shaw confessed to him that his grand resolve to devote at least four hours every day to imaginative writing was forgotten in the day-to-day work for Socialism; weeks went by with nothing to show but the trivial round of conferences and meetings but he was happy with it because it prevented him from becoming the degenerate *literateur* of the café and the brothel.

The visit had the effect of making Shaw feel a great man, there was no need for him now to wait until he was famous before he behaved as one. He demanded the right to think as he liked, live as he liked and especially to say the things others did not like.

Exuberance was the word which fitted him exactly. He was writing love-letters to seven women at a time and each one thought that she was the honoured one; he was confiding the same innermost secrets to all his friends and each one thought that he was the chosen one and honoured his confidence. He had become an incorrigible philanderer but he never refused or broke an engagement to pass a gallant evening. "If you once put off a lecturing engagement for any private consideration whatever, you are lost."

He did not hesitate to lecture each of his friends on their most intimate affairs; he cured their constipation, their financial worries and their awkward manners and taught them how to make love, how to conduct their business and how to educate the young: there was nothing too trivial for his omniscience. Life was an open book to him and he read rapidly and gauged the position quickly. As a matter of fact Shaw held chastity as the most inspiring of all the passions, and women found that they could talk to him and be with him on the basis of complete equality without fear of sex intervening.

.    .    .    .    .    .

His next engagement was at the Industrial Remuneration Conference and he brought the house down with the wittiest and the most daring statement of policy they had ever heard:

"It is the desire of the President that nothing should be said that might give pain to particular classes. I am about to refer to a modern class, the burglars, but if there is a burglar present I beg him to believe that I cast no reflection on his profession and that I am not unmindful of his skill and enterprise; his risks so much greater than those of the most speculative capitalist, extending as they do to risk of liberty and life, his abstinence; or finally of the great number of people to whom he gives employment, including criminal attorneys, policemen, turnkeys, builders of jails, and it may be the hangman.

I do not wish to hurt the feelings of shareholders or of landlords, any more than I wish to pain burglars. I will merely point out that all three inflict on the community an injury of precisely the same nature. . . ."

This witty interlude was based, of course, on the revolutionary assumption that all property was theft. His other Fabian colleagues, Sydney Olivier and Graham Wallas, saw in his humour an echo of the Union Debate. Having been themselves distinguished members of the University of Oxford, they were sorry that this clever Irishman had not had an opportunity of spilling his wit down the drain of college life; instead Shaw had settled into a perpetual adolescence, seizing every opportunity for a rag and always preferring the wild assertion to the qualified fact.

It was not long before he was asked to read a paper before the Economic Section of the British Association. These economists, after years of wandering in the Sahara of dried facts, thought that they might snatch a little fun by bringing in 'a man red-hot from the streets'. It was like a cat-lover introducing a tiger to cheer up his lonely home. They found the tiger exciting enough, for they reported that 'in a really brilliant address he sketched in the rapid series of steps by which modern society is to pass into social democracy. There was a peroration rhetorically effective as well as daring'.

In his address he prophesied alternations of industrial prosperity and decline, periodic wars of a world-shattering nature and then, the complete crash of the capitalist order.

This he had derived from his reading at the British Museum of Karl Marx, who remained to him the historian of the nineteenth century. Knowing that his audience held the typical ostrich opinions based on outworn fictions, he played havoc with these fictions, tearing them to pieces one by one, and led his listeners to believe that their academic studies completely unfitted them for their task.

A most unusual experience for an academic gathering was the sudden outburst by Henry Sidgwick, the professor of political economy and ethics at the University of Cambridge. He sprang up and shouted, "This man is a criminal and I will not countenance his presence!" and, walking off the platform, left the room, violently slamming the door behind him. Yet, Henry Sidgwick was known to be the gentlest of all people and had never in his life been known to have lost his temper.

Sidney Webb, who was disturbed by this incident, could not understand why Shaw insisted on giving an eccentric and individual twist to a purely impersonal argument. But Shaw was an Irishman, an incalculable creature, and Webb preferred to work out his moves in terms of calculable counters.

The Fabian Society was well able to hold such incompatible views within its narrow confines and Shaw liked working with people who totally disagreed with him. He was attracted to the Fabian Society just because it was possible to disagree and remain entirely friendly, and they, in spite of his extravagance of thought, knew that they could not do without him: for when he was not there the meetings lacked lustre, his half-truths were more stimulating than their arid display of fact. The Fabians, with all their advanced views, were a very respectable crowd, anchored to current fashions and sentiments, and Shaw continuously pointed out that the education and upbringing of these privileged and well-intentioned people was a serious obstacle to them, and he advised them to rid themselves of the evil effects of culture before attempting to help others. He made it his task to initiate them into the new spirit which was finding expression in the arts, but they seemed incapable of appreciating its appeal.

Under the leadership of Sidney Webb, the Fabian Society managed at least to hold together, while the Socialist League under William Morris was in a continual state of breaking-up. Shaw heard from Morris:

"I am trying to get the League to make peace with each other and hold together for another year. It is a tough job; something like worst kind of pig-driving I should think, and sometimes I lose my temper over it. It is so bewilderingly irritating to see perfectly honest men, very enthusiastic, and not at all self-seeking, and less stupid than most people, squabble so: and withal for the most part they are personally good friends together."

Shaw laughed to hear this from the exponent of 'Fellowship is Life'. "What a life!" he exclaimed.

As an art critic George Bernard Shaw started out with the notion that the private art galleries were in a conspiracy to prevent good art from being shown, therefore he was not influenced by the social status of the artist or his popularity. Famous artists found themselves ignored by him in his criticism while unknown artists were given space and appreciative comment. No doubt this attitude was due to his own failure to get his novels published, for he still believed that they were better than any of the novels sent to him for review. The Royal Academy was particularly distasteful to him, for he saw good paintings out-glared by the blazing reds and yellows, reeking from varnishing day when the other exhibitors worked up their canvases competitively to concert pitch. In his opinion such crimes made Burlington House a Chamber of Horrors.

He thought it a pathetic predicament for an artist to have to submit his works to people who felt that they could say yes or no to a painting after a fleeting glance. Years ago he had taken it for granted that the works shown at the Dublin Art Gallery had come down from heaven, but now he was actually seeing how the thing was manipulated. At Dublin he used to leave the Art Gallery with his perceptions quickened and the commonest landscape lit up before his eyes, but now, as a critic, his visits dulled his perception and he found difficulty in making his articles interesting. Art dealers would use every device to get him to extol certain artists; they did not offer him cash down for a favourable notice; it was more subtle than that. The older hands were experts in the art of humbugging the reporters, who, being only news men unable to tell a Greco from a Guido, or a Frith from a Burne-Jones, got on by praising eminent painters and ignoring beginners, were persuaded by the dealer that his latest speculation was a discovery of a new genius and the result was the usual conventional rose-water. George Bernard Shaw complained to William Morris of the tawdriness of an industry based on the sale of pleasure. As an art critic Shaw would often be asked for advice about art as a career. Roger Fry, just down from Cambridge with a science degree, told him that he contemplated taking up art and received an answer:

"I have gone into the subject of art and find there is nothing in it. It is all hocus-pocus."

Fry did not know how to retort because, like many young men, he was dazzled by Shaw's wit and deeply impressed by his stupendous experience.

William Morris, on the contrary, was attracting a large circle of artists and craftsmen whom he encouraged in every way, yet it consoled him to think of barbarism once more flooding the world, and, at last, real feelings and passions, however rudimentary, taking the place of hypocrisies. Men and women who made up the Socialist movement seemed to possess the qualities he despised; they were obstinate and vain and with an irritating cleverness. That George Bernard Shaw had these qualities to a maximum degree did not deter Morris from advising him to hold on to his art criticism because, however futile it was, it was better to have him as art critic than a mere flatterer. "Never mind failure," Morris would say, "the creative person seems to lose something with success, an indefinable something essential to the creative act. To lose the happy human touch is too bitter a price to pay for being a celebrity."

The last thing that Shaw wanted was to criticize other people's work when his own work should have been before the public, stirring the critics and arousing controversy. In many ways his position now had deteriorated since he had left Dublin, for he had come to appreciate the part that money played in life and he could not therefore throw over his work as he did as a cashier. He shuddered at the memory of his descent upon London: his ignorance, his shyness, his gawkiness, his shabbiness, but now that he had overcome all these shortcomings, the obstacles to success seemed even greater, for it was the ordinary man who rose to the top and not the genius. A moneyless condition was more frightening to him than death itself. He re-read his novels as a critic, that is, as though someone else had written them and he liked them, and saw only too clearly that it was the author's hostility to respectable thought and society which caused them to stay unpublished. He resolved that if he returned to the writing of fiction he would not be satisfied unless it drew hatred upon himself.

When he received an invitation from his Fabian colleague, Hubert Bland, to open a debate at the Blackheath Essay and Debating Society, he chose as his subject, "That Realism is the Goal of Fiction". He gave weeks of careful preparation to this lecture, writing it out in full with one eye on its effect on the audience and the other winking with amusement. He found it difficult to appear spontaneous and natural without meticulous preparation. To put his audience at ease, he addressed them as 'pestilential and uncleanly minded old fools' and warned them that he was going to mention everything that he dared not mention. He then proceeded to inform them in the gentlest manner that he despised their opinions because they thought that it was the business of the artist to please. To please whom? The same work of art could possibly please the bookmaker and the author, the navvy and the philosopher. His thesis was that the time was ripe for the emergence of an extremely unpleasant and unpalatable author, one who would tackle the large number of shams, repressions, sentimentalities, insincerities and ideals of which the English were so proud. As an example he referred to the pointed omission of the influence of the intimate sex life on the character and destiny of men and women. It was like the absence of atmosphere in respectable painting. He welcomed the Depressionist in fiction as he had welcomed, as an art critic, the Impressionists in painting.

His definition of Realism was 'that fiction, in which men and women recognized their own feelings and passions'.

He complained that fiction was so divorced from life that it played havoc with love-making because people generally gained their information about love and marriage from novels written by sedentary cowards who traded on deception, cowards who should be summarily penalized. Though Shaw was deadly serious in all he said, his lecture was greeted with convulsive laughter. When asked to name a contemporary realist, his answer was the usual modest one, 'You will not have heard of him, his work has only appeared in serial form in two minor magazines.'

Two women were now tugging at his soul and he was playing one against the other. Annie Besant first heard him speak at the Ethical Church, South Place, Bishopsgate, and went away with a profound revulsion to him, for he had held himself up as a scoundrel, a sponger and a loafer. She expressed her disgust in an article in the *Reformer* and vowed that she would take the first opportunity to show him up. A year later, in the spring of 1885, it came to her notice that this 'monster' was to speak at the Dialectical Society on Socialism and she decided to attend this lecture with the sole object of annihilating him. She was easily as good an orator as he, and Socialism to her was anathema. Instead she was converted to Socialism by his slashing rhetoric and asked him to nominate her for membership of the Fabian Society. From then he assumed the personality of a saint in her eyes. She and Shaw spent long evenings together playing duets, and she, completely unmusical, worked for hours secretly practising her parts, so that she could keep up with him. She tried her utmost to make him a likable figure in society, because she was certain that his crushing brilliance and satirical style of address prevented him from becoming the leader he was destined to be. She tried to get him to stand for the School Board where he could speak for the despairing children, but he could not work up sufficient enthusiasm for the disgusting school buildings and the work done in these prisons. She pleaded that the only alternative for these children was roaming the streets and growing up illiterate; the schools were warm and dry and a harbour from the elements. "So is prison," Shaw replied, and dismissed the subject because it brought up too many painful memories. She approached him about the creation of a new church which would include all who have the common ground of faith in and love for man, but he laughed the sardonical laugh which always repulsed her: "I am just the person to call the *righteous* to repentence."

With Kate Salt it was a desire to liberate him from dreary criticism and the over-intellectualized atmosphere about which she was always complaining. She was willing to pay for the publication of all his novels and to give him enough money to devote all his time to writing. But again he laughed, for he knew that his novels would not bring a penny and the atmosphere of the Fabian Society was necessary to him; but her pity had been aroused and she undertook to do all his clerical work for him. This he accepted with alacrity, for he could boast of having a secretary of the highest status.

The so-called progress of the country was bringing in its wake a host of evils and the greatest of these was the increasing number of unemployed. There was a spirit of insurrection everywhere and according to Hyndman and Morris the governing class was trembling in its shoes. Hyndman had a way of magnifying his importance by conveying to the crowds that every time he uttered a rebellious sentiment, it went at once to the ears of the Prime Minister. George Bernard Shaw differed from the revolutionaries, for while they were urging the people to overthrow the government, he maintained that the people were not ready to take over government and had very little understanding of what Socialism stood for.

The unemployed marched through the fashionable streets of London and generally finished up with a demonstration in Trafalgar Square. The shopkeepers and the well-to-do residents were panic-stricken and sent a deputation to the Home Secretary, Henry Matthews, with the plea that this flaunting of poverty degraded the country in the eyes of the world. When Sir Charles Warren, Chief of the Police, heard of the demonstration to be held in Trafalgar Square, he visualized the swelling of the army of the poor and the disinherited to dangerous proportions and prepared a surprise for the demonstrators.

On November 13th, 1887, contingents of the unemployed and

their sympathizers assembled at the appointed places for the great march towards the Square. The enthusiasm was immense. Shaw, sensing what might happen, appealed to his section not on any account to be provoked into violence. "If we can hold our heads, and hold them high, we'll win." The extremist leaders did not hide their contempt for him and his appeal was received in silence.

His section marched on, arousing sympathy and attracting followers all along the route. As they approached the Square, there was a sudden charge by the police who were awaiting them with uplifted truncheons. Men, women and children fell under the hail of blows. Then ensued a still more savage scene: a rattle of cavalry and up came the Life Guards, and they were followed by the Scots Guards with bayonets fixed and ready to fire.

Shaw showed great presence of mind and courage by moving on without moving off. Strangely enough it brought back memories of his boyhood days with the street fights and he felt elated that there was not an ounce of fear in his make-up on this occasion. He came out of the scrimmage neither bloody nor bowed. Afterwards he heard that Cunninghame Graham and John Burns had been arrested for "unlawfully assaulting the police while in the discharge of their duties". A topsy-turvy world indeed! These two men stole the laurels while he had to bear the reputation of coward.

The economic crisis subsided and the 'impotent windbags', as he termed the agitators, ceased to dazzle the crowd, for the movement was like a cork carried on the tide of discontent. Shaw took advantage of the lull by bringing the intelligentsia up to date in their economics and facts, for he preferred fact to millenial vision. "Clever orators who dazzle the crowd with utopian visions do not satisfy the discontented because whatever is achieved falls far short of the allurement."

He edited a book of Fabian essays compiled from addresses delivered by seven Fabians. Two of these essays were by himself: the *Economic Basis of Socialism* and the *Transition to Social Democracy*. The other contributors were Sidney Webb, Graham Wallas, Sydney Olivier, William Clarke, Annie Besant and Hubert Bland.

Shaw knew that he could not contribute much that was of an original nature but his trenchant style amply justified his inclusion in the series. His vivid examples drawn from life brought home points more successfully than theorizing would have done. For example, in discussing 'Value', an arid and confusing abstraction, he gives this instance:

"A New York lady, having a nature of exquisite sensibility, orders an elegant rosewood and silver coffin, upholstered in pink satin, for her dog. It is made; and meanwhile a live child is prowling barefooted and hungerstunted in the frozen gutter outside. The exchange value of the coffin is counted as part of the national wealth; but the nation that cannot afford food and clothing for its children cannot be allowed to pass as wealthy because it had provided a pretty coffin for a dead dog."

The point Shaw wished to make was that exchange value had become bedevilled and, instead of representing utility, only signified the cravings of lust, folly, gluttony and madness, technically described by genteel economists as 'effective demand'.

He proved an exemplary editor, correcting elaborately and repeatedly, and it was through him that the Fabian Essays maintained a high literary level. One of his difficulties was that the essayists included minds of very different types, especially perhaps those of Sidney Webb and Hubert Bland, but Shaw refused to Webbulize Bland or to Blandulate Webb, for he insisted on retaining and even emphasizing the particular approach and style of each contributor. They all agreed that capitalism was a tawdry business and that the source of our social misery was not an eternal well-spring of confusion and evil but only an artificial system capable of almost infinite adaptation at the will of man. They looked to economic science to marshal the facts and to work out solutions and then it was for the people to bestir themselves and make an end of capitalism by gradual and decisive change.

Hitherto the economists had always treated wealth as though it could be measured by exchange value. Ruskin had exposed this as a fundamental error; a profound religious, social and philosophic error, in short a damnable heresy. Ruskin had introduced the conception of 'illth' as a positive thing to be measured and dealt with as urgently as 'wealth'. Shaw thought it his duty to give new life to academic economics by bringing it into direct relation with human passion. The problem was: how were the people to bestir themselves, once they had graduated in this science of regeneration. He made it clear that all the mobs and guillotines in the world could no more establish socialism than police coercion could avert it. It would be such a slow development that it was not even necessary to use the words socialism or revolution. In fact, the Socialists and Revolutionaries had given the movement such a bad name that it was wiser to enter the other progressive parties and work through them.

Shaw complained to Sidney Webb that his own original judgements, forged in the fire of inspiration and tempered by contemplation, read as platitudes, and his comprehensive, analytical faculty was held suspect by the specialists. Only his frivolous, unthinking comments were accepted as world-shaking pronouncements by the people who did not count. But Webb assured him that the new generation looked to the Fabians for guidance, even though the popular Press never reported their speeches. It was true enough: their meetings attracted mostly teachers and technicians, typists and students, who came with a smile on their faces, knowing that Shaw would dispose of one aunt sally after another and Webb would supply the facts.

From the point of view of sales, therefore, the Fabian Essays were a great success. The first edition and the second impression sold out immediately and then the book was given over to a publisher instead of being packed and sent off from his house by the honorary secretary as the orders came in.

Strangely enough there was no essay on the Fine Arts in this series. William Morris would have been the ideal writer but he despised the Fabian Society for its drawing-room background, and the next best would have been George Bernard Shaw. This would have meant a third article by him and he had no intention of Shavianising the book. When, however, the Society was at a loss for a course of lectures, Annie Besant, impressed by the criticisms she had read of Ibsen and convinced that a writer who could be called 'bestial, cynical, disgusting, poisonous and indecent' must have some quality in him, suggested a course of lectures on the dramatist. These lectures, she hoped, would prove an antidote to the abnormal sanity and indecent respectability of the Fabians. In her view there was only one person qualified to give them and that was George Bernard Shaw, and she was ready to preside.

The effect of Shaw's lectures on the packed hall was overwhelming. Annie Besant thought that she was listening to an oratorio: it was pure undiluted Shaw. He had set out to discover Ibsen and landed on the New Woman, a much more desirable prospect. He meant to reveal the soul of woman and to point out, with all the vigour at his command, that man must wake up to the perception that, in killing women's souls, they were killing their own. How many women would marry if they had known as much about marriage a week before the wedding as they did six weeks after? The world suffered from a lack of frankness, as if it were afraid that hell would be revealed if the truth were told. A Karl Marx was necessary, a Marx with his terrible powers of invective and analysis.

These lectures were extended into a book and published under the title of *The Quintessence of Ibsenism* after he had toyed with the thought of calling it *A Guide to Woman*. This book became the banner of the emancipated woman. Ibsen had always declared that he had no special mission but that he was a poet and so to be judged, but Shaw read a social mission into his works and was also able to read his own ideas into the works of Ibsen. If Ibsen had read this book he would most certainly been shocked to find himself associated with ideas that had never occurred to him.

George Bernard Shaw could not help feeling, as he launched the book, that he was making possible, the devil knows who, someone of whom he would vehemently disapprove. Hyndman criticized the book for praising 'a portentous purveyor of commonplaces log-rolled by Archer and Shaw into being considered a genius'. In Shaw's opinion it was only because there was not a sensibly organized theatre for adults where the darkest tragedies of this modern life could be dealt with frankly, that he had to spend his precious days extolling the obvious.

Shaw claimed that he had put Ibsen on the map in this country, and this time not by denunciation but by praise. Even Henry Irving had to admit that Ibsen was in the air. Janet Achurch, a conscientious but unsuccessful actress, went to Irving and asked the great actor for financial help because her husband, Charles Charrington, and she were anxious to put on a comedy, *Clever Alice*, at the Novelty Theatre. Irving at once sent her £100 with which Janet Achurch and Eleanor Marx-Aveling put on *A Doll's House*. Irving made no comment and actually went to see the play and was depressed by the performance.

Charles Charrington was a mild Irish idealist with an enthusiasm for whatever was fine in literature and the drama and it was he who produced Ibsen's play, mainly, in this instance, to bring out his wife as a great actress, for he believed that she would compare favourably with Ellen Terry and might even make a greater name for herself, because she was brave enough to do unpopular plays. The play was talked of and written about as no play had been for years and the performances were extended from the usual seven to twenty-four, and the Charringtons lost only £70.

William Archer, the translator of Ibsen and dramatic critic to the *World*, was taken aback by the howl of protest from his colleagues. He became gloomy and pessimistic and gradually convinced himself that the play must have run for about three nights only amid 'a hail of dead cats, sixteen a shilling eggs, brick bats and ginger-beer bottles and that on the fourth night there was no audience whatever'. He complained that Shaw was an Irish lunatic, whose head was turned by his first acquaintance with a pretty actress. That Shaw had fallen for this actress, Janet Achurch, was known to everyone, for he presented a miserable spectacle of infatuation. In his own words, "I found myself suddenly magnetized, irradiated, transported, fired, rejuvenated, bewitched."

This infatuation inspired him to write a sequel to *A Doll's House* which Archer read and begged him not to publish because it was 'slosh, rubbish, dull, dreary, philistine stuff and not even comic'. He also advised Shaw never to attempt creative work when infatuated.

Shaw was appalled by the ignorance of the dramatic critics and wrote to Janet on 21st April, 1892:

"They look at plays, *Lady Windermere's Fan* is an instance, in which there is one actress supported by a crowd of people, not one of whom is better than a fairly good walking gentleman or a lady; and they write columns about it without one line to show that they have perceived any shortcomings. Therefore dont attend to any of them; but listen with the greatest respect to *my* opinion."

From that moment he took Janet Achurch in hand and taught her the art of acting. He begged of her to cultivate the beautiful, reposeful, quietly expressive, infinitely inflectionable normal voice, neither raised nor lowered, which is the great charm of a fine speaker.

"I am not to be propitiated by any increase in tragic power, however striking. Anybody can be tragic if they are born so; but that every stroke shall be beautiful as well as powerful, beautiful to the eye and ear; that is what I call art."

He told her that he goes to the theatre to be *moved*, not pained, and warned her that he was writing a tragedy for her.

Within a short time he informed her that he cried off the tragedy because he could write nothing beautiful enough for her, and that he could no longer allow himself to be in love with her because "nobody short of an archangel with purple and gold wings shall henceforth be allowed to approach you".

Instead of writing a play, Shaw reviewed his own works of fiction for the *Novel Review*. Because of the extreme difficulty of finding anyone else who had read his novels, he had to do it himself. After a long and rather tedious analysis of his novels, he concluded:

"On the whole, after having more than once considered the advisability of consigning the four novels I have mentioned to the oblivion which shrouds that desperate first attempt which has never seen the light I have come to the conclusion, based on some experience as a reviewer of contemporary fiction, that Mr. Mudie's subscribers are very far from having reached that pitch of common sense at which they can decently pretend that my novels are not good enough for them. From their point of view the business of the fictionist is to tell lies for their amusement. Middleclass respectability, out of the depths of the unspeakable dulness of its life, craves for scenes of love and adventure . . . but there are readers who have sufficient experience and sense of reality to require a much higher degree of verisimilitude from fiction if it is to produce any illusion for them."

He recommended to them the works of his youth "in spite of their occasional vulgarity, puerility and folly". Then he wound this up by a plea to publishers:

"If any publisher is in search of a novelist whose popularity is advancing by leaps and bounds, it is possible that a handsome offer might tempt me back to the branch of literature which I originally cultivated."

# Chapter Six

IN spite of William Morris's advice, George Bernard Shaw threw over his art criticism when an article by him was shelved and instead there appeared, under his own name, a note obviously written by the wife of the proprietor of the paper, expressing her high opinion of artists unknown to him, who had won her gratitude by their generous hospitality. The ecstatic little raptures were obviously the result of invitations to fashionable studio functions. The shelved article merely stated that "the Impressionists are finding that their particular form of naturalism is as natural as light itself, while we in England insist that all things that matter should be kept *dark*".

It so happened at this time that a fellow Irishman, T. P. O'Connor, had started an evening paper called the *Star* and was on the look-out for promising journalists, and George Bernard Shaw was invited to send an article. This was a heaven-sent opportunity to do what he had always longed to do, that is, castigate everybody and everything in the political world. The sample article sent a cold shiver down the Editor's spine, because it would have killed the paper in one blow. Since Shaw was without employment, the Editor asked him for another suggestion and the reply came, 'Music criticism at two guineas a column'.

It was agreed that Shaw should fill a column every week with a pot-pourri of tomfoolery with genuine writing and to call it 'musical criticism'. He signed his articles by the Italian for the basset horn, *Corno di Bassetto*, and this gave his articles an aristocratic air, and, since it was written by a foreigner, an air of authority.

Corno di Bassetto was soon regarded by the readers as a privileged lunatic, and his fierce unwarranted criticism of English customs and institutions were only tolerated because they were written with wit and humour. The readers had to admit however that he showed a remarkable knowledge of music.

Once, in a meeting with Dr. Francis Hueffer, the music critic of *The Times*, Shaw declared that English society did not care about music and did not know good music from bad. Hueffer replied indignantly that Shaw knew nothing about it and that nobody had ever seen him in really decent society; he accused Shaw of moving only amongst cranks, Bohemians, unbelievers, agitators and generally speaking riff-raff of all sorts; and that he was merely theorizing emptily about the people whom he called bloated aristocrats.

This was a reference to William Morris, Sidney Webb, Henry and Kate Salt, Joynes and Annie Besant, Sydney Olivier, Graham Wallas and Prince Kropotkin, who were all summed up under the generic title of 'riff-raff'.

Music was Shaw's native world but he never felt at home in a concert hall. Poor Corno di Bassetto went to the St. James's Hall, where the concert-goer went for everything; there were the popular classical performances at the Crystal Palace; there were the provincial festivals with their eternal round of dreary oratorios, and there were the strictly social occasions when he was supposed to ignore the programmes entirely and refer only to the dresses worn by the celebrities. His response was not always predictable, for when invited to attend a Salvation Army Festival, where forty trombones played together and got effects which had never been excelled, he rose in defence when these bands were attacked by other critics and he declared that he looked forward to the time when the churches would ring with brass and people would dance and sing in them. He went as far as asking General Booth, the head of the Salvation Army, to attempt acting little plays at his services and offered to write one. General Booth unfortunately informed him that the writing of a cheque would take far less time and would be more acceptable. This was beyond even Shaw's ability.

His sister Lucy was ashamed of her brother posing as an expert in music, and whenever she was asked what he was doing, her answer was: "Nothing." She could talk like that because she was playing at last in a popular success, a light opera called *Dorothy*, of which her brother said, "Nothing but the most ghastly and widespread starvation of the affections could make such poor fare marketable." Mrs. Carr Shaw read the column by Corno di Bassetto on music without discovering the identity of the writer and it established at last a subject they could agree about, for both concurred in denouncing the outrageous sentiments and thoughts expressed by the irresponsible critic, but she was pleased to read that this music critic visited schools and wrote careful and sympathetic criticisms of the choirs.

One reader of the *Star* called Shaw an Ass and received this modest reply:

"Sir Isaac Newton confessed himself an ignorant man; and though I know everything that he knew, and a good deal more besides, yet relatively (relatively mind) I am almost as ignorant as he. The term ASS I take to be a compliment. Modesty, hard work, contentment with plain fare, development of ear, under-

Dr. Gurly

Dr. Edward Aveling

William Archer

Harley Granville-Barker

1904. The Court
Theatre period

estimation by the public: all these are the lot of the ass and the last of the Bassettos."

It was discovered that this columnist was the Shaw who talked Socialism to the dockers, who went down to Bow to help the match-workers when on strike, who travelled a hundred miles to address a meeting of a half a dozen miners, and who was the President of the Local Government Board at the Charing Cross mock Parliament (not to be confused with Westminster). And it was he who declared in his Preface to the *Fabian Essays*:

> "There are at present no authoritative teachers of Socialism. The essayists make no claim to be more than communicative learners."

*Learner* he certainly was, for while others seemed to have come out of their cultural discipline with, at least, a code of conduct, there was no such code in his case. He wrote to Webb, "Morality means custom; and it is custom that tyrannizes over most people's minds." His belief in the super-personal force threw him entirely on his own resources, causing him to build up his spiritual reserves and his knowledge as he went along, often denuding him of all sense of right and wrong and leaving him with cunning only to help him through impasse after impasse. Webb knew exactly what he wanted others to do, knew how to use people to further his schemes; the thought of a sentimental association was utter waste to him. With Shaw an intimate relationship was necessary and he yielded to Webb and permitted himself to be used to the last inch by him. The dominance of Webb, the one-track mind over a comprehensive character like Shaw, amazed those outside the Fabian coterie, for they now heard Shaw refer to artists as vagabonds, to administrators as the salt of the earth, to blue books as the only readable literature and that the people needed tracts and more tracts, not romance but statistics.

There was a large humiliated element in him, due no doubt to his early life, and by his abject failure as an artist, the one vocation he had desired. He would fight like a giant and as suddenly retreat like a coward. When told that his writing was beautiful, he felt like the lady who disfigured her face to repel her admirers.

Throughout this period he suffered from periodic headaches, and all his efforts to get rid of them failed. He fasted, stopped eating pulses and potatoes and ate only dates and nuts but to no effect. He put it down to his helpless years in Dublin when he fed with the servants in

F

the kitchen. Now at last, because the first vegetarian restaurant had been opened, he could have a meal more to his liking. Shaw was not a heavy eater, preferring tasty tit-bits and especially wholemeal bread buttered very thickly, for this reminded him of those very rare occasions when his mother took it into her head to feed him as Lee advised her.

To all appearances, Shaw was now a successful man. The jaunty air, the dogmatic utterances conveyed an assured and integrated person with no inner conflict or tension; he personified what he stood for: the New Man, liberated intellectually and physically, who could talk about politics, art, music, drama, sex and science, cooking and dress with an air as if he had invented these things. Tomorrow might bring new ideas, and if they contradicted all he had expressed the previous day it did not matter, for like Emerson, he held himself above such trivialities as consistency and fashion.

The Shaw family was well in the limelight, for Royalty had visited the North London Collegiate School in the person of the Princess of Wales, and Lucy was being acclaimed in the provinces as a success in *Dorothy*. Every night at the stage door titled young men greeted her with offerings of flowers and jewels, and more than one provincial blood dreamed that it would be paradise to live with her. Then she discovered a man, also playing a minor part in *Dorothy*, and agreed to marry him because he was the antithesis of her brother. She announced her marriage to her mother and to her brother after the event. According to Lucy her mother-in-law was the ideal person, for she was an adept at conventional behaviour and so was able to give Lucy the social training she had always craved for. She learned to distinguish what was nice from what was not nice, what was correct and what was not correct, who were the right people and who were the wrong people to know.

It did not take her long, however, to discover that her pretty husband drank and gambled and had other loves. Lucy walked out of her house, sought a divorce, obtained one and then, after a while, permitted her ex-husband to break his loneliness by her fireside.

George Bernard Shaw was now offered £5 a week to act as music critic to the *World*, and he persuaded himself that this paper would give more scope for his technical knowledge; he dropped his pseudonym and signed his articles by the mere initials G.B.S. In this paper there now appeared at the same time William Archer on the Drama and Shaw on Music.

A miraculous invitation came from an Anglo-Dutch Ibsen enthusiast who had started the Independent Theatre, convinced that there were in England hundreds of dramatic masterpieces shunned by the commercial stage. He had discussed the matter with the Charringtons and they suggested that George Bernard Shaw might be approached, for though this music critic knew nothing about dramatic construction, he might be persuaded to permit William Archer to dramatize *An Unsocial Socialist*. J. T. Grein approached Shaw and was promised an original play within a few days guaranteed to set London on fire.

The play was slow in arriving, for Shaw found, as always, far too many distractions and could find time for writing only when travelling on buses or waiting to address meetings. The whole world conspired to prevent the completion of the play: there was the General Election when Webb and he had to provide a policy for the Liberal Party; there was the marriage of Sidney Webb to an heiress, Beatrice Potter, a fact which threatened to break up his friendship with Shaw, and there was the death of Lord Tennyson and the scheming to get William Morris to accept the Poet Laureateship.

He had not mastered the art of finishing a play. He was at a loss to know what to do with his characters if he was to avoid murder, divorce and a sensational climax. Ibsen gave him the clue: the discussion. For the first time in his life the characters he had created would leap off the paper and become incarnate. Inspired by this vision, he fished out the old play he had started with William Archer, added a third act, called it *Widower's Houses* and handed it to Grein with the warning that it would mean the death of the Independent Theatre as it depicted middle-class respectability and younger son gentility fattening on the poverty of the slum as flies fatten on filth.

Shaw made no effort to introduce a ray of hope into the play and it was only too obvious to Grein, when he read it, that all the characters would be hissed off the stage. They found it impossible to get an actor to play the part of the rent collector, a part as difficult to fill as that of a prostitute. During the rehearsals over a public house in Maiden Lane, a young man poked his head in by accident and Grein at once asked him to read the part of Lickcheese, and was so pleased with the reading that he felt that the play might be redeemed after all. James Welch, the man who had strayed in, threw up the part when Shaw was present because he could not stand the man in the light-grey stockinette one-piece suit. Grein had to assure him that this 'one-piece' man was not a character in the play.

The first performance provoked a sensational mixture of applause and hooting. The author came forward on the stage in his dazzling Jaeger suit and stunned the audience into the belief that he was not of this world at all, but had descended from the moon. The second and last performance brought a different audience entirely, an audience that listened intently and seemed to consider it a great occasion. The author now felt like a god who had created human beings and found them bad.

"Would the world ever have been created," he asked Grein, who was depressed about the failure of this effort, "if the Maker were afraid of making trouble? Making life means making trouble."

The critics took the easy course of comparing him with Ibsen and always to Ibsen's advantage. They now found much to commend in Ibsen. Ibsen had humour, Ibsen had a good dramatic story to tell, Ibsen had theatre technique, for every stroke led up to the climax; but with Shaw the play rolled all over the place and the characters failed to interest. Even his Fabian colleagues preferred to ignore the play. While his novels remained unpublished they liked to think of him as an unacknowledged genius, but now this play proved him, according to the critics, a dabbler in a medium alien to him.

Shaw on the other hand felt that he had found his true vocation at last and vowed that if he had to give twenty years to it he would master the technique. He considered Ibsen the end of an era, while he trumpeted in the beginning. The praise of Ibsen coincided with the praise of Shelley whom they were at that moment celebrating at Horsham on the centenary of his birth. Shaw heard Edmund Gosse declare:

"Encouraged by universal public opinion and by dignitaries of all professions, yes, even by prelates of our national church, we are gathered here as a sign that the period of prejudice is over, that England is in sympathy at last with her beautiful wayward son, understands his great language, and is reconciled to his harmonious ministry."

Small wonder that Shaw made the suggestion in the *Albemarle Review* that Shelley be represented on a bas-relief in a tall hat, Bible in hand, leading his children on Sunday morning to church.

With the hissing of his play still in his ears, he went to see his dying friend Joynes at West Hoathly. For the first time in his life, the thought of death did not make him chuckle. Joynes was one of the few people with whom a frank interchange of opinion was possible.

"It doesn't matter if I go," Joynes said to Shaw, "we have achieved what we set out to do; we've started the world moving in the right direction at last. I'll be forgotten and you'll be forgotten but the world will carry something of us."

"If a dozen of us could go on for a hundred years or so we'd change life beyond recognition," Shaw answered.

On what did they base their optimism? Certainly not on statistics. The Fabian Society did not number more than two hundred; the Social Democratic Federation numbered a thousand perhaps and the Socialist League half that number, and yet they all felt that they were winning through: every failure at the polls was a moral victory and every rebuff was an 'extra nail in the coffin of the capitalist class'. They were certainly not a mutual admiration society: to hear William Morris talking about Hyndman and Hyndman about Shaw caused one to wonder what kind of bed could possibly hold such fellows together? They were all united in stirring up the needs and wants and wishes of unhappy men.

The second play would be an exposure of Ibsenism. It was written in response to a challenge from Florence Farr, the actress who played Blanche in *Widower's Houses*, that it was a simple matter to expose economic evils for they were there for all to see, but would he have the courage, like Shakespeare, to expose his soul to the world? In answer, Shaw built up Charteris, the chief character in his second play, *The Philanderer*, and made him a contemptible, cynical, heartless young man who attracted one woman after another and many at the same time because he behaved towards women without the respect due to their sex. Charteris regarded advanced views as merely a fashion, picked up and followed without understanding.

The effect of this play was even more devastating than the first. William Archer took this play as a personal insult; Janet Achurch refused to act in it and Florence Farr did not want to hear the brutal callous words uttered in her presence. It had no artistic merit to compensate for its brutality. Grein found it impossible to find an actor to take the part of Charteris and once more George Bernard Shaw failed as a dramatist. Yet Shaw wanted this play produced and persisted in finding a stage for it, for he loved this play as a mother loves her mongol child. He wrote to Janet Achurch:

"Never was there anything so heartless. I will complain of you to Charrington. I will have satisfaction, I will tear up by the roots all the fibres you have stirred in me, I will throw away my heart and soul and have my inside fitted with brass machinery and millstones."

The new drama in his opinion demanded new intellectual speech channels which must at first seem strange and artificial, even immature and disgusting. As a genius he was privileged to utter sedition, to blaspheme, to outrage good taste, to corrupt the youthful mind and generally to scandalize one's aunts and uncles. The audience must simply get accustomed to his iconoclasms, seditions and blasphemies.

His mind was a noisy workshop, working perpetually on the ideas he was gleaning on all sides. There was no escape from that brain of his. He was convinced that he had nine brains to compensate for the lack of one heart.

Sidney Webb's marriage upset the balance of the nine brains. George Bernard Shaw found nothing whatever to object to in Beatrice Potter, his friend's choice: she was very handsome, their interests were identical and her temperament was complementary to Sidney Webb's. For six years prior to her marriage she had devoted her free time in obtaining an inside knowledge of the homes and workshops of manual workers. Although she had an independent income of a thousand a year and was groomed to become the wife of a Prime Minister or of an Archbishop, she worked as a rent collector, and then as a sweated worker in the slums of London, and also collaborated with Charles Booth in his great enquiry into the *Life and Labour of the People*. She was the first of the Fabians to make Shaw feel an outsider, for she regarded him as a slum child picked up by Sidney from the gutter. At first she meant to take him in hand, but after reading *The Philanderer* she advised her husband to drop him, for it was obvious to her that Shaw was only seeking a flashy reputation. Her husband persuaded her that Shaw was useful to him and she had to admit that there were disabling gaps both in herself and in Sidney, for neither had the time to give to music or drama, to brood over a literary work or visit galleries. They had to admit: "Such dim inklings as we have of these great human achievements reaches us second hand through our friendship with George Bernard Shaw."

No one came forward to tell Shaw that he could write a play. William Archer expressed publicly, and his opinion carried great weight, that Shaw would never succeed as a playwright because he was hopelessly destitute of dramatic faculty. Webb, in the friendliest manner, warned him that such plays might well damage the hard-won reputation of the Fabian Society. Shaw confessed to himself that he really had no facility and had to slave and plod for bare life to make himself at all current.

Beatrice Webb could not get herself to like Shaw. She watched the two friends: Sidney had no glow of satisfaction at public applause while Shaw went out of his way to court it, even when he claimed that he despised it; Shaw was the ideal man on the platform, Sidney was the ideal man at the desk; Sidney sought an academic reputation of solid worth, Shaw sought a flashy reputation. Sidney was born for success in whatever he undertook, Shaw was doomed to failure. The only thing to do was to get the 'Sprite', as she called him, married off. He would not be an easy husband, tending to philander, to posture, and to poverty. She pondered on all the eligible middle-aged ladies she knew and classified them according to their interests, abilities and wealth. There was always this and that obstacle: now it was his diet, here it was his acute Bohemian temperament, then there was the insuperable obstacle of his dislike to be hampered by passion. Nobody could fall in love with a Sprite, she concluded.

This was the second time he had come across a truly perfect marriage. In the case of the Salts it was a sexless companionship, but with Beatrice and Sidney it was perfect because both hammered at the same anvil and forged the one sword. Shaw was in a dilemma: he wanted to partake of the happiness and at the same time to break it up. He had begun his life as a subtle disintegrator of households and now he admitted to himself, with all his cynical love of fact, that his genius for breaking up unions was working to full capacity. He accompanied them on their holidays at home and abroad, making himself indispensable in a thousand different ways, led the pair into argument and extended the difference of opinion to bursting point. This trait he called the 'female element in my make-up'. Sidney, for example, never felt the least need for religion, but Beatrice could not do without prayer. Shaw, as a mystical atheist and a free-thinking Protestant, knew exactly how to lead the argument to the precipice of misunderstanding. In his defence he would argue that the world was full of precipices and if these lovers were determined to walk into them, it was of no use trying to hold them back: over they must go. Then again, Sidney was tolerant about the infidelities of men like Hubert Bland and Edward Aveling, but Beatrice was a Puritan in such matters and so Shaw could watch the smoke turn into fire. Always the pacifier, Shaw was appreciated by both as such.

Beatrice Webb had never met a person like Shaw before. She had heard of artists, of course, but held all the prejudices of her middle-class Puritan upbringing. Artists were, to her, without regularity or system, extravagant and licentious, undependable and unpredictable. When she was invited by G. F. Watts to sit for him, she refused because she thought that to be painted was a form of vanity. She boasted that she had never a desire to go to the Royal Academy, and when told that William Morris was an artist she felt she understood why she could never read his works. She explained that she had not read Karl Marx because she had once met his daughter Eleanor and found that she showed signs of an unhealthy excited life kept up by stimulants.

Shaw was accustomed to triangles. He could claim that the world was not round because he was always involved in a triangle and that therefore the world must have been created in that shape. The *ménage à trois* of his childhood habituated him to it and so he was not ashamed of falling in love with Kate Salt and Janet Achurch and Florence Farr. He had to face the fact that marriage intensified his interest in his friends. When, for example, he met May Morris, he appraised her as a suitable wife for himself, but he said nothing and did nothing about it, until he heard that she had married Mr. Sparling, and then he foisted himself on both, living with them for quite a time, until the very patient husband complained. But this Webb business was different because his love was entirely on the male side: it was Sidney he could not do without.

She did not succeed in getting rid of Shaw and so did the next best thing and treated him as a domestic pet. She believed in propaganda through personal contact and the brilliant Shaw was used as a bait when she entertained the influential people of the day. The 'Sprite' might not have had a perfect social training but he could be relied upon to be extremely entertaining. He had a nasty habit of swallowing his food in record time, giving an adverse opinion on the cooking, tilting his chair to breaking point, refusing alcoholic beverages with a little lecture on their evil effect on clear thinking. He would come out with intimate confidences and treat the most important people as infants. This was disconcerting, but he was such a wonderful talker that an invitation to the Webbs was rarely refused when it was known that Shaw would be there. He did not mind singing to prove a point in music and reciting whole speeches from plays, and he did not hesitate to tell the visitors how to run their bodies as well as the body politic. A subject had to be mentioned and off he went: he talked about clearing the bowels with the same enthusiasm as clearing the slums, about public lavatories as well as public schools, about the conception of children as well as the creation of peers.

The interests of the Webbs were limited; when either of them started with 'we think', Shaw knew that he was not included, although all three were heavily afflicted with the bug of world-betterment. The lovers went on solving all the social problems at their dinner parties and giving Shaw material *ad lib* for his future plays. The Webbs did not know that Shaw while entertaining others was entertaining himself, for he wanted to meet the characters thrown up by the new world and all his thrusts and confidences were aimed at bringing out the essential nature of the guests. He preferred meeting these people to becoming involved in literary and artistic coteries where the gossip went on endlessly about adulteries and royalties.

The Webbs spoke as if they were the State, but Shaw spoke as if he were God Himself. Jealousy was out of the question with him: his father was not jealous of Lee under more provocative conditions, and he had never felt the least jealousy of the husbands of the wives he adored. He wrote of Beatrice Webb:

"If only she were a perfectly free woman, I could put forth my subtleties and bring her to a point of view where we could really understand one another; but that would involve an intimacy even closer than Webb's."

"It is only by holding my edge steadily at the most delicately felt angle to her grindstone that I can avoid becoming hateful to her. The strain on my attention is as fatiguing as writing two articles a week."

"I, George Bernard Shaw, have actually suffered from something which in any one else I should call unhappiness. I would give anything for a moment of really sacred solitude."

Like Hamlet, he could come to no decision. Circumstances almost did it for him and he could only ascribe the accident to a strong death wish in him. How he avoided death on this occasion he could not explain. It seemed that the Life Force had work for him to do before he could be dispensed with entirely.

Sidney Webb, Bertrand Russell and Shaw went for a cycle expedition on the Chepstow Road; Shaw wished to prove how daring he could be on the machine; with his feet on the rests he went at a speed which took the machine miles beyond his control. Bertrand Russell was ahead of him and Webb well behind him. Shaw gave himself up to a headlong tearing toboggan down the steep hill. At that moment, Russell jumped off his machine and turned it right across Shaw's path in order to read the signpost. Smash! Shaw flew through the air for several yards and smote the ground like a thunderbolt. Statistically, if all three had been killed it would have meant three fewer people in a world of millions, but it would have meant a spiritual catastrophe of the worst order.

Shaw had an opportunity of describing this incident in a letter reminiscent of his father's description when, as Bob, he had fallen through a window-pane and the result, fortunately, was no worse. In his subtle analysis of his relationship with Beatrice, he overlooked one simple but important consideration: he could not take her life in hand as he had done with the others. He never wrote long letters to her, telling her how to do her work, how to conduct herself in company, how to behave with Sidney, operating on her as he did with the others, because she had no need, neither would she have permitted it.

While staying with the Webbs in Monmouthshire, Shaw wrote his third play: *Mrs. Warren's Profession*. Here in this active and very serious atmosphere the play progressed bravely. Every morning he sat down without an idea in his head, having no knowledge what his characters had been doing with themselves while he left them alone, but he had to lift his pen and at once they began to talk. There was hardly a person among them whom he wanted to know and if they were alive he would have gone miles to avoid them. Yet here, in this amazingly beautiful place, his imagination had to conjure up a number of extremely disagreeable people to make his life tolerable with the spooning Webbs. Why, he asked himself, must I create a mother, a deplorable old rip? Shaw did not mind the daughter because he had always been fascinated by mathematicians and she was one. The plot, in so far as there was a plot, was that the mother, uncertain of the girl's father, kept all the old men at bay by telling each one that he was the parent. There had to be a grand discussion with both sides equally matched, in this case between the daughter and her mother.

Beatrice Webb was not sorry to hear that the play was banned. He had read the play to them as a change from discussing endlessly the people they knew, or amusing themselves with self-analysis. She had warned him that people would be attracted by the vice and not the wisdom and called him the master of the Immorality play. Sidney, who understood Shaw better, had to contradict her by agreeing with her entirely, but "all the same there is something in Shaw's method of inoculating the people with their own poison". He reminded Shaw that it didn't do to enquire too deeply into the source of a parent's wealth. Most of the members of the Fabian Society sprang from the new rich who managed by their illgotten gains to send their children to the University.

"Why," Beatrice asked, "do advanced people consider the mere mention of the word, prostitution, a mark of emancipation?" and waited for the answer with a bland and innocent face.

Jack Grein, who had also read the play, exclaimed that Shaw had shattered his ideals, and William Archer disowned Shaw because, as he said, "Shaw could not touch pitch without wallowing in it."

Shaw enjoyed the position of being a banned author immensely. Instinctively he was drawn to the subjects that were considered too low to mention and he gloried in laying bare the most sordid aspects of life. He alone could argue that the white slave traffic was an economic problem; since brothels paid larger dividends than respectable hotels, capable business women could make more money as procuresses than as ordinary shopkeepers. Morality did not come into the matter.

His next play would deal with horrors which the world would consider entirely virtuous and moral. Graham Wallas, his brilliant Fabian colleague, criticized a book by Auguste Hamon, entitled *La Psychologie du Militaire Professionel*, and put forward the point that heroism was a form of hysterical cowardice. Shaw, recalling 'Bloody Sunday' at Trafalgar Square, saw in this thought an explanation of his own action on that occasion. Slum property and prostitution were unmentionable themes, but war, which involved the slaughter of human beings, was, in the eyes of humanity, a courageous and ennobling profession. He had met a Russian refugee, Stepniak, with whom he discussed the play he had in mind and was advised that Bulgaria was the most appropriate setting, for it was a country full of comedic possibilities; there soldiers won by running away and every innkeeper was an amateur general. Shaw at once thought of placing his friends, Sidney Webb, Cunninghame Graham and Annie Besant, in this comedic setting. As a genius without a success to his name he felt he had the right to guy his friends and expect them to take it in good heart.

He had no doubt whatever now that he was a genius and he studied the psychology of genius to place himself in the right category.

"There are two sorts of genius in this world" (he wrote to Florence Farr) "one is produced by the breed throwing forward to the godlike men and the other is the mere monster produced by the accidental excess of some faculty. I am a genius of the first order."

He knew where the file dealing with him would be found in the ultimate classification: "I know my order and the price I must pay for excellence."

While engaged on this, his fourth play, *Arms and the Man*, he had a rare visit from Oscar Wilde, the other Dubliner who had taken London by storm and was reputed to be making £8,000 a year and spending ten thousand pounds. Wilde called for a little chat which extended for hours. The two Irishmen watched the twilight turn to dawn and they were still talking. They discussed the failure of Shaw's plays and Wilde insisted on calling them an 'infamous success' and asked Shaw why he considered it necessary to give his characters a trade or profession. "The unpleasant necessities of the world need not throw their shadows on the stage," Wilde argued. "I go out to amuse the dead, while you go out of your way to pain the living. In a choice between pain and pleasure few have the knowledge that pain is more beneficial."

Shaw gave Wilde the usual avuncular advice about the passion for chastity and abstinence, the two greatest passions, in his opinion: "Indulgence makes me less critical of my work."

Wilde was unimpressed. "An author must not be in a condition to criticize his work; he must be carried away by it."

Shaw accepted this as being true of Wilde, for while he himself worked hard at his humour, Wilde played with everything, with wit, with philosophy, with drama and with actors and audience, in fact with the whole theatre.

"Think," Wilde added, "what a great literature we might have had if it were not for the reading public and what great dramas would have been written if there were no theatres. The author or dramatist becomes self-conscious and therefore not at his best when he is mindful of the public!"

He implored Shaw to throw over Ibsen and to stop humouring the workers. "Work at humour by all means, but always avoid fashion if you do not wish to be out of date within six months."

Shaw countered with the opinion that Ibsen's reputation grew with every failure. He had himself in mind when he talked in Ibsen's defence; he spared no pains to make known that his plays were built like Ibsen's to induce, not voluptuous reverie, but intellectual interest, not romantic rhapsody, but humane concern about immediate problems.

"I am far too much in advance of the time to be interested in fashion," Shaw replied.

Oscar Wilde could only shrug his shoulders and suggest that, in the ultimate analysis, success went only to those who could prove that they were well-connected and quoted from *Widowers' Houses*: "You have nothing but that Norfolk jacket. How are they to know that you are well-connected if you do not show it by your costume?"

It was probably the only sentence in the play that Wilde remembered and he must have awaited his opportunity to quote it. Shaw wished to suggest a course of colonic irrigation to Wilde, for as the evening wore on he became more and more conscious of the flatulence from which the opulent dramatist suffered. Beatrice had prescribed such a course of treatment for her husband and it made a world of difference to him. Oscar's need was very much greater for though his mind sparkled, his body was losing its buoyancy. Shaw led to the subject of diet and Wilde was amused, for to him it seemed that his fellow Dubliner had sentenced himself to a life of hard labour: he expressed obliquely that he would rather die than live without pleasure or happiness of any kind except the satisfaction of failure and 'progress'.

"I derive my horror of eating vegetables from the reading of Wordsworth and Coleridge, bless their souls, for it is they who taught me in my youth that plants had deeper feelings than animals. You say, my friend, that the creative appetite created Man as its particular organ. That is no particular compliment to the appetite. I would have stopped at flowers and vegetables for I have never seen the necessity for man. You and I are not men, *we* are *Artists*."

Their conversation naturally included references to Ruskin and to William Morris, for both these men were great influences in their lives.

"Ruskin made a point when at Oxford," Wilde said, "of turning ode-makers into roadmakers and in that way put me against work for the rest of my life, but William Morris was wiser, for he turned roadmakers into makers of odes and I worship him for it. You see, all four of us writhe under the lash of inconsequence because we dreamt of becoming painters and had to wake to the fact that we were only fitted to write."

Wilde left by cab and Shaw settled down to the completion of his war play. This visit of Wilde's animated him in a strange way: for while Oscar Wilde was sitting in the hygienic bamboo chair and he lay flat on the hard bedstead, the Wilde spirit had entered him and it came to him that unconsciously he had been translating himself into an Englishman and he laughed unconsciously at the thought, for he could see nothing in the world so exquisitely comic as an Englishman's seriousness. Yes, he had been taking himself far too seriously. Now, as he wrote, he laughed to himself and he seemed to hear Wilde laughing at his side. He was working off the reputation he had made on Bloody Sunday by dethroning heroics and heroism. After the strong and alert front he had to present to Beatrice, this exercise in humour was a great relief. When he read the play to the Webbs they were not amused: the placing of the scene in Bulgaria made it appear too remote and almost abstract; for them ideas began at home and finished there and they did not concern themselves with foreign affairs. In England men were sent across the Channel, or even the Atlantic Ocean, to defend our interests but war was a by-product and of no account. When Shaw suggested that his ridicule would abolish war from the face of the earth, Beatrice could only say: "Why do you concern yourself with such utterly frivolous matters? None of us will ever have to face a war."

"It is my work to think of the unthinkable," Shaw answered.

William Archer, on the other hand, was most impressed and told Shaw that he had redeemed his reputation as a dramatist. He thought the play the funniest he had ever read and confessed that it made him laugh hysterically.

"A man who can create such laughter," he said, "is worth his weight in gold."

## Chapter Seven

GEORGE BERNARD SHAW cultivated actresses of repute. He knew that the writing of a play was not enough, and that even a bad play well acted could be lifted to importance and a good play ruined by bad acting.

Florence Farr was producing modern plays at the Avenue Theatre with money provided by Miss Horniman, and he wanted her to put on *Arms and the Man*. He wrote to her:

"This is to certify that you are my best and dearest love, the regenerator of my heart, the holiest joy of my soul, my treasure, my salvation, my rest, my reward, my darling youngest child, my secret glimpse of heaven, my angel of the Annunciation, not yet herself awake, but rousing me from a long sleep with the beat of her unconscious wings, and shining upon me with her beautiful eyes that are blind. . . ."

He had to plead again and again: "It is by jingling the jester's cap that I, like Heine, will make people listen to me. All genuinely intellectual work is humorous. . . ."

Florence Farr put on *Arms and the Man* at the Avenue Theatre on April 21, 1894, with James Welch, who had appeared in *Widowers' Houses*, as Major Paul Petkoff and herself as Louka. It ran for eleven weeks, an enormous success in Shaw's eyes, and then it was put on by Richard Mansfield at the Herold Square Theatre in New York in September of that year. This helped to establish George Bernard Shaw in America as a dramatist to be watched.

Shortly after the run of this play, Shaw was asked by his American agent to write another play with an eye on box-office receipts, for the agent intended to groom this new playwright into a success like Pinero and Wilde. The answer came:

"What do you mean by giving me advice about writing a play with a view to box-office receipts? I shall continue writing just as I do now for the next ten years."

He mapped out a new play for Janet Achurch. *Candida* would be the story of a truly happy marriage and it would be the first play ever written to show understanding of a woman's soul. What a contrast it would be to his other plays. It would not have a cynical word in it and would be frank woman worship inspired by the Madonnas.

The action took place in a district never associated with ecstasy, Bethnal Green, a place inhabited by the poorest in London. Shaw knew Bethnal Green very well indeed for he had often addressed meetings in Victoria Park, where the folk were more responsive to philosophic argument than those in Hyde Park. If Hyde Park was a windbag's Paradise, Victoria Park was a poet's hell, for the very trees exuded misery and the grass was turned to mud before it could display its green. It was by the law of opposites that Shaw chose this place as a background to the play, for Candida grew in his brain in the glowing sunshine of Italy. It was a wise choice, for it would bring out the portraiture as in a Rembrandt painting.

He read it to different groups of friends. To Edward Carpenter and the Salts on one occasion, to the Webbs on another, to the Charringtons when he could get them both alone. With Carpenter the response surprised him. After the reading was over there was a long silence and then an exclamation which sounded like a 'boo'. "It wont do, it wont do!" Carpenter shouted and walked out.

With the Webbs the reception was even more derogatory, for it seemed to have hit right across Beatrice's Puritanism. " 'Tis pity she's a whore!" she exclaimed. "You seem to like them." She saw in Candida a commonplace woman, the usual unsatisfied wife who sought to recapture youth in her middle life by using feminine devices to humiliate both her husband and the romantic victim.

Shaw himself thought it the greatest play of the day, if not of the century. The Charringtons agreed with him, for they saw a great part in Candida and the making of Janet.

Shaw now set himself to mould Janet into the proper shape and he worked upon her as a sculptor until she would personify the person she was to portray. He would have her fast and meditate over the meaning of his sentences until they expressed the greatness he intended. He must train her voice which had become harsh since her tour in Australia and make it tender and yet all-pervasive, reaching to the hearts of the furthest seat in the gallery. When it was ultimately arranged to produce the play in New York, he wrote to Janet:

1904
Charlotte Shaw

I took this at Maybury Knoll, Woking early in the century — probably somewhere round about 1906.

It was evidently taken without a filter on the lens, as the values are all wrong, and the result is a dark man instead of a fair one.

As the hair is all disarranged I by the focusing cloth I must have been experimenting and not aiming at a portrait.

G. Bernard Shaw 1/12/30

**GEORGE BERNARD SHAW**

*From a photograph taken by himself and printed by F. H. Evans*

The keen photographer

20th March, 1895.

"You must part your hair in the middle, and be sweet, sensible, dignified and Madonna-like. If you condescend to the vulgarity of being a pretty woman, much less a flashy one, you are lost. Observe, Janet Achurch, what you have to do is to play the part. You have not to make a success. New York must notice nothing: it must say 'Of course', and go home quietly. If it says 'hooray!' then you will be a mere popular actress, a sort of person whom I utterly decline to know. You must confine yourself strictly to your business, and do that punctually and faithfully, undisturbed by any coveting of success for yourself or me or the play. It does not matter whether the play fails or not; it is sufficient if you gain the respect of the public and your fellow-artists."

In spite of this excellent advice he could not resist playing one actress against another. To Ellen Terry, with whom he was corresponding, he described the Mother play, and when she asked for just a peep at it, he informed her coldly that he could not take 'Janet's one ewe lamb from her'. More eagerly than ever Ellen Terry claimed that her own motherhood entitled her to read a Mother play and she was not inspired by a competitive motive. But he amused himself by threatening Janet that the great Ellen was after the part and she, Ellen, had no need for the spiritual transfiguration that Janet required. Ellen could walk into the part as she was already the Mother Perfect.

Meanwhile Florence Farr became interested in the part and Shaw arranged to meet her in Richmond Park. He taunted her about her frightful vacuity, her vulgarity, and her lack of religion. He informed her that Janet Achurch was cut out for the part of Candida because she had all the qualities necessary for it.

Shaw was completely unprepared for Richard Mansfield's refusal, at the last moment, to put on the play with Janet Achurch as Candida, for he wanted an American actress, Minnie Selingman, to take the part, and was willing to make Shaw a very good offer to be allowed to do so. Shaw replied:

"Offer declined. Nothing can be done at present without Achurch."

Mansfield then informed Shaw that *Candida* was not a play but was all talk and lacking in all essential qualities. He felt called upon to remind Shaw that the stage was not for sermons and that the

G

American public would not stand for it. The letter was interspersed with the most pathetic expressions of eternal friendship and admiration and ended with a note of encouragement: 'Go on, Shaw. We want a great work from you.' Shaw's reply was:

> "My dear Mansfield,
>      . . . The hour of vengeance has come. I have not the slightest respect for you; and your acquaintance with my future plays will be acquired in the course of visits to other people's theatres."

Shaw escaped from this disappointment into the fantasy of political propaganda. The Fabians were deceiving themselves into the belief that they were influencing the course of events because they were welcomed with benevolent smiles by the governing classes. It became clear to Shaw, however, that they were being used for electioneering purposes, to be thrown aside when they were no longer necessary. Shaw published a Manifesto in the *Fortnightly Review*, entitled: "To your Tents, O Israel":

> "The heroic speeches made by the Liberal leaders, when, rallying to the revolutionary flag, blazoned with payment of members, death by taxation to the ground landlord and royalty owner, home rule for London and the municipalisation of every monopoly under the sun, they hauled it to the high top-gallant of the great Liberal Party amid the inspiring strain of 'We are all Socialists now', are not usually alluded to at present having also served their turn; and it is not for the Fabian Society to spoil a stirring page of political history by bringing the public behind the scenes to see those eagle-eyed statesmen carried to the platform, kicking, screaming and protesting in the arms of the collectivist Radicals of London, who offered them the alternative of saying as they were told or spending another seven years in opposition."

H. W. Massingham, the political editor of the *Daily Chronicle*, lost his temper with his friend Shaw on account of this Manifesto.

> "It is not easy" (he wrote) "to discuss seriously a Manifesto chockful of levity, of unreal and insincere argument, of unverified statements and of purposeful exaggerations."

He accused his friend of 'perpetrating a schoolboy jest'. This letter made Shaw ask himself why it was that when most serious he was always accused of levity, that when he went out of his way to discover the facts, he was accused of exaggeration and when he was most logical in his reasoning, with not a flaw to be found in it as far as he could see, he was accused of unreal argument? He now deliberately accepted the charge of the committee-rooms in New Cross Road, South London, where Sidney Webb was seeking re-election with a far-reaching programme of municipal socialism. In a dismantled shop, without a fire, and with the light of heaven obscured by election posters, Shaw sat, day after day, addressing envelopes, interviewing constituents, explaining subtle points in economics and by homely example opening the eyes of those 'H'less' proletarians who regarded Webb as a symbol, a mole working unobtrusively to undermine the existing social order. Sidney Webb staked his hope on an elite of experts who would make no claim to superior social status but would content themselves with exercising the power inherent in superior knowledge and administrative experience. Strangely enough this belief in the administrator as the god-substitute was accepted by Shaw in all earnestness. He despised doctors and schoolmasters, but the administrator, the product of Webb's romantic imagination, was laughter-proof.

For Sidney Webb had a vision of a school specializing in the training of administrators by attracting a group of dedicated spirits. It was a vision and Webb treated it as such, tentatively talking about its possibilities with Beatrice, Graham Wallas, who was now lecturing for the Extra-mural Departments of Universities, and of course with George Bernard Shaw, who responded, to what seemed an impossible suggestion, with a loud and decisive "Why not?"

This vision was to be realized in a most unexpected way. Beatrice and Sidney Webb, Graham Wallas and Bernard Shaw were staying at Godalming, when a letter arrived, informing Sidney Webb that, by the will of Henry Hutchinson, he had been given the duty of directing the expenditure of £10,000.

Henry Hutchinson had been an early member of the Fabian Society and had occasionally been of great help to it financially, but would always include with his cheque querulous letters about Shaw's ill behaviour.

Shaw at once suggested that the money be used to subsidize Fabian candidates for Parliament, but the Webbs thought that what was most needed was hard thinking and research, and therefore part of the bequest was used to found a school on the lines of the École des Sciences Politiques, Paris. Shaw pointed out that as they were men and women with outrageously heterodox opinions they would never win the sympathy, financial or otherwise, of the most reactionary elements in the country, and it was these elements that had the power. Webb answered that this would depend on the Director elected for the School. Shaw immediately plumped for Graham Wallas with his Oxford credentials. Webb found it difficult, under the circumstances, to say exactly what he felt, but his attitude was that they must not permit a cranky taint to this 'college', for it must achieve a reputation of complete impartiality, so that in the near future it was granted a university status. To which Shaw replied:

"By impartial you mean reactionary!"

The Webbs remembered an incident at the Bodleian Library, Oxford, and this determined their choice of Director. They had gone to the Bodleian for certain documents in connection with their *History of Trade Unionism* and had been received with downright rudeness. Disturbed and wondering what to do, for they knew that the documents were there and were essential for their research, a young man approached them and offered to help them in every possible way. This young man was not an official of the Library but was himself doing research there. He had already published a book called *English Trade and Finance chiefly in the 17th century* and had been giving a course of lectures on Social History. It was this young man, W. A. S. Hewins, who became, on the strength of this strange meeting, the first Director of the School. At first it was housed at 9 John Street, Adelphi, but was quickly transferred to 10 Adelphi Terrace. They managed to obtain more financial help for the School from a wealthy Irish lady, Charlotte Payne Townshend, who subscribed £1,000 to the Library and endowed a woman's scholarship, and besides that she rented the two top floors, not required for school purposes, for £300 per annum. This lady had been introduced to Beatrice Webb as socialistically inclined, although she knew very little of what it stood for. On account of her wealth, Beatrice brought her into the Fabian conclave.

The Webbs were only too conscious of the claim to the Directorship of Graham Wallas. To propitiate him, Beatrice, when she discovered that this Irish lady was tired of her spinsterhood and was fond of men, had a wonderful idea of uniting Graham Wallas and Charlotte Payne Townshend, and thus, at one stroke, doing a good turn to both.

Miss Charlotte Payne Townshend was an endless subject of discussion among the Webbs and Shaw. As she was plain, plump and not too intellectual, they had to find hidden depths to explain her generosity, and Shaw had to point out that if one studied any human being sympathetically, one found a good deal in him or her.

"When you have said that Miss Payne Townshend has so much in her, depths unfathomable, you have said nothing at all; any mother will plead the same for her ugly duckling and plead it truthfully too; for we all have depths unfathomable in us, since it must have taken millions of ages for the Life Force to have evolved even a human idiot. The question is whether she will hold her own among exceptional people."

At no point was it suggested that Charlotte Payne Townshend would be suitable for Shaw as a wife. It was concluded by all that he had decided to marry Bertha Newcombe with whom he was seen everywhere. Bertha Newcombe was an artist with a studio in Cheyne Walk and she was at home equally with intellectuals, artists, dockers and navvies. He visited her studio almost daily and was always threatening to take the business side of her work in hand because she was too idealistic and had no commercial sense. He advised her on how to price her paintings: so much per square inch, so much for a full-length figure, so much for a head and shoulders, and never to give her work away for nothing because it "was throwing it away".

Bertha Newcombe described their relationship:

"Frequent talking, talking, talking of the pros and cons of marriage, even to my prospects of money or the want of it, his dislike of the sexual relation and so on, would create an atmosphere of love-making without any need for caresses or endearments. ... Shaw has not a gift of sympathetic penetration into a woman's nature. He employs his clever detective power and pounces on weaknesses and faults which confirm his preconceived ideas. He imagines he understands but I object to my emotions being divided into compartments and still retain my opinion that the emotion of love can be a fusion of body, spirit and mind."

He introduced her to Janet Achurch who professed sympathy with the friendship between her and Shaw. She described Janet Achurch:

"I immediately succumbed to the charm. She was so accessible, generous and responsive. She was largely made, though not tall. There was no prettiness but loveliness and beauty ... But she wanted a wide stage to extend herself upon, otherwise, as I remember in the *Doll's House* she seemed immense and gave one an uncomfortable feeling of elephantine grace."

When Shaw became aware that he was expected to marry the artist, he asked himself whether she was strong enough and disorderly enough for a lawless life. He now denounced her to all his friends as a Bohemian anarchist yet continued his association with her, explaining to his friends that it was "to prevent her worrying herself into a state of broken-heartedness". Bertha Newcombe wrote to him:

> "I feel dazed and must rearrange my ideas and take you away from the position you have occupied in my life. . . . But knowing that you really admire and wish to do just and honourable things, that you should choose the lower way of life, *that* I do not understand. You say this and you *preach* that and then I hear all that I have heard from Janet. What can I think? How is it possible to think of you as anything but a hypocrite and to feel anything but contempt for your writing? Nevertheless I acknowledge now that the hand of Providence with Shaw's consent and guidance intervened with good results on his behalf in warding off any possibility of a marriage with me."

His reaction to being held in contempt and being considered a hypocrite was to re-establish his character by rebounding into a world of fantasy where he identified himself with Napoleon. He described him as:

> "Imaginative without illusions, creative without religion, loyalty, patriotism or any of the common ideals. Not that he is incapable of these ideals: on the contrary, he has swallowed them all in his boyhood, and now, having a keen dramatic faculty, is extremely clever at playing upon them by the arts of the actor and stage manager. Withal, he is no spoilt child. Poverty, ill luck, the shifts of impecunious shabby-gentility, repeated failure as a would-be author. . . ."

Writing *The Man of Destiny*, his one-act play, gave him a great opportunity to get it out on the English:

> "It is impossible to live in England without sometimes feeling how much that country lost in not being conquered by Napoleon as well as by Julius Caesar."

He was feeling increasingly alien in England, a complete outsider and only happy and at home in the world of painting, literature or science. He was drawing away from Beatrice and Sidney Webb and looked to the type of genius as exemplified by Napoleon or Caesar to take the country in hand and purge it of all obstacles in the way of advancement.

He believed that this one-act play would bring Henry Irving to the realization that there was a dramatist alive who could write parts for him and was 'the best theatre tailor' in the world.

He persuaded Ellen to act as mediator but Henry Irving rejected the play because he could not see himself uttering sentiments like these:

"There is nothing so bad or so good that you will not find Englishmen doing it; but you will never find an Englishman in the wrong. He does everything on principle. He fights you on patriotic principles; he enslaves you on imperial principles; he bullies you on manly principles; he supports his king on loyal principles; and he cuts off his king's head on republican principles. His watchword is always duty; and he never forgets that the nation which lets its duty get on the opposite side to its interest is lost."

It was failure number ten. He was beginning to think that the greatest obstacle to his success was himself. But unfortunately he was necessary to the writing of his plays. Shaw knew that he had very few friends. Even in the socialist movement, where he might have achieved a reputation for complete unselfishness at least, he was accused by Robert Blatchford, the most popular socialist writer of the day, of 'being a man made after supper out of one of Ibsen's plays'. Shaw admitted that his own mother was certainly out of *A Doll's House*, for she had banged the door on her husband before 'door-banging' became fashionable.

Shaw had public friends whom he despised in private, private friends whom he disowned in public, useful friends whom he discarded when they were of no further use, and all of them meant little more to him than the pennies jingling in his pocket. He even boasted that Oscar Wilde said of him:

"An excellent man! He has no enemies; and none of his friends like him."

When Edmund Yates, the Editor of the *World*, died, Shaw left the paper and was invited by Frank Harris, the Editor of the *Saturday Review*, to become the dramatic critic. According to Shaw:

"This man Harris groomed and boomed and soon loomed as a great man in the literary world. . . . He had returned to England with the morals, manners and conversation of a buccaneer combined with a voice and elocution that gave him an imposing personal distinction."

Shaw was fascinated by his new Editor and encouraged him in his boastings of villainy and reprobate virility. Like Shaw, Harris had also been nurtured on the soap box and therefore their conversations were a competition in exaggerated wit, humour and exploit. Shaw was given a free hand in his criticism with the advice to 'let it rip!' and for this 'ripping' activity he was paid £6 a week. Frank Harris enjoyed meeting him, praising his "perfect unconstraint, his devilish look, his consciousness of his ability, very direct, very sharply decisive", although he understood perfectly well that it was all put on for his benefit.

Shaw preferred dramatic to music criticism because drama was a much less segregated cult than music, and it therefore reached a much larger public, in this case, probably the most intellectual element in the country, for among the other writers were D. S. McColl, Chalmers Mitchell, Cunninghame Graham, Arthur Symons, Walter Pater, Oscar Wilde and H. G. Wells.

He handed in his contributions punctually, his proofs were corrected carefully and heavily and he was always conscientiously provocative. Now he had a platform from which he could dethrone the idol of the theatre world, Henry Irving, and to destroy for ever the 'well-made play'. He defined the well-made play as:

"The kind of play which amuses only the surface of the mind and gives no satisfaction whatever to the soul. There is all the semblance of satisfaction and amusement, but once the theatre is left, a realization comes as having been the victim of a mechanical joke."

A stranger reading his dramatic criticism in the *Saturday Review* would be led to believe that Shaw, by his omniscient air, knew not only all there was to know about the theatre, but also about everything else. Actresses and actors read his column in fear and trembling. One actress, playing Lady Macbeth, described her feelings as follows:

"The performance of Lady Macbeth is ever memorable to me. Half way through, the producer came with exciting news: a well-known critic, one who had written a play and had had it acted, was in the front row: 'He has got red hair, a red beard and a white face but he wont eat you. He's a vegetarian.' "

Theatre managers tried to get round him as subtly as they could: they consulted him as an expert on the advisability of producing some foreign play of which they had purchased the performing rights. If he had thought well of it, he could translate it and be paid £50. Sir Henry Irving changed his mind about *The Man of Destiny* and offered to accept the play without committing himself to a date for production, intimating that if any time he desired an advance on royalties it could be arranged. At the Lyceum, Irving's temple, the stage was cleared after the first-night performance and a banquet was spread for privileged critics and friends. Shaw accepted the invitation as a courteous tribute to his influence but he never went.

If he could deride Henry Irving, he could at the same time feel that he was the only one in the country who could appreciate the subtle humour of his fellow-Dubliner, Oscar Wilde.

"The critics laugh angrily" (he wrote) "at his epigrams, like a child who is coaxed into being amused in the very act of setting up a yell of rage and agony; they protest that the trick is obvious, and that such epigrams can be turned out by the score by anyone light-minded enough to condescend to such frivolity. As far as I can ascertain, I am the only person in London who cannot sit down and write an Oscar Wilde play at will. The fact that his plays, though apparently lucrative, remain unique under these circumstances, says much for the self-denial of our scribes. In a certain sense, Mr. Wilde is to me our only thorough playwright."

The whole world was soon to howl at Oscar Wilde though he was at the height of his popularity, and he was to go through the terrible ordeal of a trial for homosexuality at the Old Bailey. A day before the trial, Frank Harris and George Bernard Shaw pleaded with Wilde to fly the country in order to avoid the sentence which would surely be passed on him, but Oscar Wilde preferred to face his trial. Shaw was a little anxious about this trial for a personal reason, for his well-intentioned mischievousness had set more than one story going through the wagging tongue of Frank Harris, who was always ready with his booming voice to take up any whisperings.

When Oscar Wilde was sentenced it was impossible for a long

time to mention the word sex without being suspect. Edward Carpenter's *Love's Coming of Age*, a book for the guidance of the adolescent, stopped dead; Walt Whitman's *Leaves of Grass* was discovered to be homosexual and Shelley and Ibsen became once more the basest of immoral writers. It seemed to Shaw a satanic climax that Irving's knighthood was announced simultaneously with Wilde's conviction.

# Chapter Eight

IT was the custom for the Webbs to take a country house for their holidays and to invite friends to stay with them, and it was always taken for granted that the 'Sprite' would go with them. With Graham Wallas still on her mind, Beatrice invited him and Charlotte Payne Townshend. Shaw discussed with Bertha Newcombe, whom he still visited, the advisability of joining the Webbs because he was weary of these earnest Fabian discussions and the eternal Fabian gossip. He told her that he would give anything for a moment of silent communion. Bertha Newcombe was also invited because Beatrice Webb wanted Graham Wallas and Charlotte Payne Townshend to be thrown together. Shaw advised Bertha not to go for it would be good for her to be away from the Webbs and to give her attention to her own work.

Shaw joined the party in the usual way, because, as he put it, it would give him an opportunity to take Wallas under his wing as he was presenting an anxious problem, threatening at any moment to throw over the bonds of socialism.

Within a short time the Candida situation was unrolling itself in a Suffolk Rectory. The wealthy Irish lady was well disposed to Graham Wallas although she found him too academic, but she was highly entertained by the exuberant Shaw who came forward on every occasion with the vocabulary of rebellion and cynicism so dear to her heart. They soon disappeared out of sight on long bicycle expeditions and Charlotte became convinced that it was he, the impecunious, lonely dramatist, who needed her more than the benign scholar. She handed him the key to her Adelphi Terrace flat and invited him to come and do his writing there.

The next play was written for her entertainment. Every sentence was calculated to win her approval. *You Never Can Tell* portrayed a new kind of love-making: Gloria is brought up to be above sentimentality and romance and to be guided by reason alone. She is wooed by a dentist in the 'scientific' way and yet they reach the same emotional entanglement as the rest of humanity, and to Gloria's disgust she rather enjoys it. The waiter in the play has the last word about marriage:

107

"Cheer up, sir, cheer up. Every man is frightened of marriage when it comes to the point; but it often turns out very comfortable, very enjoyable and happy indeed, sir, from time to time."

Charlotte Payne Townshend, new to the world of the theatre, was entranced with the play and prophesied immediate success. Cyril Maude, the popular actor-manager, actually put the play into rehearsal after she had promised to recoup him for any loss, but two of the leading members of the cast walked out and the project had to be abandoned.

Until now he had avoided all talk of finance with Charlotte, but after this failure he felt it imperative to put all his cards on the table and to tell her that he would never be able to make his plays bring in money. He wanted her to realize the disparity in their circumstances and he made it clear to her that he could never consider marriage until he had earned a thousand pounds at least. Charlotte agreed to live with him without legal marriage. She believed in him, for to her he was a 'genus' and a genius needed protection against the buffeting of a callous world. As a little girl she had once announced to her parents that she was going to marry a 'genus' when she grew up and now that she had met a genius who behaved like one, she came forward with this proposal: she was prepared to form a syndicate to finance his plays if he would promise to give up his journalism, his political work and his association with cranks. It would also mean leaving his mother and the squalid room in Fitzroy Square but she was prepared to make a generous settlement on both his mother and on his sister, Lucy.

He disliked conditions being attached to their association because he felt that it would twist him out of his shape and force him to behave, not as led by the Life Force, but at the bidding of another person. His whole life had been a protest against this very thing. She went for a holiday on the Continent and he was left to portray himself as a reprobate and an outcast in a new play he was writing, *The Devil's Disciple*. It was inverted melodrama where the villain did all the heroic things by the law of his own nature. He makes Dick Dudgeon, the Devil's disciple in the play, utter these words:

"I have been brought up standing by the law of my own nature; and I may not go against it, gallows or no gallows. I should have done the same for any other man in the town or any other man's wife. Do you understand that?"

Do you understand that? This question was significant because he knew himself to be the only one to understand that spirit and he considered it his fate to knock his head against the wall of dark, uncomprehending minds. He would never admit to himself that real life was too much for him, that he was afraid of being alone in it, and to escape that fear he filled his world with grotesques. He was more at home therefore with the characters of his own creation than with the people about him. The people, however, were necessary to his playwriting, especially the women. If it was not Florence Farr, it was Janet Achurch, if it was not Janet Achurch it was Bertha Newcombe and now it was Charlotte Payne Townshend. He admitted to each in turn that his strength was gained by feeding on their regard for him. He awakened in each the sense of the maternal by playing the completely exhausted man, the weary, heart-broken man:

> "I am really" (he wrote to them) "only fit for intercourse with sensitive souls when I am broken and weary. Mrs. Archer has been relaxing me, joint by joint, but I am still hardly safe without a chain and muzzle."

And again:

> "I shall never have a home, but do not be alarmed: Beethoven never had one either. No, I've no courage: I am and always have been as timid as a mouse."

He expressed this, and off he went to exhaust himself still further in political work. As an acknowledged genius he could now declare to an audience of enthusiastic socialists that, if it were not for socialists we would have had Socialism; he could announce at a Humanitarian Conference that humanitarians were the most quarrelsome humans on earth; and he could defy the atheists who wanted him as a leader by stating his conviction that without religion people were cads. "Why," he asked himself, "was I given nine brains and only one tongue?"

In 1897 he permitted himself to be co-opted on to the St. Pancras Vestry and he soon discovered what he always knew to be there, that the borough was culturally moribund and politically corrupt and that the Vestry was dominated by local shopkeepers. The squalid facts stared them all in the face but it was impossible to do anything about them because of the vested interests. There was an Irishman who always began his speech with, "This is one of the most stinking scandals that ever disgraced the annals of St. Pancras . . .", but he was an Irishman and therefore not to be taken seriously.

Shaw had a strong supporter in the Reverend W. Ensor Walters. The friendship between the 'blasphemer' and the clergyman was reminiscent of the relationship between Voltaire and John Fletcher of Madely. Shaw shocked them all by his denunciation of slum landlords, swindling shopkeepers, and manufacturers of dirty foods, and by his pronouncement that if he had his way, all these people would be immediately exterminated.

Again came the old plea to his friends: "It is good for me to be worked to the last inch while I last."

He had built up a topsy-turvy life for himself in which his sensitivity to beauty had sent him into the ugliest places, in which his love of laughter had sent him into dens of misery, in which his love of power had sent him into a place like the Vestry where he could achieve nothing. It was as though the earth had once toppled over and human beings were compelled to adapt themselves to topsy-turvy conditions. The only one on the Vestry who knew that Shaw was a critic of note, a playwright, and the man who had answered Dr. Max Nordau and had sliced him into a thousand pieces, was the Reverend W. Ensor Walters.

Dr. Max Nordau was a scientific mouse who strayed into the virgin field of experimental psychology and came out sprinkled with a deadly poison which he proceeded to spread over a large book called *Degeneration*. This deadly poison was to eliminate the arts. He became the pet of the Victorian Philistine and the dread of the aesthete.

Dr. Max Nordau had studied under Lombroso, the criminologist, and had come out of it with the theory that the criminal was only too often of a degenerate breed. He had experimented on degenerates and had found that they had certain reactions in common. Then he went one step further and expressed the view that the artists, musicians and writers of the day showed all the same signs of degeneracy, and he proved his points with much evidence. The leaders of the artistic world of the day, Tolstoi, Ibsen, Wagner and Rossetti, were exposed to the fiercest psychological analysis and were found debased.

No one came forward to answer him because his scientific verbology was so impressive and his field so comprehensive that others feared to tread on unknown territory.

Benjamin Tucker, the editor of an American journal, *Liberty*, remembered that there was one person who had not been overawed by the new scientific language and who had sufficient knowledge of the arts to answer this scathing indictment. He offered to pay George

Bernard Shaw any figure he cared to name for an article reviewing *Degeneration*. This was an opportunity which Shaw would not have missed. He asked not a penny and devoted careful study to the writing of his answer.

"The severity of artistic discipline" (he wrote) "is produced by the fact that in creative art no ready-made rules can help you. There is nothing to guide you to the right expression for your thought except your own sense of beauty and fitness; and, as you advance upon those who went before you, that sense of beauty and fitness is necessarily often in conflict, not with fixed rules, because there are no rules, but with precedents."

This gave him his opportunity to state his faith in the sanity and discipline of art and its necessity as both an instrument and an object of culture. Yet, in spite of the *tour de force* there was more of the Max Nordau in him than he cared to admit to himself. He envied the Webbs their immersion in prosaic statistics for they had embarked on the laborious task of investigating the evolution of the Trade Union Movement; happiness had certainly not dulled the inspiration of his two friends, nor had their work reduced the sheer poetry of their mutual life. The difference between the Webbs and himself came home to him when he happened once to make exactly the same remark as Sidney Webb. When Webb spoke all were impressed by his veracity, but when Shaw said the same thing later on, there was a look of cynical disbelief on every face. It was because Webb never dramatized himself and stated the fact without emphasis, while Shaw was now an acknowledged genius and therefore suspect because he was different in kind to the ordinary person. Those whom he wanted to please laughed at him, while those for whom he did not care followed him with a solemnity that palled on him. A genius might achieve notoriety but never any influence. He tried to work out the place of the genius in society, the place of the artist-philosopher in a philistine community: how much selfishness, for example, how much pretentiousness, how much laxity should one stand for the sake of his exceptional gifts?

He concluded that it was necessary for the genius to be given special privileges on the chance of his being right in the long run. Dr. Max Nordau obviously took, for all his learning, the short-sighted, utilitarian view.

The lesson he learnt from his Vestry work, and it took him a long time to absorb it, was that human beings could become accustomed to anything, however disgusting; for example: he worked hard to get women's lavatories installed in the district, but as the subject was un-mentionable in this highly moral atmosphere, he found himself de-nounced as a sordid monster. When Shaw demanded to know what women did in urgent moments there was a stunned silence and the problem had to be shelved.

Beatrice and Sidney Webb tried to persuade Shaw to take the cultural life of the new school in hand. The School of Economics, as it was now called, concentrated on utilitarian subjects like Methods of Statistics, Commercial Law and Currency and Railway Economics, and it was suggested that a little futility would add to the life of the School. Through Sidney Webb's cunning manipulation, the School had every hope of a place in the University of London, and it was felt that the intensive culture might be too one-sided and the product therefore ill equipped for his tremendous responsibility. This was but the beginning and it was hoped that a whole series of social institutions would be built up, vitally affecting human behaviour and be a veritable framework of prevention. Shaw shocked them with the pronounce-ment that he had no use for formal education and competitive examina-tions because they produced invincible ignorance and moral imbecility as a result of the unnatural abuse of the apprehensive faculty. He was willing, however, to lecture but there was no demand for culture in the School.

Mrs. Carr Shaw did not like Beatrice Webb because of her habit of taking flowers from a vase and crushing them while she talked; this act seemed to her to denote a person fit for stratagems and murders. Besides, Beatrice had once come knocking at her door looking just like a gipsy, carrying great bunches of wild flowers which were already dead in her arms. Beatrice explained that she had only just returned from the country and had not yet put herself straight.

"Straight with whom?" Mrs. Carr Shaw asked severely.

Grant Richards, an enthusiastic but not too successful young pub-lisher, approached Shaw with a view to publishing his plays and this time it was Shaw who felt that he was being teased. This publisher had been following his criticism since the *Star* days and had not missed a speech or debate of Shaw's in London.

When they met, Shaw made him feel like a schoolboy, teaching him the significance of margins, how to eliminate mutton quads and how to make printed pages pictorial in themselves.

The labour of preparing the plays for the Press assumed unexpected and colossal proportions, for Shaw had to replace simple stage direc-tions intended for actors and actresses by vivid descriptions for the benefit of the general reader. Thus the plays became transformed into conversational novels with descriptions of the places and penetrative character sketches. Grant Richards argued that these plays were bound to sell because thousands of intelligent people regularly read the debates in the House of Commons and would be much more interested in the debates that went on unceasingly in Shaw's mind.

Shaw complained that the labour of creating actors and actresses to interpret his plays was so great that he had decided more than once to stop writing plays, especially as they were limited almost entirely to the West End of London where playgoing had been turned into a dress parade and an after-dinner relaxation.

He was also engaged on the compilation of *The Perfect Wagnerite* to educate the English Public in ideas to which they were not accustomed.

"The combination of music with an interest in politics is not common in England; and as I seem so far to be the only publicly articulate result of it, I venture to add my commentary to what has already been written by musicians who are no revolutionists, and revolutionists who are no musicians."

George Bernard Shaw was extremely worried about his health, for he remembered that every man of genius had a critical illness round about forty. Schiller and Mozart died at that age, while Goethe survived though he nearly followed Schiller into the grave. Added to this, Shaw had his own personal dread of forty: for it was at that age that his father had married and it was at that age that his mother had left him for England. When he was advised to have an operation on his foot, he took it heroically and wrote to all his friends giving vivid reports of every stage of his progress.

"11th May 1898.

Dear Janet,
They were all frightened out of their wits by the doctor who wants to cure me of my vegetarian follies and says that I am in a critical condition from undernourishment, I say from overwork. Anyhow when he got down to the bone it was carious, which certainly shows that I have been overdoing the superhuman.
G.B.S."

We next hear of four doctors treating him, including an eminent surgeon gouging 'a pound or two out of the instep'. Shaw was certain that the diagnosis was wrong. Charlotte, who had heard of his state and had returned to England, was taking him in hand and paying for

H

all the medical attention. She told him that the alternative in his case was a long spell of disablement and being confirmed in the habits of an invalid. One doctor, to Shaw's great amusement, diagnosed locomotor ataxy.

The illness speeded up an event which he had put off for as long as he could, the marriage with Charlotte Payne Townshend. As she was insisting on his removal to a house in the country under her care, being so shocked at the pathetic condition of his home in Fitzroy Square, he thought it wiser to marry and thus make the whole thing respectable.

Mischievously he invited Graham Wallas and Henry, the husband of Kate Salt, to witness the marriage at Caxton Hall on June 1st, 1898. G.B.S. arrived at the wedding on two crutches and was mistaken for a person expecting alms.

It had gone around that Shaw had thrown over all his principles now that he was wealthy: that he had thrown over his vegetarianism because it had reduced him to a pitiable condition; that he had thrown over his independence by yielding to an heiress; that he had capitulated to the doctors; and when very ill, had asked for the benefit of religious consolation.

This brought an immediate retort from G.B.S. in a letter to the *Academy*, a journal he selected because it had announced the forthcoming book by him as *The Complete Wagnerite*.

"15th October 1898.

I see you have been announcing a book by me entitled *The Complete Wagnerite*. This is an error: you are thinking of an author named Izaak Walton. The book, which is a work of great merit, even for me, is called *The Perfect Wagnerite* and is an exposition of the philosophy of *Der Ring des Nibelungen*. It is a G.B.eSsence of modern anarchism, or neo-Protestantism. This lucid description speaks for itself. As it had been written on what the whole medical faculty and all the bystanders declare to be my deathbed, it is naturally rather a book of devotion than one of those vain brilliances which I was wont to give off in the days of my health and strength. My situation is a solemn one. Life is offered me on condition of eating beef-steaks. My weeping family crowd round me with Bovril and Brand's Essence. But death is better than cannibalism, not to mention that I would not change my hat, much less my diet, on the evidence.

I know that I am mortal, which in my *Saturday Review*ing days I had come to doubt. My will contains directions for my funeral, which will be followed, not by mourning coaches, but by herds of oxen, sheep, swine, flocks of poultry, and a small travelling aquarium of small fish, all wearing white scarves in honour of the man who perished rather than eat his fellow creatures. It will be, with the single exception of Noah's Ark, the most remarkable thing of its kind yet seen.

Should we not meet again, my dear Editor, farewell, and forswear sack and sausages.

George Bernard Shaw.

P.S. I have just strained my ankle in trying to master the art of bicycling on one foot. This, with two operations and a fall downstairs, involving a broken arm, is my season's record so far, leaving me in excellent general condition. And yet they tell me that a vegetarian cant recuperate."

Charlotte, in sympathy, stopped eating meat and fish, but she soon gave up as she had difficulty in finding a cook who knew how to prepare vegetarian dishes and so G.B.S. had to sit down to his table with a 'cannibal'.

Dr. Gilbert Murray, who visited him on this occasion, described the visit as follows:

"I went to see him at Hindhead and took for granted that he would be in bed, but was told that he was in the garden in a hammock. I went to look for him but saw no one, but presently I heard a chuckle behind a large holly bush. Guided by this I found him, unconscious of my presence, unconscious of pains, swathed in bandages, writing away with his unbandaged hand and laughing with sheer enjoyment."

G.B.S. had a very clear idea as to the kind of life that Charlotte and he were going to live. To sleep in the same room, let alone in the same bed, would lead to impossible situations. Which party, he argued, would decide whether or how much should the window be opened? How many blankets should be on the bed, and at what hour should they go to bed so as to avoid disturbing one another's sleep? They were both middle-aged and had settled, more or less, into fixed habits. His friends watched the process of domestication with amused interest. Charlotte found it much easier than she expected because she was helped by his helplessness. G.B.S. felt like a duke without the social burdens of wealth and position. He asked himself what he would have done without a fortune: it would have meant a hospital, an amputation, and no income, for he could not have gone on with his theatre criticism. As always the word *State* was the magical solution to every difficulty: a State Medical Service.

When he threw away his crutches he became a different man: imperious, impatient and inaccessible to outsiders but appreciative and very attentive to his wife. G.B.S. remained if anything abnormally ascetic, liking to sleep on a hard bed with the minimum of blankets in the winter and with the window opened wide. If his sleep were disturbed at night his temper and work suffered next day, for work came before everything. Charlotte on the other hand went to bed two hours before her husband and enjoyed the indulgence of a feather-bed and a warming pan. She told everybody that fusion without understanding had played havoc with young lives, while in their case there was understanding without fusion and that was the basis of permanence. She held up a mirror to him in which he could see a noble image of himself, and the image that he saw, and she wanted him to see, was of Caesar: a man who could estimate the value of truth, wealth and success quite independently of convention and moral generalization. He was turning the excitement of the marriage to intellectual advantage: the healthy, self-possessed ecstasy which it irradiated flowed into his writing.

She collected the press cuttings and classified them in coloured bags, destroying all adverse or lukewarm notices and gloating over adulatory ones. She would not have anyone whisper a word against the genius. She would see to it, with all the wealth at her disposal, that the whole world would recognize him as such. She carried about with her a notebook in which she jotted down any memorable sayings by her husband, the names of her husband's friends who were of no further use to him and therefore must be gently brushed off, and a note of the people whom they must cultivate for the good of his career.

They returned at the earliest moment to 10 Adelphi Terrace to take up their residence there, and G.B.S. asked for not a single bit of furniture to be added or taken away on his account.

Beatrice Webb visited them and wrote:

"Sidney and I meet the Shaws on Thursdays in Charlotte's attractive flat over the School of Economics. They have settled down into the most devoted married couple, she gentle and refined with happiness added thereto, and he showing no sign of breaking loose from her dominion. What the intellectual product of the marriage may be, I do not feel so sure: at any rate he will not become a dilettante, the habit of work is too deeply ingrained. It is interesting to watch his fitful struggles out of the social complacency natural to an environment of charm and plenty."

When his old friends and flames complained of neglect he had a ready formula:

"You do not understand the nature of Charlotte's objection to you. It is not a question of like and dislike in the ordinary sense; she has exactly the same objection to my mother and sister and everybody who forms part of the past in which she had no part. The moment you walk into the room where I am, you create a world in which you and I are at home and she is the stranger. That was the real difficulty of marrying at forty."

His problem, consummate actor that he was, was to remain the same person when he was several persons. He was Morell, facile, cheery, spontaneous and bumptious; he was Dick Dudgeon who pitied the Devil and championed him, now he was Caesar, amiable, magnanimous, yet powerful. Whom had she married after all?

Shaw was engaged on a historical play and his difficulty was the minor one of having no historic sense: all he could do was to dress himself and others in fancy dress and make them say things of contemporary significance. He could only present the world in the light of his own time, or, as he would have it, in the light of the future, for he considered himself a ghost of the future. In the writing of *Caesar and Cleopatra* he refused on any account to play on sexual infatuation and to treat Caesar as a hog; here he would give the world an exhibition of how a great man behaved, a man who never lost his head in an emergency, the scholar-ruler par excellence.

The play turned out to be an inverted *Candida*. Shorn of locality and period, it had basically the same situation: a middle-aged person, in this case a man, in love with a young person, young enough to be his daughter. It was a situation which haunted Shaw, for he was in his early forties and regarded it as old age. He knew only too well that in the world of youth he would soon be brushed aside as an old fogey.

Charlotte had shown him the part wealth played in the affairs of life and what a protective covering it made. The simple life was an extremely expensive way of living and he could now live up to his convictions without anxiety. Once when due to give a lecture, he had missed his train, and without a second thought he hailed a cab which cost him five times as much. He spent most of his evenings at Adelphi Terrace playing and singing to his wife and rarely going to a theatre. He wrote regularly every morning and those moments she considered 'mystic, wonderful', and she would sit within call. When women of talent asked her for advice as to how one lived with a man of genius, her answer was:

"A man does not want a women with whom he enters into personal relationship to be either intellectual, original, independent, self-willed, courageous or public-spirited. He wants to feel in his own house that he is not only master but lawgiver and deity."

This was not an easy statement for her to make because she had intended to live in the manner of Beatrice and Sidney Webb, but when she found that he vehemently rejected her ideas and criticism, she withdrew into herself, only to find that all she had suggested had been incorporated as his own. It was she who was consulted on every aspect of the business side and it was she who suggested Mrs. Patrick Campbell as Cleopatra for the first performance of the play at the Theatre Royal, Newcastle-on-Tyne, in March 1899. The play misfired hopelessly; the audience could make nothing of the plot or the humour. This angered Charlotte beyond measure and she could only blame Mrs. Patrick Campbell for the failure due to a purely physical sexual interpretation of the part: she had made her into a vampire instead of the innocent child being moulded into a Queen by wise and patient guidance. Charlotte loved the play even more than *You Never Can Tell* because she felt that there was more of her husband's great intellectual power in it, and it proved that the Life Force he believed in so ardently was as real to him as gravitation or magnetism. She, herself, could not understand this faith, but it seemed to fit the Genius like a glove and she accepted it as part of him.

Charlotte had a younger sister, married to a military man, who was so shocked that Charlotte had married an atheist, vegetarian and a socialist, and worse than all these, a man who did not hunt or shoot, that the couple refused on any account to meet them. Charlotte, however, felt that if she could get the two men together they would both find that they had much in common for they were both doughty fighters and both did their fighting best when sitting down. When they met G.B.S. put himself all out to charm his relatives; he acted the part of the perfect gentleman, proved an extraordinarily knowledge-able person in military affairs, avowed that the best text-books on

Generalship were: *Arms and the Man, Man of Destiny* and *Caesar and Cleopatra*, all of which were unknown to his new relative. G.B.S. was charmed with his sister-in-law, Cicely Cholmondeley, especially as she manoeuvred her firebrand of a husband with tact and success. After the meeting he made these notes:

"A slave state is always ruled by those who can get round the masters. The slavery of women means the tyranny of women. No fascinating woman ever wants to emancipate her sex: her object is to gather power into the hands of Man because she knows that she can govern him."

"A cunning and attractive woman disguises her strength as womanly timidity, her unscrupulousness as womanly innocence, her impunities as womanly defencelessness: simple men are duped by them."

"It is only the proud, straight-forward women who wish not to govern but to be free."

The outcome of this meeting was a play with such a lady as the heroine. The part was made to fit the great Ellen Terry so that she could live in it easily and happily. He gave it the ugly but arresting name of *Captain Brassbound's Conversion*, and the heroine was named Cicely. Ellen Terry did not however relish the part of a female tactician using her feminine wiles among a lot of barbarians and also she did not think that the play would do for the stage. She suggested Mrs. Patrick Campbell, telling Shaw that she felt sure that he must have had her in mind when he wrote it. This shocked G.B.S. and in anger he lectured her on her lack of understanding:

"Listen to me, woman with no religion. I tried to show you fearing nobody, and managing them all as Daniel managed the lions not by cunning but by moral superiority. Here you get far beyond Candida, with her boy and her parson and her suspicion of trading a little on the softness of her contours. Here is a part which dominates the whole play because the character it represents dominates the world. In every other play I have ever written I have prostituted the actress more or less by making the interest in her partly a sexual interest, in Lady Cicely I have done without this and gained a greater fascination by it."

This was a remarkable confession on the part of G.B.S. about his previous heroines, and Ellen Terry was more convinced than ever that Lady Cicely was also prostituted to make a feast for the stalls. It was Janet Achurch who played the part of Cicely after all, at the Stage Society production in 1900. Again, as in *Candida*, he took Janet in hand to train her in the art of 'ladyship'.

> "A lady is one who never shows real excitement, or loses her distinction and immense self-conceit and habit of patronage . . . she might be childish and make little jokes and puns that only courtiers laugh at; she might do forty-thousand things that no woman who was either above or below suspicion would do; but in everything external she would be distinguished from the middleclass woman, who lives her whole life under suspicion and shortness of cash."

Money, in his eyes now, put a person immediately on a different plane, for the views which he had expressed before out of sheer bravado he could now utter as a matter of course, as a man of the world. All the same he kept in contact with the Vestry work at St. Pancras, where they were up against a shocking problem. An epidemic of small-pox had risen to such alarming proportions that victims were carted off to isolation ships anchored down the Thames, many to be returned to their families in coffins. It looked like a recurrence of the Black Plague.

Shaw opposed vaccination, the generally accepted treatment of this vile disease, and made himself thoroughly unpopular by denouncing it in speech and article. The wealthy especially hated him for this attitude for they feared that the epidemic would, if not stopped by vaccination, spread to them. Sidney Webb complained again that by putting forward these trivial and contentious ideas Shaw was making the Socialist movement ridiculous. But Shaw saw further than Webb and insisted that inoculation did not deal effectively with the causes of disease; it was essential that dirt, poverty and overcrowding should be tackled and removed to prevent another occurrence. He expressed this at a great demonstration at Queen's Hall, London:

> "My lord, ladies and gentlemen, in addressing an audience like this to-night, an audience whose applause has shown it to be strongly possessed by the passion of humanity, and which is, I hope, typical of the great nation to which it belongs, I have to admit, if we look facts in the face, that the English Nation is not in the

habit of allowing considerations of humanity to interfere either with its interests or with its pleasures.

We are all in the doctor's power when we are ill. I myself have been vivisected. And why? Because I had to accept the doctor's word that it was necessary. He had me, as much as any doctor ever had, a guinea pig in his power. I submitted; and the sole ground for my submission was my faith in that man's dealing with me honestly and mercifully. But if he had begun to argue in my presence I could not have helped asking: 'Why should not this man sacrifice me if he thinks he can confer a benefit on humanity or advance science by doing so?' The doctor may say quite logically and in this case truthfully: 'Here is a person who never will be missed. If I perform and experiment on him in the interests of science, and anything comes of it, that man by his death will have done more for the world than he would if I merely cured him.'

I never talk sentiment to a doctor. I always say: 'If you are to acquire knowledge at all costs, go about your investigation in a ruthlessly scientific spirit: for instance, suppose you were to take a woman's child and burn it alive before her eyes! What a lot you would find out.' . . ."

His point in this speech was that science should be pursued under the same moral and legal restraints as any other activity. Any other activity barring war, of course. The Boer War had just broken out and it split the Fabian Society into four conflicting sections: there were the Pacifists who were opposed to all war; there were those who were opposed to this particular war; there were those who thought that now we were in it we must go on with it to the bitter end; and finally there were those who welcomed the war as a necessary blood-letting. It may seem incredible that the person who had given this humane speech at Queen's Hall, could follow it with this letter to Henry Salt:

"12 March 1900.

I delight in the war more and more. It has waked up the country out of its filthy wallowing in money, blood is a far superior bath; and it has put fourpence on the income tax which will never come off if the Fabians can help it; so that old age pensions will be within reach at the end of the ten years repayment period, if not sooner. . . . Charrington calls me a Tory because I declare for Imperialism as our social theory. . . ."

This was the first time that Shaw was called a Tory, and this by an admirer of his, the husband of Janet Achurch and the founder of the Stage Society. Shaw could well feel this scientific and detached interest in the Boer War, for his only personal connection with it was Cicely's husband, Colonel Hugh Cholmondeley, who went out with the City Imperial Volunteers.

As editor of *Fabianism and Empire* he maintained that the Liberal and Tory politicians had proved themselves too incompetent to continue the task of Government, and that it was the destiny of conscious socialism to create a party with a purpose and a faith, then 'English Statesmen will once more have a craft and master it'.

The first real rift in opinion between Shaw and Charlotte came over the Boer War, for she was an out and out pacifist, declaring that people should refuse to participate in wrongdoing. She had hoped that the Genius would have seized the opportunity of becoming the spiritual leader of the day by declaring as vehemently against war as against the horrors of poverty. G.B.S. would not accept this suggestion, for, as he said, he was not an archbishop and could not pretend to pass his life on one plane and in one mood, and that on the highest plane. He argued that, after the apathy of the ruling classes to pressing problems, anything that waked the country was welcome to him. He had been trying to wake it for twenty years and the country seemed to be shuffling backwards instead of forwards.

In these tense moments she argued as heatedly as he.

> "Genius should be uplifting and therefore should devote all its energies to the portrayal of good triumphing over evil. The good characters should be so outstanding that ordinary people would be inspired to model their own lives on them."

Shaw could not agree that soot and whitewash were the only colours to smear on men's souls. And he could not agree that people tended towards that which was good; if it came to that they were far more fascinated by evil. He had learnt very early in his political and social life that it was only as a bad man that he could ever get a hearing. Hundreds of men and women were now doing good only because he had given it all the fascination of evil.

He felt a sense of rejuvenation with the coming of the new century. The nineteenth century had been a benighted period and all a genius could do was to tell the purse-proud people its own villainous history. He hated the nineteenth century because it had turned the mystic that he was by nature into a harsh realist, had caused him to cling to Sidney

Webb when he would have lived with Blake, had caused him "to be a Swift when he would rather have been the first swallow announcing spring". Pondering on his life he could not understand where the faith came from to carry him through the failures and humiliations of his early years in London to his self-discovery as a dramatist. He wrote to Kate Salt: "Who could account rationally for the Life Force, the evolutionary appetite, the Divine Providence? It had just to be accepted as a so far inexplicable natural fact." This was his constant source of vitality.

What would the new century bring after its blood bath? He had got youth at his feet at last. The largest halls were always packed when he was announced to speak. At one meeting, when he was to speak on Darwin, Alfred Russell Wallace, Darwin's fellow pioneer in evolutionary thought, came as a humble member of his audience and honoured him with the title of 'Meta-biologist'.

# Chapter Nine

GEORGE BERNARD SHAW noted these events in the first years of the twentieth century:

(1) That he saw a young actor, named Granville Barker, make his first appearance in the Stage Society's production of *Candida* and he was fascinated by his performance of Marchbanks.

(2) Samuel Butler was present at a private performance of *Mrs. Warren's Profession*, and although this celebrated author was known to frequent prostitutes, he would not tolerate any serious discussion on prostitution on the stage.

(3) When *Mrs. Warren's Profession* was produced in the United States, it was taken for granted that as it was refused a licence in England, it must therefore be of incredible indecency and so the worst elements came in enormous crowds and fabulous prices were paid for seats.

(4) That his plays went down better at matinées than at evening performances because the audiences were ten to one female, the sermon, lecture-loving rather than pleasure-loving kind.

(5) He received twenty begging letters a day and every time he hardened his heart, Charlotte opened her purse.

(6) He received three proposals a week from young women who had read or seen his plays and to these Charlotte never responded.

All these added up to the fact that he must somehow write a play demolishing Woman; in other words, make Don Juan the quarry instead of the huntsman. He decided that such a play could not help being a success because women like nothing better than seeing their own sex shown up.

As always, in the writing of his plays, it was his friends who unwittingly handed him many of his wittiest speeches: he might be at a loss, and, out of nowhere as it were, the connecting link would be forged. He did not think these occurrences accidental: Nature always arranged for a vacuum to be filled.

For example, when the Webbs and they dined on Thursdays together, G.B.S. happened to say, "I would rather have my mob all

Caesars instead of Toms, Dicks and Harrys," Beatrice Webb took him up on this and asked, "Where do the Anns, Marys and Joans come in?"

"They dont come in at all," Shaw answered, "because they are too conventional."

Beatrice, taking this to be an attack on her sex, handed him this little speech: "We must be conventional or we are so cruelly, so vilely misunderstood. Even you cannot say what you think without being vilified."

A special gift worth all the others came from Sydney Olivier, who innocently remarked, after a long absence, that Shaw looked gloriously happy.

The denial was immediate: "I solemnly say that I am not a happy man. I may be triumphant, successful, victorious, the price for which I sold my happiness. On the day we married we both renounced happiness." This speech was extended and altered and given over to Tanner in *Man and Superman*.

Charlotte was hurt at first that he would never admit happiness in his marriage, but then she consoled herself with the thought that a genius was like that: a sublime altruist in his disregard of himself, and an atrocious egotist in his disregard of others. He gave her the feeling that he was a bird in a gilded cage and her happiness sprang from the fact that she had succeeded in trapping the singing creature. One evening when she remarked that she admired Arthur Balfour, the Prime Minister, for putting the philosophic instead of the military man on the map, her husband looked up and beamed at her gratefully. He wrote:

> "I sing, not arms and the hero, but the philosophic man: he who seeks in contemplation to discover the inner will of the world, in inventions to discover the means of fulfilling that will, and in action to do that will by the so-discovered means. Of all the other sorts of men I declare myself tired."

When he read *Man and Superman* to Charlotte she felt that it was not as good as *Captain Brassbound's Conversion* in which Woman was enthroned and not made a bird of prey. The men were more or less the same, for all his heroes seemed to have one speech, the eternal Shavian creed; but Woman was still a mystery to him, and he seemed to study her as dispassionately as Darwin studied the worm. When Brassbound talked, or rather preached at Cicely, it might have been Tanner laying down the law with Ann:

"Look you: when you and I first met, I was a man with a purpose. I stood alone; I saddled no friend, woman or man, with that purpose, because it was against law, against religion, against my own credit and safety. But I believed in it; and I stood alone for it as a man should stand for his belief, against law and religion, as much as against wickedness and selfishness. Whatever I may be, I am none of your fairweather sailors that'll do nothing for their creed but go to Heaven for it. I was ready to go to hell for mine. Perhaps you dont understand that. . . ."

No one was supposed to understand these very high-sounding sentiments and heroic gesturings. Charlotte hoped that one day she might get him to write a play where the woman not only understood these sentiments but was herself a superman.

Shaw made fun of Charlotte's reaction to *Man and Superman* in a letter to Henry Salt:

"The play is one of the most colossal efforts of the human mind, and contains several passages which you will find congenial and which will make Kate blush for having gradually argued herself into a conviction that I am a lost soul.

As a matter of fact I go on much as I used to, except that my pecuniary circumstances are embarrassed. My wife has at last become a convinced vegetarian and she now eats nothing but birds and fish which are not 'Butcher's meat'. She is also converted to simplicity of life for although we have both a town and country residence we keep no horses and spend hardly £3000 a year on our housekeeping. She has great hopes of reducing this ultimately to £2500, especially as Charlotte is never happy except when we are staying in some grubby public house out of reach of the servants and the two residences. Is there any chance of seeing you again? Charlotte says you dont like the food at Adelphi Terrace. Or is it you dont like *her*?

G.B.S."

Shaw tried very hard to interest other literary sages in political reform, especially when these authors were very popular. He asked for Conan Doyle's help in getting a minimum wage for all workers and appealed to him as a business man, as Managing Director of an important firm as well as a specialist in detective fiction. He received the following letter:

May 26, 1902.

My dear Shaw,

I am not a managing director and have no practical interest in the working of any firm, but my general feeling about low wages is that where it is unskilled work if you raise the wage on humanitarian grounds to benefit the worker, you drive the whole trade to Germany or elsewhere and leave the unfortunate worker in a worse position than ever. I dont see how this can be avoided. Much of our card and printing trade has already gone.

With all thanks and goodwill,

Yours very truly,

A. Conan Doyle.

This simple letter made Shaw think hard, and it made the Fabians think. A great threat was looming up and dare not be ignored: Germany as an economic competitor. The Fabians had treated all their problems as English problems, even when they sent their delegates to International Socialist Conferences. Here was a country growing rapidly and ready to throttle England. It was true that the Socialist Movement was strong there but it was not powerful enough to check the anti-English spirit which revealed itself during the Boer War. At the International Conference, Shaw found the Germans very responsive to his clever jibes at England.

But then he laughed at the Irish as well: all national habits were a butt for his humour. He considered himself, since his answer to Dr. Max Nordau, a licensed cosmopolitan or nothing.

When William Butler Yeats asked him to write a play as a patriotic contribution to the repertory of the Irish Literary Theatre, Shaw knew that the last thing Yeats wanted was an uncompromising presentation of the real Ireland. He saw no earthly reason for having to love the country of one's birth; a genius, in his opinion, was immune from such banalities. So he settled down to a play which would make the Irish laugh at themselves, though he knew that all he would get in the end was a howl of disgust and indignation.

He despised Ireland for having given him the thing he hated most in himself: the eternal dreaming which he had had to struggle against all his life.

G.B.S. did not hesitate to preach religion, his own particular religion, where the State was the Church and the Church the People, three in one and one in three:

"It is a commonwealth in which work is play and play is life; three in one and one in three.

It is a temple in which the priest is the worshipper and the worshipper the worshipped; three in one and one in three.

It is a godhead in which all life is human and all humanity divine; three in one and one in three."

As a reaction to the dreaming Irishman with no hold on reality, he stood, in 1904, as a Progressive Candidate for the London County Council, and he meant to succeed by telling the truth, the whole truth and nothing but the truth.

No candidate did more to destroy his party. He was a great draw; people came from everywhere to hear him but they left not knowing which way to turn, feeling that the signposts had been interfered with and were all pointing in the wrong direction. He was brazen, incorrigible and shameless, flinging pearls of wisdom without stint, running down schools as prisons, calling the poor, criminals, and putting doctors in the same category. He slashed brilliantly to the right and to the left among his own supporters, and made enemies everywhere.

"I am myself an owner of property and therefore not likely to be indifferent to the interests of property," he announced, and bang went the proletarian vote.

"It is better to pay a shilling more to the rate collector than a couple of pounds more to the doctor," he claimed, and bang went the votes of the ratepayers and the doctors.

"May I remind you, in all earnestness that there is nothing more dangerous than the conscience of the bigot?" he declared, and bang went the Free Church vote.

Sidney Webb, whenever he could spare the time, tried hard to undo the mischief his friend was doing, but what was the use if the people he canvassed told him that the candidate had advocated something totally different on the day before?

Needless to say Shaw was not returned and his defeat assured him of one thing: that he would never be selected as candidate again by any constituency where the Progressives had an earthly chance. On the whole he had enjoyed acting the part of Superman at the election and told everyone that he even preferred it to the writing of plays.

Elsewhere the Progressives romped in. G.B.S. compared himself with Napoleon who could never have won a local election in France because he had too clear a realistic knowledge of public affairs, nor would Caesar, an honourable man, have succeeded with the rabble

Dr. Albert Einstein            Sidney and Beatrice Webb

Rodin and Charlotte Shaw in France, 1910

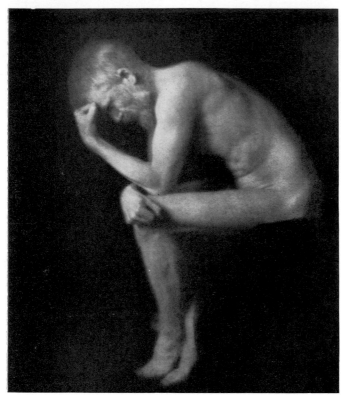

After Rodin's "Thinker"

Inspired by Charles
Doughty's "Arabia
Deserta"

because he knew exactly what was wanted and was never turned from his purpose.

So successful was the Stage Society production of *You Never Can Tell* that six matinées were given, and Max Beerbohm, his successor as dramatic critic of the *Saturday Review*, wrote:

> "Why are the commercial speculators so obtuse as not to run Mr. Bernard Shaw for all he is worth? I assure them that he would be worth a great deal to them."

Like St. Francis, Shaw could only say about the election, "I have lost all save honour," for the dramatic critics were at last shaking down to a firm opinion of him, the favourable ones playing up strongly. Max Beerbohm seemed to have come out as one of his supporters but G.B.S. refused to think of Max's blessings as anything but thinly disguised curses. For had he aimed at the commercial speculators he could have succeeded without standing on his head. Six matinées of *Candida* were given at the Court Theatre in 1904, with Granville Barker again playing Eugene Marchbanks, and as a result of this success the Vedrenne-Barker partnership came into being, and its main object was to magnify George Bernard Shaw as the Shakespeare of the age. From now Shaw could shovel his plays red-hot on to the stage; the only difficulty was to compose them quickly enough.

Granville Barker, as a producer and actor, supplemented Shaw in a remarkable way. That he was not entirely English and had Italian blood in his veins made him extremely acceptable to the dramatist. Shaw knew too well by now that however much he liked managing people he always failed in the attempt.

> "I can only manage schemes and ideas; the moment I have to deal with people who dont like me and people I cannot win over the limits of my tact make themselves felt. I play the deuce unless I can win by brute force of brains."

Barker, on the other hand, was patience and understanding personified; he was a genius at managing men and women; he had few ideas of his own but co-operating with another made it easy for him to excel in the representation of intellectual emotions. Barker's success in this direction made it possible for Shaw to achieve success in a kind of play unknown as yet to the Stage. At last, discussion and long speeches were given full dramatic significance.

I

G.B.S. was now compared with Shakespeare. He would not have it and wrote to Tolstoi's representative in England, Vladimir Tchertkoff:

"As you know I have striven hard to open English eyes to the emptiness of Shakespeare's philosophy, to the superficiality and secondhandness of his morality, to his weakness and incoherence as a thinker, to his snobbery, his vulgar prejudices, his ignorance, his disqualifications of all sorts, for the philosophic eminence claimed for him."

In the *Daily News*, April 17th, 1905, he again pitched into the fray with another attack on Shakespeare:

"Shakespeare's weakness lies in his complete deficiency in that highest sphere of thought in which poetry embraces religion, philosophy, morality. . . . His characters had no religion, no politics, no conscience, no hope, no convictions of any sort."

He knew when he was writing this that Tolstoi had expressed his own reaction to Shakespeare in a similar vein:

"I read Shakespeare" (he wrote to G.B.S.) "with repulsion, weariness and bewilderment."

Shaw had to overlook the fact when he received this note that Tolstoi also expressed disgust with 'the cravings of Beethoven and the ravings of Wagner'. He impressed upon Barker, with all the modesty at his disposal, that there were two orders in literature:

(1) The first order consists of those works in which the author accepts the current morality and religion ready-made, without any question as to their validity.
(2) The second order consists of those works in which the author writes from an original moral standpoint of his own, thereby making his book an original contribution to morals, religion and sociology as well as to *belles lettres*.

Granville Barker guessed correctly that Shaw was, in his own opinion, of the second order, while Shakespeare was of the first.

Although G.B.S. had more than his share of the plays produced at the Court Theatre he encouraged other authors to write plays for it. He selected for these invitations novelists of standing and in this way brought John Galsworthy to the fore as a dramatist. John Galsworthy interested Shaw because he saw a clash of personal emotions in society and not, as with Sidney Webb, the clash of impersonal institutions. It was a point of view which Shaw found abhorrent, especially with Galsworthy's plea for generosity and mutual understanding among opposing forces. He sensed in Galsworthy a love of the aristocrat and a contempt for the bureaucrat, and without a moment's hesitation wrote a long letter to the author of *The Silver Box*:

> "The aristocratic idol who does not earn his worship is an impostor and a robber; and it is found in practice that whereas an aristocracy which really governs can maintain its supremacy even when its members are in their personal conduct what we should call infernal scoundrels, aristocracies of the most charming ladies and gentlemen imaginable who do not govern finally collapse and are trampled out with every circumstance of violence and insult by the mob. By the mob I mean, the unidolized. And when I say idolized aristocracy I include its latest form which is an idolized bureaucracy of experts. All the fears expressed that socialism will produce a huge increase of officialism are quite well-grounded: under socialism we shall all be officials actually or potentially."

The new critics, instead of acclaiming Shaw, used his own weapons to denounce him. "The stage," they wrote, "is too fine an instrument for the expression of life, to be suited only to pointless satire and intellectual buffoonery." Or, "His plays will be forgotten as rapidly as they have become fashionable."

The whole of fashionable society, aristocratic as well as bureaucratic, flocked to see his plays, and G.B.S. expected as a result of his success the tables turned on him by the younger critics whose custom it was to decry the established. King Edward VII went to see *John Bull's Other Island* and was seen shaking in his seat and laughing aloud. Beatrice Webb noted in her diary:

> "The smart world is tumbling over one another in the worship of G.B.S. and even we have a sort of reflected glory. It is interesting to note that the completeness of his self-conceit will save him from the worst kind of deterioration. He is proof against flattery. Where it will injure him is in isolating him from serious intercourse with intimate friends working in other departments of life. Whenever

he is free there is such a crowd of journalists and literary hangers-on around him, that one feels it is kinder to spare him one's company and that it will be the instinct of many of his old friends engaged in administration, investigation or propaganda. What a transformation scene from those first years I knew him; the scathing bitter opponent of wealth and leisure, and now the adored one of the smartest and most cynical set of English 'Society'."

G.B.S. maintained that he was not interested in success as such. He wrote to Janet Achurch:

"Success was a thing that came to you, took your breath away as it came to Byron and Dickens and Kipling. What came to me was repeated failure. By the time I wore it down, I knew too much to care much about either failure or success."

He pleaded with his friends not to put him on the topmost shelf bound in plush and reserved for successful entertainers of Royalty but to go on treating him as a 'playwright in the process of becoming and with the worst yet to come'. . . . To Florence Farr he wrote:

"I am getting quite maddened by the business that my recent boom has brought on me. It is enough to make one curse the day I ever wrote a play."

To Ellen Terry he wrote:

"I dread success. To have succeeded is to have finished one's business on earth, like the male spider who is killed by the female the moment he has succeeded in his courtship."

To the world at large he reported that the enterprise had only succeeded because of team work: producer, actor, and playwright worked as one, and all were inspired by an audience that hungered for something new and significant. But 'Society' had its own way of dealing with new and significant ideas by treating them as playthings, by laughing and passing them round as the latest jokes and his quips and digs at themselves caused the greatest amusement; they all fought for his attendance at their At Homes. He had his ready reply to their invitations: for instance, when Lady X informed him on a card that she would be At Home on Thursday at 3 p.m. his reply was written on the other side: "So will G. Bernard Shaw."

George Bernard Shaw needed above everything else a Tormentor, one whose special prerogative it was to attack him on every possible occasion. In 1903 Bernard Shaw and Graham Wallas had innocently introduced a successful author, H. G. Wells, into the Fabian Society, and it did not take him long to become the leader of the *avant garde* of the Society. He charged the members with playing up to George Bernard Shaw, with having developed a private way of joking, with creating a lot of little Shaws who were affecting icono-clasms when they were really leading conventional little lives in suburbs. Wells incited the younger members to go into the large world, away from the drawing-room, setting service before gain, order above disorder and fact above personal advantage. He accused the Fabians of being poor, small and sluggish when they had a cause which should have made them the most powerful organization in the country, and he put it all down to the Shavian influence which had drugged them into a sense of power by words and phrases. He was ten years younger than Shaw, exuberant, enthusiastic and over optimistic. He had contempt for Shaw's tactics in misrepresenting what others said and belittling their motives. It was obvious to all who had watched Shaw in debate how cunningly he reduced the other side's argument to something completely false or ridiculous, some-thing for which he had a ready answer, relying more on his voice than on his mind, and more on his sonorous periods than on his reasoning. Wells, worked up to a temper by Shaw, fell into the language of a street brawl and this was just what Shaw had intended. In his fury Wells called G.B.S. a liar, a trickster, a reactionary and even an enemy of humanity. To his astonishment Shaw gladly admitted to all these defects and confessed to being even worse, for he declared himself to be also a coward and a thief!

It was a simple matter for Shaw to answer Wells, for funda-mentally he agreed with him about the Fabian mentality, for he too was an artist and knew how difficult it was for the impatient artist to work in that *milieu*, but he preferred to stand by the anti-artist because in his clerical soul he feared the artist in himself. From that moment Wells appointed himself as *The Tormentor* and opposed Shaw on every possible occasion. On the question of the Life Force, for example, Wells charged him with turning Evolution into a benevolent, soft and bright deity, and all because Shaw preferred the literary style of Butler to that of Darwin. At a by-election in Manchester, H. G. Wells supported the Liberal candidate because Shaw had spoken for the Socialist.

This recrimination had a background other than political or

aesthetic: the Fabians prided themselves on their exceptional frankness in sexual matters. Hubert Bland confessed to Wells one day that he was a student of illicit love. Wells passed on this information to Bland's handsome daughter, and she jubilantly reported it back to her father. Bland mentioned this betrayal to Webb and Olivier, who passed on this information to George Bernard Shaw, who interpreted the word betrayal in the one way which lent a dramatic quality to it and warned everyone that Wells was a fearful roué and not to be trusted with young females. It was this which caused Wells to act in this hysterical fashion.

Gossip was second nature to Shaw and by putting forward his own confidences, often created on the spur of the moment in mischievousness, he elicited the most daring confessions, especially from wives of friends, who only saw through him after they had succumbed to his irresistible humour. Mrs. Bland, one of the first to succumb, described him as the grossest flatterer she had ever met, "horribly untrustworthy as he repeats everything he hears and does not always stick to the truth. . . ."

Meanwhile Herr Siegfried Trebitsch, an Austrian author of repute on a visit to England, was treated by William Archer to a melancholy talk on the parlous state of the theatre in this country. Herr Trebitsch was interested in Culture and was not surprised to hear of the lack of response to High Art in 'commercial England'.

> "Take our Mr. Shaw for example" (William Archer said), "he has to make do with matinées at experimental theatres. No commercial theatre is prepared to speculate a penny on him."

Herr Trebitsch had never heard of Mr. Shaw and regarded the experimental theatre as a sign of failure. He visualized immediately a poverty-stricken genius living in a garret with a cupboard full of plays, all unwanted except by a few cranks. What greater service to humanity could a cultured writer perform than to discover a neglected genius? To him England was cut off from the cultured world by a barrier of sea and language; it would be worth his visit to England if he could add another illustrious name to those of Goethe, Heine and Molière! Archer thereupon handed him the published works of this 'neglected dramatist' and Herr Trebitsch seized the first opportunity to read one of his plays. He dipped into *Candida* and was entranced, never dreaming that anyone but Goethe could have created a character like Eugene Marchbanks, with a soul so sensitive, so refined, and so unhappy.

He obtained an introduction through Archer and met the Shaws at 10 Adelphi Terrace and found when he saw the dramatist that 'his features showed how the dreamer had given up the unequal struggle with the thinker. . . .'

Herr Trebitsch, in a prepared speech, disclosed to Shaw that he was determined to translate his plays into German with a view to conquering the German public for him, and was amazed by Shaw's answer: "I am a dusty relic of the day before yesterday. I belong to the world of Yellow Books, Keystone Novels and Aubrey Beardsley." Then he referred his visitor to Charlotte. "She thinks me the greatest of all dramatists, past and present, such is the bias people have towards their property." He jumped up and called out, "Charlotte, here is a young lunatic Archer sent me: come down and help me fling him out of the window!"

She came, smiling and apologetic, and quickly recalled her husband to business. "He is quite right," she said, "why should not the German theatre do to you what it has done to Shakespeare, naturalize you into a German dramatist?"

The upshot of this visit was the signing of an agreement in which Herr Trebitsch was given a year in which to translate three of Shaw's plays and to get them performed. When Trebitsch left Adelphi Terrace with the agreement, Shaw said to his wife:

"That's got rid of him. He'll never do it because no German has a sense of humour."

Within the year, *The Devil's Disciple*, *Candida*, and *Arms and the Man* were translated and in the hands of a publisher, and arrangements had been made for the performance of *The Devil's Disciple*. George Bernard Shaw had got a foothold in German-speaking territory, for in Trebitsch's words:

"It was one of the most remarkable first nights I have ever experienced: one could feel a breath of something alien in the air; one could feel the impact of a new atmosphere."

The other two plays were even more successful and yet Shaw considered this success in Austria as a flash in the pan and wrote to Trebitsch that he would much rather have been a triumphant failure. Trebitsch found it far from simple to work with him: "Shaw was tempestuous and I was steadfast; he wanted to *demand* and I wanted to convince."

At the same time Shaw had to deal with another temperamental clash nearer home. Vedrenne became more and more thrifty, almost to the point of stinginess; while Barker, warmed by his growing reputation, became increasingly extravagant in his demands, having only perfection in mind. Shaw backed Vedrenne to the point of refusing to pay more than £5 a week even to Ellen Terry who had now agreed to play the part of Lady Cicely. She was very sweet about it and addressed the dramatist whom she had never met as "Dear Silly", which G.B.S. kept as a token of his conquest at last.

All reformers now placed George Bernard Shaw's name on the top of their lists as the person who could help, by his writing, to eradicate their particular evils. The number of articles from his pen were legion. All his articles were not only widely read but eagerly discussed; articles on such subjects as 'Flogging in the Navy', 'Fiscal Policy', 'Vivisection', 'Egypt', 'Spelling Reform', 'Minimum Income', 'Regulations in Hospitals', 'Publishers' Methods', 'The Czar's Visit to England', and of course 'The Medical Profession'. Somehow the evils still seemed to remain and he put it down to the fact that his suggestions were too logical and reasonable. He complained that it was a ghastly business to get anything done: one had to shout and lie, mock and plead, make a fool of oneself generally to find in the end that things had receded. There were moments when he was ashamed of the whole business of propaganda and would throw it over and try to understand himself rather than humanity at large.

Writers of all kinds were now writing articles about George Bernard Shaw. In his fiftieth year, Charlotte was pasting into her scrapbooks articles on: 'The Rise and Decline of George Bernard Shaw', 'His Woman Wooers', 'Jester to the Nation', 'Is He among the Prophets?', among hundreds of others, and she was disturbed by the intimacy and audacity of the matter. The G.B.S. projected on the world was a fiction, in her opinion, and there was no way of stopping it. The G.B.S. she preferred to know was still the Genius of her dreams and not the author of *Major Barbara* and *Mrs. Warren's Profession*.

It became clear to many of his friends that the real, the basic Shaw was a lover of power and wealth, and that the artist in him was a superstructure imposed upon him by the coming into the Shaw household of an alien influence in the person of Vandeleur Lee. Beatrice Webb wrote this of *Major Barbara*:

"G.B.S.'s play turned out to be a dance of devils, amazingly clever, grimly powerful in the second act, but ending as all his plays end (or at any rate most of them) in an intellectual and moral morass. . . . I doubt the popular success of the play: it is hell tossed on the stage with no hope of heaven."

G.B.S. felt it imperative to hasten and express the antithesis of this view by introducing an artist in *The Doctor's Dilemma*, who, on his deathbed, expresses his credo:

"I believe in Michelangelo, Velasquez and Rembrandt, in the Might of Design, the Mystery of Colour, the Redemption of all things by Beauty everlasting, and the Message of Art that has made these hands blessed. Amen, Amen."

He was rehearsing this play with Granville Barker playing Louis Dubedat, the artist betrayed by the specialists, and his eyes were bubbling with merriment and mischief, laughing aloud at his jokes against the wealthy medical men, laughing too at the audacity and poetry of the artist, fascinated by the multi-coloured shower of epigrams, when at the death scene, there was a sudden transfiguration, a sense of unlimitedness, and for once he was conscious that he had expressed something beyond even himself, not a belief in power and wealth, but in beauty, the redemption of all things by beauty.

The legendary G.B.S., the mountebank, the swashbuckler, the philanderer, the lover of power and wealth, was now caught unaware by his own art and was moved to tears.

Shaw was soon to know from actual experience the thoughts that come to one on point of death. He was on holiday at Llanbedr and was enjoying his daily bathe when he found himself carried away and in danger of drowning. There was no pier, no boat, nor any mortal means of help. He swam as best he could although he was being whirled round, until the exhaustion of fighting the waves caused him to surrender entirely, and then he became conscious of being submerged. With death confronting him, he could think of two things only: that Charlotte would be worried if he was not back in time and that he had not put his agreements with his translators in proper form. At this point he discovered that he was miraculously standing on firm ground up to his waist in water. He had been carried on to a sandbank.

# Chapter Ten

THE shock of being alive brought with it an obsessive sense of urgency: he would pass into history at all costs. He resented the reputation he had gained as Jack of all Tirades and Master of none. He admitted that none of his plays had, as yet, earned the crown of immortality, and he meant to write play after play until at least one would stand out as the work of a master mind, the greatest intellect of the twentieth century.

In spite of his plays the old ideas and sentiments persisted: In *Man and Superman* the meaning of life was written in the skies for all to see; in *Candida* he had exploded the mad rage for happiness; in *The Devil's Disciple* he had shown that love was not necessary to inspire great deeds, and yet the world behaved as if his works had never been written.

He knew from the tempo of his inspiration that the play he was writing, *Getting Married*, was not going to be the masterpiece, but he meant to go on to the bitter end in case something of great moment came to him, like the Hell scene in *Man and Superman*, the death scene in *The Doctor's Dilemma*, and like the trial scene in *The Devil's Disciple*. He was letting this play write itself and shape itself and he did not see what he was driving at. He hoped, as in *You Never Can Tell*, he might yet introduce a decisive character in the last act to bind the whole play together and to give it significance. He complained to his friends:

"The more I try professional art the greater becomes my horror and weariness of it. I'll make my new play impossible in point of length and subject. No division into scenes and acts but permitting for short intervals for a rest and a drink."

He came to the conclusion that his other plays had proved ineffective, except from the box-office point of view, because the plots obscured the issues; *Getting Married* would have no such subterfuges, it was to be a dramatic tract, a pamphlet almost, in which a discussion on marriage was to take place with frankness and good humour so that the most puritanical of eavesdroppers could listen without embarrassment. To give it authority he introduced a Bishop. But

Shaw's Imp was also at work when he introduced the Bishop's sister and made her declare to her suitor that her only reason for marrying would be to have a child and then the father of it would have to be cleared out of the house for two years because at such times "he was superfluous, importunate and ridiculous". The Imp was on the verge of supplying 'a Sunday husband' as being the more potent factor in a child's upbringing. In spite of Shaw's unsentimental approach to this subject he found himself introducing an ecstatic love song, a Song of Solomon:

"When you loved me I gave you the whole sun and stars to play with. I gave you eternity in a single moment, strength of the mountains in one clasp of your arms, and the volume of all the seas in one impulse of your soul. A moment only; was it not enough? Were you not paid then for all the rest of your struggle on earth? . . ."

There were the usual digs at English life, when the Bishop explains, for example: "This is not quarrelling, Lesbia, it's only English family life," and in the inevitable Preface he decried sentimentality by giving his beloved Ruskin's childhood as an example:

"Ruskin's mother gratified the sensual side of her maternal passion not by cuddling her son, but by whipping him when he fell downstairs or was slack in learning the Bible off by heart, and this grotesque safety valve for voluptuousness, mischievous as it was in many ways, had at least the advantage that the child did not enjoy it and was not debauched by it, as he would have been by transports of sentimentality."

This was the time when Shaw came across the writings of Sigmund Freud and his attitude to this psychologist was the same as to all pioneers: "I have said it all before him."

*Getting Married* was to be put on at the Haymarket and Shaw found it extremely difficult to make his actors and actresses play it as he had intended. This was a static play and static it had to be whether the theatre crowd would like it or not. While with his other plays he encouraged the exaggerated, flamboyant style of Grand Opera, here he had to train them to converse quietly and not to permit stage business to interfere with the words. He told them that one day he would write a play which consisted of talk without movement, with nothing happening except the ecstasy of thought and the tragedy of it. He explained Ruskin's insanity as entirely due to his failure to make himself understood: everybody paid him lip service and none but a few choice spirits understood him. Shaw was too sane a person to be driven out of his wits; he meant to perfect the means of communication between dramatist and playgoer by the subtle bond of thought, even if he became thereby the chipping block of all the bright original spirits of the rising generation.

He was also working at the same time on a Preface to *The Sanity of Art*, now to be published in book form. Although thirteen years had passed since he had perpetrated his assault on Dr. Max Nordau, he did not feel like changing a word of the argument, but with the squeamishness of advancing years, he softened one or two expressions which struck him as being uncivil to Nordau. He was at last becoming sensitive, alas, to good manners. In the Preface he again asserted his belief in journalism as the highest form of literature

> "The writer who aims at producing the platitudes which are not for an age but for all time has his reward in being unreadable in all ages."

Without any squeamishness on his part he confessed that although he dealt with all periods he had never studied any but the present which always showed a chaotic front to the people of the day.

> "Written history stops several decades back; and the bridge of personal recollection on which older men stand does not exist for the recruit. . . . Dont forget that the race is only struggling out of its dumbness and that it is only in moments of inspiration that we get out a sentence. All the rest is padding."

Unfortunately for him, the world had gone on since he first wrote his article for *Liberty*, and as he himself looked at the New Art, the New Poetry, the New Drama and heard the New Music, he felt inclined to write a book similar to *Degeneration*, for he could make nothing of Post-Impressionism in art, Imagism in poetry, and Expressionism in drama. "They say that they are expressing themselves," he said of Cézanne, of Ezra Pound, of T. S. Eliot, of James Joyce and of Eugene O'Neill, of Stravinsky and of Schönberg, of Wyndham Lewis and Picasso, "but they obviously have no selves to express!"

Charlotte had her own way of assuring her husband's immortality: she lodged £1,000 to Rodin's credit on the undertaking that he was to be under no obligation whatever in respect of it, and might, if

he so desired, make a bust of her husband. She dearly wanted Rodin
to do it, and knew, that once the money was there, he would
put her husband in a line with Balzac whose bust had turned her
head; she had had her education 'finished' in France and had fallen
for Balzac's work. The sculptor made enquiries as to who this Englishman was and could find out nothing about him in France. That he
was a man of substance, a *bourgeois gentilhomme*, was obvious, but
Rodin had no time for mere wealth: it was character and romance
and thought he was interested in, young love and old wisdom, the
passionate embrace and the dispassionate thought. The Shaws went
to France, called on Rodin but the sculptor was not impressed with
the face of the proposed sitter. Charlotte informed Rodin that her
husband was the Voltaire of England, showed him proof of his fame
and at last Rodin agreed. Rilke, the young German poet who acted
as Rodin's factotum, watched her fluttering round her husband during
the sittings, like 'a spring breeze playing through the fleece of a he-
goat', urging the sculptor all the time to immortalize her husband.
She complained that all the caricaturists and the photographers aimed
at making her husband a sort of suburban Mephistopheles and stressed
that G.B.S. really had the face of Christ, did he not think so? Rodin
replied:

"I know nothing of Mr. Shaw's reputation but what is there I
will give you."

Like a good Frenchman he could not hurt this 'charming lady with
the boorish husband', and he agreed that there was something of the
Christ face in him!

Rodin's technique interested Shaw, who had never before seen a
sculptor at work: the mechanical, unsentimental way he plied his
callipers, measuring his features with them. To Charlotte it seemed
barbarous when the sculptor, unsatisfied with his work, cut off un-
ceremoniously the nose or the ear and with the quick movement of
the hand replaced the organ to his satisfaction.

When it was finished, G.B.S. was not very happy with it because
it robbed him of his eyes and made him look blind. Charlotte however
was satisfied and bought the head of Balzac to go with it in her sitting-
room. She could not understand her husband's criticism because she saw
the eyes as looking inward and she wished him remembered like that.

"Well," G.B.S. summed up this adventure, "I'll be known to
posterity as the man who sat for Rodin, if for nothing else."

Granville Barker thought the bust unnecessary because Velasquez's
portrait of Pope Innocent was obviously based on Shaw and that
should have been enough.

By this time the two Shaws were tired of flitting from one country house to another, or staying at hotels, and when told that the house they were inhabiting would be sold with some of the furniture they bought it because it would have cost as much in time and trouble moving to another house. G.B.S. liked to think that he was led to Ayot St. Lawrence, a tiny village in Hertfordshire, because there was an aura there which he had not sensed anywhere else in his travels. Charlotte could not work up any enthusiasm for the place, but it would at least keep him away from London for the week-ends. It was as well that he could be in the country because he still suffered from headaches; to her this was a mark of the exceptional person for she was told that Carlyle, G. F. Watts and Charles Darwin were addicted to this recurrent malady. Here in this village he would at least be free from doting females and male bores.

It soon went round that the new people were not gentry, for they did not shoot, nor hunt. The squire's wife called on them and suggested that they contribute something to the village school, an annual prize, for example.

"I am prepared," G.B.S. answered, "to give a handsome prize to the worst-behaved child, for I was that at school. And look at me now!"

He was invited by the Rector to address the Sunday School and was only too glad to do it. This was the first time he had ever addressed children. He started by telling them that he was a very old man but that they must not be overawed by mere age. When he was a little boy he thought that his father was infallible, but when he grew up he found that his father had every possible weakness except amiability. In the same way, when they grew up they would also scrap all that they had been taught, to discover that one person at least was worth listening to because he was different from everyone else. This modest reference to himself brought the only laugh.

Charlotte became aware of the fact that her husband was pursued by females even in this unapproachable village and it demanded all her tact to keep them off, for he had a way of encouraging them by answering their letters and even arranging to meet them. A man of fifty, she knew, was a dangerous animal, and it was wiser not to let this recrudescence of adolescence take hold of him. However, there was one young woman who was more persistent than the others, would not be put off in any way and actually obtained a motor-bicycle that she could come often to Ayot St. Lawrence. She claimed that she alone understood the great man, and that he understood her. Both were above such vulgar things as sentimental love. She would arrive at ten or eleven o'clock at night and assume that the New Rectory, as the Shaw house was called, was her home, and that Shaw was her husband. She had established a hold over G.B.S. or he of her, and they seemed to have come to a mutual understanding. When Charlotte would not permit her entrance into the house she camped in a field at the back, or lodged in a nearby farm. G.B.S. would meet her at the local inn, however, and at last Charlotte had to appeal to Granville Barker to intervene. Charlotte had, more or less, adopted Granville Barker, and begged him to help her in her predicament because her life had been made a mockery in the village.

Granville Barker, who spent many week-ends at Ayot St. Lawrence, urged Shaw to stop seeing this person because he was harming the girl as well as his wife.

"She is an exquisite sort of person with talent and through her I do not feel so completely out of touch with the young, for she knows Rupert Brooke quite well and can talk about everything modern and can be indelicately frank," G.B.S. informed G.B.

Granville Barker threatened to shoot her and make Shaw clear away the mess. "Marriage is loyalty or nothing," he pleaded.

"Dont on any account be melodramatic with her for it will only amuse her. She is above that kind of thing; she is the Super-woman."

The association with her was amplified and exaggerated into Shavian proportions, he assuming the double role of Lord Summerhayes and Tarleton, and the result was the dullest of all his plays so far, *Misalliance*.

> LORD SUMMERHAYES (to Hypatia): "I'll put it as bluntly as I can. When, as you say, I made an utter fool of myself, believe me, I made a poetic fool of myself. I was seduced, not by appetite, which, thank Heaven, I've long outlived: not even by the desire of second childhood for a child companion, but by the innocent impulse to place the delicacy and wisdom and spirituality of my age at the affectionate service of your youth for a few years."

Superimposed on this play was a running commentary on the relationship between parents and children, for according to G.B.S. parents never knew their children or what to do with them, and children regarded their parents as anachronisms. As to schooling, it was high time, he believed, that we fitted the school to the child and gave up the barbarian practice of fitting the child to the institution.

He had to assure himself that even the lowest form of human being could be roused to a generous act, otherwise he saw no hope for the human race. It meant therefore the writing of another religious play in terms of the dregs of humanity and prove that the Life Force had a way of getting even these, suddenly and unawares. As a reaction to the conversation piece *The Showing Up of Blanco Posnet* was full of action and incident. It was set in a wild outpost in the U.S.A. and dealt with a horse thief.

Blanco Posnet had just stolen a horse and knows, that if caught, hanging will be his fate. As he is riding it away, he is stopped by a woman in great agitation, who pleads with him to lend her his horse with which to take her dying child to the doctor. He does so and is thus left on foot twenty miles from anywhere. He is arrested and charged with the theft of the horse. A woman of ill fame declares that she had seen him on the horse and when he is about to be convicted, the woman who had borrowed it is brought into the court and denies that the rider was Blanco Posnet, thus saving his life. The prostitute is touched by the story of the dying child and confesses to her perjury. Shaw puts his own message in the vulgar tongue of Blanco:

> "He's a sly One, He's a mean One, He lies low for you; He plays cat and mouse with you. He lets you run loose until you think you are shut of Him, and then, when you least expect it, He's got you. . . ."

No one could possibly regard this cat and mouse image of the relationship of God and man as attractive but it represented Shaw's own relationship with the Life Force at the moment. The Censor of plays did not object to the use of the prostitute or the atmosphere of brutality and all the crudity of the backwood, but all he asked for were certain innocent alterations to make the Almighty seem more respectable. Shaw refused to comply and permission for performance in England was refused. It was however produced at the Abbey Theatre, Dublin, and the audience, strangely enough, treated it as a comedy and overlooked the religious aspect of it. Small wonder that G.B.S. in giving evidence before the Joint Select Committee of Enquiry into the Censorship claimed to be 'a conscientiously immoral writer'.

Shaw sent the play with a covering letter to Count Tolstoi and expressed humbly his debt of gratitude to the person who was the first to open up a new mine of dramatic material. He pleased Tolstoi

G. B. S. the Orator
(André Maurois behind
the microphone)

The self-appointed
Tormentor of G. B. S.:
H. G. Wells (with J. B.
Priestley on his left)

*Pygmalion:* the film, 1938. G. B. S. with Wendy Hiller, Leslie Howard,
Gabriel Pascal and Anthony Asquith (*My Fair Lady*
is the 1956 musical version of *Pygmalion*)

Party at Malvern Festival, 1932, with J. T. Grein, extreme left, front row (*standing*),
and Sir Barry Jackson, extreme right, front row (*seated*)

by declaring that he was not an Art for Art's sake man and would not lift a finger to produce a work of art if he thought that there was nothing more than that in it, and ended with an ironical jest that "if the world was one of God's jokes, would you work any the less to make it a good joke instead of a bad one?"

Shaw had gone far from the days when he first arrived in London, singing to himself:

> "Life is a jest, all things show it
> I thought so once, now I know it."

Tolstoi's reply came many months later for he was at that time deeply involved in a domestic tragedy:

May 9th, 1910.

My dear Mr. Bernard Shaw,

I have received your play and your witty letter. I have read your play with pleasure and am in full sympathy with the subject and your remark that the preaching of righteousness has generally little influence on people. Young people regard as laudable that which is contrary to righteousness is quite correct but it does not however follow that such preaching is unnecessary. The reason for the failure is that those who preach do not fulfil what they preach, i.e. hypocrisy.

I cannot agree with what you call your theology. You enter into controversy with that in which no thinking person of our time believes or can believe: with a God-Creator and yet you seem yourself to recognize a God who has definite aims comprehensible to you. 'To my mind,' you write, 'unless we conceive God as engaged in a continual struggle to surpass Himself, as striving at every birth to make a better man than before, we are conceiving nothing better than an omnipotent snob.'

Concerning the rest of what you say about God and about evil, I will repeat the words I said about your Man and Superman namely that the problem of God and evil is too important to be spoken of in jest. And therefore I will tell you quite frankly that I received a very painful impression from the concluding words of your letter. . . .

Yours sincerely,<br>Leo Tolstoi.

Tolstoi's letter moved him deeply, for the faint praise cheered him more than the resounding applause of the theatre or the

K

appreciative laughter of an Albert Hall audience. It was a realization of a hope in those far-off days of failure that one day he
would win the approval of William Morris and Tolstoi, both of
whom had shaken the world with the majesty of their spirit. Tolstoi
was not the first person to rebuke him for his jesting, but it was
physically and artistically impossible for him to exclude laughter;
it was part of his make-up inherited from his father, his words
shaped themselves in that way and no effort on his part could
check it.

If the preaching of righteousness had little influence on people, then
the only alternative was to preach downright wickedness, and that
must be the theme of his next play.

He threw off a play rapidly to teach that "the young had better
get into trouble to have their souls awakened by disgrace". The theme
was not inspired by Tolstoi this time but by Samuel Butler. The
play wrote itself and it was the old, old cry that conventional people
with all their respectability and all their piety have no way of telling
right from wrong because their fixed social habits had shut out all
promptings coming from the Life Force.

> "Nowadays we do not seem to know" (G.B.S. wrote) "that
> there is any other test of conduct except morality; and the result
> is that the young had better have their souls awakened by disgrace
> . . . than drift along from their cradles to their graves, doing what
> other people do and knowing nothing of good and evil, of courage
> and cowardice. I hate to see dead people walking about: it is
> unnatural."

This play, *Fanny's First Play*, swam forward in the tide for two
and a half years. It paid to preach 'disgrace'. It was put on by Lillah
McCarthy, the wife of Granville Barker, and she was glad to find
that Shaw was no longer the idol of the few who had worshipped at
the shrine of *the Court* but had become the Jesting Apostle for the
many. The shopkeeper, shopgirl, the suburban mother and the kindly
old gentleman who played bowls in Wimbledon discovered him to
be a jolly amusing fellow!

George Bernard Shaw had also become an amiable old gentleman
who went for walks with his wife. He was the successful playwright
who knew how to turn out a well-made play and was linked up by
the critics with the very dramatists whom Shaw had once denounced.
If people wanted an amusing harmless evening they went to a Shaw
play, and there was always one to be seen. He was invited to lecture

to Churches of all denominations, to distribute prizes at school and
to address meetings on the same platform as peers and Tory Members
of Parliament, who considered him as one of them. The Universities
of Oxford and Cambridge invited him to address the students, and
as the London School of Economics had now become a flourishing
concern he was canonized there along with the Webbs.

He accepted an invitation to lecture at the New Reform Club and
he chose as his subject *Modern Religion*, refusing on any account to
give a talk on the Drama, because, as he put it, "I am weary at the
thought of my association with it."

His first words at this lecture made his audience shudder, for they
might have been uttered at the Moody and Sankey revivalist meeting
he had attended in Dublin:

> "One of the reasons which has induced me to take up this
> subject of late years is the simple observation that people who have
> no religion are cowards and cads. We must have a religion if we
> are to do anything worth doing to get our civilization out of the
> terrible mess in which it now is."

He confided that the purpose of his life was to make people more
and more conscious of their souls and the purpose which has evolved
the soul as its special organ. How different were the impressions he
made on different people: the preacher, the Utopian, the man of
common sense, the expert, the man who believed in exaggeration, the
artist, the philistine, the immoralist and the saint. He had become the
universal subject of conversation and each found that he or she was
talking about an entirely different person. At this meeting they heard
him say:

> "All English men and women are eager to be ladies and gentle-
> men; yet the things we do to become ladies and gentlemen are
> just those that steep us in the basest caddishness and the deepest
> irreligion. If you allow people who are caddish and irreligious to
> become the governing force, the nation will be destroyed. We
> are to-day largely governed by persons without political courage,
> and that is what is the matter with us."

What did Shaw mean by a religious person? An atheist in his view
was not a man who had no religion any more than a professing
Christian was necessarily a person who had a religion. He meant that
a religious person was one who conceived himself or herself to be the

instrument of some purpose in the Universe which was a high purpose, and was the motive power of Evolution, that is, of a continual ascent in organization and power of life, and extension of life. Any person who realized that there was such a power and that his business and joy in life was to do its work, and his pride and point of honour to identify himself with it, that person was religious.

There were not many such religious people but the Life Force had a way, as described by Blanco Posnet, of getting people even when they were certain of having escaped it. And because Capitalism was enforced irreligion, whatever its power and pretensions, it was already crumbling before the trumpet call of the few.

Shaw always ended on a note of optimism because he felt that the Life Force would not have given him the vision of Utopia unless it were within the reach of man. First the vision, then the urge and then the achievement, all the three stages bridged by reason and common sense. In his case there was no ritual, no renewal through prayer, no fasting, no trance: it was his own particular private religion and that was enough.

It demanded no self-sacrifice, his vegetarianism was not a form of self-denial but almost epicurean in its delight: he found that he could work longer and with greater intensity than ever before. It was so natural to him that he had almost forgotten why and when he had become one. Charlotte remained a cannibal and so when the Bishop of St. Albans invited them to dinner, Shaw had to reply that he was the only lion that lived exclusively on grass.

G.B.S. always got on extremely well with all the people whom he denounced: teachers flocked to his meetings, doctors sought his friendship and wealthy capitalists loved his humour. The only people he preferred not to meet were the Shavians, for they brought with them the feeling of shame and failure.

His fame had spread throughout the whole world and he was therefore not surprised to receive the following letter from William Rothenstein, an artist of repute, a collector of saints, mystics and geniuses:

July 1st, 1912.

My dear Shaw,

I want you to meet Rabindranath Tagore, as you have not met many saints in your life, and perhaps as few poets. He too must see, is seeing clearly, that England is not Anglo-India, and you must come up and talk with him. He represents all that is religious, literary, democratic, scholarly, aristocratic in Bengal. If there were no other representative we should look upon India as the most perfect country in the world. This sounds like too youthful enthusiasm, but our gifts lie in power, tact and vitality rather than in personal perfection, and you will each give the other an insight into qualities suspected but not actually experienced perhaps. . . .

Yours always,

W.R.

G.B.S. did not reply to the letter at once. He read it and re-read it and found in it the usual misunderstanding of his life. He had met saints and had worked with them: William Morris, Charles Bradlaugh, Prince Kropotkin, Annie Besant, Joynes, Sidney and Beatrice Webb and the countless anonymous people who rose out of their circumstances and breathed nobility of character. He had met many poets, not the least of whom was the tramp W. H. Davies whom he had recognized from the very beginning. And there was the 'noble Savage', Edward Carpenter, besides Yeats and Wilde, William Morris and Francis Adams. And what about Swinburne whom he had frightened out of his life? And George Meredith, who was pushed aside by his family because they wanted to hear Shaw and no one else? As for personal perfection, he did not want to meet perfect people unless they were aware of their imperfections.

This letter chilled him but Charlotte was attracted to all things Eastern and they accepted.

G.B.S. worked out his conversation with Tagore. He dipped into his verse and found it as unreadable as Whitman, rehearsed a few good stories and read up a little about Gandhi, who had come to the front as a politician of the first order in his own country.

Charlotte reminded him, as they set out, to let Tagore get a word in occasionally.

"I must make a good impression on India. He's probably never heard of me."

Shaw started talking as soon as he sat down and ate almost nothing. This made it easy for him to go on without interruption. He told Tagore exactly what religion meant, that Gandhi was religiously inspired by Tolstoi, Thoreau and Henry Salt, that he had known saints to be rogues and many rogues to be saints. "In India you revere saints, but in this country a person like myself is a figure of scorn. I have to conceal my thirst for holiness as my father concealed his thirst for drink."

When tea was served, Shaw refused it with the remark that the three most civilized poisons came from the East: Tea, Culture and

Refinement, and to this Tagore replied that the West had sent over deadlier poisons in the shape of Science, Industrialism and Competition. At once there was a head-on collision about wealth, Shaw insisting that money was the most important thing on earth and the universal regard for it was the most hopeful fact in civilization. But Tagore could not take this seriously and praised the virtues of poverty, humility and simplicity.

Shaw put down his failure to impress the Indian poet to the fact that he was overawed by the wonderful beard, for it was blue-black and of the softest silky texture. He had always been overawed by these bearded godlike men and he secretly cherished the hope that his own beard would one day prove equally impressive: he was already converting the Mephistophelean aspect of it into something approaching the beards of the Michelangelo ancients.

There were also two other ambitions that he privately nursed: one was to be the first author to amass a million, and the other was to live to two hundred.

# Chapter Eleven

On February 19th, 1913, his mother, Mrs. Carr Shaw, died at the age of eighty-three, twenty-eight years after the death of her husband and thirty-six years after the death of Agnes. G.B.S. had to make all the arrangements for the funeral and he decided upon a cremation and a Church of England service, knowing full well that she would have preferred earth burial because she had a dread of fire and a love of earth. Shaw was a fire-worshipper and looked forward eagerly to going behind the scenes on the day of the cremation to watch the flames. It was a purely aesthetic experience, strangely impersonal in its relationship to his mother. He realized that he had troubled very little about her in her lifetime and that this was the end of a relationship thrust on him through birth. He asked Granville Barker to accompany him because the actor had played Dubedat and had played so beautifully that scene in which a burning was described:

"Louis: Such a color! Garnet color. Waving like silk. Liquid lovely flame flowing up through the bay leaves, and not burning them. Well, I shall be a flame like that. I'm sorry to disappoint the poor little worms; but the last of me shall be the flame in the burning bush."

Shaw was not disappointed with the effect and Barker watched his look of ecstasy as the coffin burst into twirling rhythms of soaring flames. On the way out Shaw became quite frivolous, hummed and even spoke of the financial release. Granville Barker had to remark, "You certainly are a merry soul, Shaw," and shrunk from his contact, leaving him at the earliest moment.

Shaw himself drove down immediately to Beachy Head where the Webbs were giving a week-end party to inaugurate the *New Statesman*, a weekly review to propagate the Fabian viewpoint. He arrived late and explained that he had been delayed by his mother's cremation and as he settled down on the sofa in front of the fire he remarked that the military understood well the kind of music that was wanted at a funeral:

"On the way to the grave a solemn dead march, and on the way back from it, a gay and rousing tune." Then added, because he noticed an unsympathetic silence, "Don't think that I am a man who forgets the dead."

His whole behaviour, however, conveyed to the others that he took death more lightly than all but the very heartless. He took it upon himself to lecture them:

"One has to be practical and unsentimental with matter out of place, it's of no more use, so away with it."

It was a strange interlude for an inauguration. They arranged for G.B.S. to write a weekly article on current events but it was to be anonymous, because as the Editor, Clifford Sharp, callously put it: 'Responsible people were in the habit of discounting whatever Shaw wrote under his name and it was the object of the *New Statesman* to attract the responsible and to repel the irresponsible.' The Editor was a man in the twenties, married to Hubert Bland's daughter and had no particular respect for the opinions or writings of G.B.S.

When the journal was launched G.B.S. found that his article had been mercilessly slashed, in fact he could hardly recognize his own contribution. He did not complain but explained that he was much worse when in the twenties:

"I never permitted anyone to get a word in. In this article there are at least a dozen words of mine permitted to stay. I have always treated disrespectfully what was treated by others with reverence, so why should I expect to be treated otherwise?"

It was his opinion that people who had a religion could laugh their way through anything, even the flames of Hell. He was working at a play, a new and highly original play, he thought, incorporating this view. Shaw was having a high time with martyrs as figures of fun. The original object of this play was to show that kindness to animals pays, but the moment he put his pen to paper, the whole theme went right off the rails and there was no controlling it, although the moral originally intended shone through. Ultimately it was the old theme which obsessed Shaw, this time served up as a religious pantomime, established morality and law doing the most unjust and immoral acts to suppress the propaganda of a new spirit which they feared. The play was based on one of the Roman persecutions of the early Christians when two parties were conveyed to the Coliseum for martyrdom. The Centurion remarks as he watches these Christians:

"That's what we have to put up with from these Christians every day, sir. They're always laughing and joking something scandalous. They've no religion, that's how it is."

*Androcles and the Lion,* when produced on September 1st, 1913, was generally considered as an adolescent bit of buffoonery and perished miserably under the storm of ridicule. Reverend Thomas Yates came forward in its defence with a solemn declaration: "I protest that I prefer this direct challenge to the power and reality of the Christian Religion to that sickly exploitation of Christianity for theatrical purposes of which *The Sign of the Cross* was a nauseous example."

Instead of the Government exclaiming, "Send the inconceivable Shaw to the stake," the authorities accepted him as a matter of course. When the miners struck, when the military were called out in labour disputes, when Mrs. Pankhurst was put into prison in her militant campaign, a brilliant letter in the Press from George Bernard Shaw clarified the issue and everything went on as before. Shaw was not surprised therefore to receive a request from Madame Tussaud for permission to include a wax model of him and he did not ask whether he was to stand among the respectable celebrities or in the Chamber of Horrors. His face was so familiar through the thousands of photographs, caricatures and drawings appearing almost daily in the papers, that it was hardly necessary for him to give a sitting.

In spite of a sustained effort to get himself accepted as a religious leader, inspired as the saints of old, by direct communication with the Life Force, there was little response to his impersonal religion. Even his old friend Beatrice Webb had to explain where he went wrong in his plays and in his morality:

"In his complete ignoring of religion. By religion I mean, the communion of the soul with some righteousness felt to be outside and above itself. This may take the conscious form of prayer: or the unconscious form of ever-present and persisting aspiration, a faith, a hope and a devotion to a wholly disinterested purpose. It is this unconscious form of religion which lies at the base of all Sidney's activity. . . .

Not one of G.B.S.'s men or women have either the conscious or unconscious form of religion. The abler of these puppets of their thoughts deny it, the stupider are oblivious of it, a few are blatant hypocrites. And that being so, there is nothing left for them to be but intellects or brutes, and for the most part they are both."

Beatrice coupled Granville Barker and H. G. Wells with Shaw and prayed that the former would somehow gather the strength of mind to emancipate himself from the influence of G.B.S. and find his own soul. Granville Barker waited his moment however, for he was longing for an opportunity which he had never had, to make a thorough study of the interpretation of Shakespeare who had always been his inspiration. As he had been on the stage since boyhood he could not feel detached enough to break away from the artificial world in which G.B.S. reigned supreme, and continue with his own writing. G.B.S. was fully aware of Barker's ambition to devote himself entirely to writing and to tease him had hinted that a poor man could only achieve his ambition by marrying an heiress, and it was his conviction that two geniuses could never live together.

But Granville Barker was particularly depressed because in spite of every effort of Lillah McCarthy, William Archer and himself to found the National Theatre, it made very little headway and he saw no future in this country for himself without such a theatre. He was still a poor man living among wealthy people, for the success of the Court Theatre and his Shakespearean productions at the Savoy Theatre had practically ruined him financially though these had given him a legendary reputation as a producer.

Granville Barker's cynicism and socialism were an adaptive colouring which he could dispense with at a moment's notice and which he did dispense with in the presence of Charlotte, for there was a rare sympathy between them. She liked his sensitivity, his shrinking from giving pain, his patience in understanding other people's points of view, his hesitation in asserting his own; and she regarded these qualities as something to be treasured and encouraged.

The whole world was on the brink of a catastrophic war, but one could not tell this from the frivolous plays that were amusing the theatre crowds. England was being warned against the militaristic aims of Germany and Shaw was heard to declare in private that in the event of a war he was all on the side of Germany, which he regarded as his spiritual home. Like Lowes Dickinson, the Cambridge don with whom he compared notes, he was appalled by the smallness of the minds of English statesmen, "Little puppets knocking away with lilliputian hammers the last stays that restrained the launch of that great death-ship, War".

Shaw regarded the address he was to give on 'The Case for Equality' as one of the most important events of his life. It was to be given on the 1st of May, 1913, at the National Liberal Club and he knew that it would be attended by many important politicians, economists, authors and journalists. He meant to get down to realities, to bring to the surface the fundamental causes of the evils that beset mankind, the unmentionable causes. It was surprising that even in the world of science, certain fields remained untapped because a moral code of some kind based not on humanitarian grounds but on taboos, made it impossible to create the necessary vocabulary. In sexual matters, for example, psychologists found verbal difficulties at every stage. G.B.S. insisted that it was necessary to speak out without reserve or modesty. He now had a new label for himself: Artist-Biologist, and his workshop was the whole universe as far as he could comprehend it, including consciousness, purpose, mind, creation, choice and everything else staring us in the face. There had been biologists before but they were not artists; there had been artists but they were not biologists. Even on the edge of a precipice it was imperative to go on thinking to the bitter end, with laughter like the Christian believers in *Androcles and the Lion*. The Christians, however, were dying for a cause they believed in but the youth of the world were being led to the slaughter for something they knew nothing about.

Equality of Income, he knew, appeared fantastic in a world where there was a mad scramble for high profits and large incomes. But as all sensible schemes were considered hopelessly Utopian, he had great hopes that his views could be made impossible enough to have a chance. He meant to prove that the war which all could see coming had its roots in the inequality of income, that the social friction set up by this inequality was intense and was the cause of the smashings, the stoppages and the explosions.

The audience at the National Liberal Club was soon in his grip and was entranced by his argument that equality of income would have the effect of making the entire community intermarriageable and this would lead to a vast improvement to the race.

"We are a stupid people, and we are a badlooking people. We are ugly; we have narrow minds; and we have no manners. A great deal of this is due to the effect of being brought up in a society of inequality. . . ."

The audience was surprised that the unromantic Shaw came down so heavily on the side of love and free biological selection:

"I see a woman who takes my fancy. I fall in love with her. It would seem very sensible, in an intelligent community, that I should take off my hat and say to this lady: 'Will you excuse me; but you attract me very strongly; and if you are not already engaged, would you mind taking my name and address and considering whether you would care to marry me?' Now I have no such chance at present. Probably when I meet that woman, she is either a charwoman, and I cannot marry her; or else she is a duchess, and she will not marry me. . . . The result is that you have, instead of a natural evolutionary sexual selection, a class selection, which is really a money selection. Is it to be wondered at that you have an inferior and miserable breed under such circumstances?"

His new play was dealing with an aspect of this very subject. The problem he set himself was: given free biological choice, there would still be the obstacle of speech and manners. It was inconceivable that a cultured well-spoken man should be willing to spend his life with a badly spoken flower girl, however beautiful he might think her. This idea congealed into the distinctive Shavian shape: the male with the super-personal passion for phonetics, the female interpreting this passion as love for herself. The task was made easier for him because he was building up the two main parts round star performers, Beerbohm Tree and Mrs. Patrick Campbell. Tree saw in this play a literary scaffold on which to exhibit his own creations. *Pygmalion*, this new play, was a howling box-office success at His Majesty's Theatre and it was felt by everyone that it was Mrs. Patrick Campbell who made the play. It was common knowledge that the actress and the author were very great friends and were so much together that Charlotte had to object. The Webbs regarded this infatuation of Bernard Shaw's "as a clear case of sexual senility" and thoroughly disliked the actress. Perhaps Bernard Shaw felt that he must emulate Anatole France who had once informed him that 'French authors, however saintly, are forced to include in their retinue ladies of ardent complexion with whom they are supposed to live in sin'.

When George Bernard Shaw lectured at the University of Oxford on the origins of the Drama he found it an easy task to prove that "the apostolic succession from Aeschylus to myself is as serious and as continuously inspired as the younger institution the apostolic succession of the Christian Church". The University turned up in full force; one undergraduate, Cyril Joad, described the effect of this lecture:

"As the tall erect figure, stiff as a ramrod, came striding down the central aisle, the place shook with applause. Glowing with hero worship, I gazed with rapture, more particularly upon the hair which still bore traces of red, the rampant moustache and the beard, every hair of which seemed to bristle with vitality. . . . I make a frank avowal that the combined effect of the figure, the voice, the intonation, the accent and the gestures was to sweep me off my feet so completely that, where Shaw is concerned, I have never succeeded in getting convincingly on them again. . . ."

Not for a moment, however, did Shaw feel that he had got hold of the young in spite of the enthusiastic reception at the universities. He knew that their professed devotion to his principles was only a mask for their idolatry of an eminent person. For his own soul's good it was his wont to translate every success, and the successes were mounting to immense proportions, as deepening failure.

"If I am to be no mere copperwire amateur but a luminous author, I must also be a most intensely refractory person, liable to go out and to go wrong at inconvenient moments, and with incendiary possibilities."

He confessed to his friends that he almost looked forward to an incendiary outburst, a war to pull the world together, to realize the value of our strength and pluck. The physical being urged forward the very thing his soul revolted against; the insane bloodletting to heal the world.

Though the war had been foretold it came as a great shock to everyone. So much for Capitalism, Undershaft's Utopia that dazzled fools into believing that through wealth and science life would grow secure and happy. The Shaws were stunned into silence after its declaration and then came his *Commonsense about the War*, after the *Great War* had run its bewildering course for three months. In this he stated fearlessly that the Junker class was as predominant in England as in Germany, that the Foreign Office was nothing but a Junker Club and that the Kaiser himself was a victim of English Junkerdom. Shaw was obviously torn between two conflicting thoughts: one, that it was better for England to be conquered by Germany; for it always benefited from such a conquest; two, that England was correct in fighting for the privilege of misgoverning herself. The very small minority opposed to all war were appeased when he refused to see the Germans as dragons and devils but as fellow creatures. *The Commonsense about the War* was published as a supplement to the *New Statesman* and although Clifford Sharp, the Editor, had little sympathy with Shaw, he could not resist the increased circulation which he knew that this supplement would bring and he was brave enough to print it without altering a word.

Shaw's Tormentor, H. G. Wells, lost his temper completely after reading it and violently attacked him:

"Shaw is like an idiot child screaming in a hospital."

John Galsworthy thought the article showed lack of taste because it threw salt on open wounds, but Keir Hardie, the Leader of the Labour Party, wrote a letter which almost compensated for the universal abuse:

"Its inspiration is worth more to England than this war has as yet cost her, in money I mean. When it gets circulated in popular form and is read as it will be by hundreds of thousands of our best people of all classes it will produce an elevation of tone in the national life which will be felt for generations to come."

Shaw's answer to all his critics was: "We must tell the truth unashamed like men of courage and character."

In contradistinction to other Allied authors, Shaw's plays were the only ones permitted to be performed in Austria and in Germany because he had never said or written a single hostile word about the Central Powers, and so *Candida*, *Pygmalion* and *Man and Superman* continued to entertain them and to 'fortify them in their determination to extinguish the degenerate English'. One day his loyal and devoted translator, Herr Siegfried Trebitsch, who was keeping him informed of events, received a summons to the Ministry of Foreign Affairs in his country and was summarily ordered to abandon all attempts at correspondence with 'enemy alien Mr. Shaw'. This command referred only to correspondence, but Shaw's plays could still speak to the enemy. The play that had amused King Edward was now having the same effect on the Kaiser.

Shaw complained that there was not much of him left for the War had already killed eight of his lives and there were "only a few crumbs to be swept away". He could not find any consolation in the kind of patriotism which felt that it had made a good bargain when the slaughter of one Englishman was followed by that of two Germans. It was imperative for him to write a new play to convey the drift that had led us into the war. This play must be of cultured, leisured Europe before the war. But he could not get himself to concentrate because humour would creep in and he never could eliminate it. He re-read some of the books he had venerated in his early years: Dickens and George Eliot: not a ray of hope in them; Swift and Shakespeare fell into the bottomless pit of an utterly discouraging pessimism.

"One knows now" (he wrote to Henry Salt) "why Shake-speare and Swift were so bitter. Have you read the articles by men who had written about Shelley and Wordsworth and patronised Tolstoi. Horrible! . . . the mud bath and the blood bath . . . the intellectual spiritual looting. . . . We two have survived our wounds so far; but we shall always be revenging them. . . ."

He saw the closing of art galleries, the stoppage of cultural activities, the churches becoming centres of hate, and everywhere an open defiance of morality and decency. He would rather we went back to the rigid codes of the Victorians than watch the mad demand for happiness and more happiness till death shut out the possibility of it. It would need something more than a god and much more than six days to turn the darkening chaos into order and light.

His article in '*Killing for Sport*', a book of humanitarian essays, edited by Henry Salt, was taken very badly because he argued that he would have all those who had not the sense of the importance and glory of life carefully sorted out and eliminated, starting with the sportsman and finishing up with the politician to whom the destruction of life was an exciting amusement. He went even further:

"Men must be killed and animals must be killed; nay whole species of animals must be exterminated before the earth can become a tolerable place of habitation for decent folk."

Three incidents drew him out from his philosophic meanderings. The first was the news that Granville Barker had been bewitched by a wealthy American lady and wished that a divorce could be speedily arranged between Lillah McCarthy and himself. Shaw was asked by both parties for advice and help and felt in many ways responsible for this tragedy. It was obvious that Granville Barker had taken his teasing to heart both about money and genius. Instead of making the slightest effort to bring them together again, he now carried on the same tactics with Lillah McCarthy. He wrote to her:

"Quite seriously, I have come to the conclusion that you had better get rid of Harley. He has gone to France; and I have now no belief that you and he will ever patch it up again. If I am right, the sooner you set yourself free the better for you. . . . I was struck by the way in which, when he went off to America, you immediately recovered your health and looked five years younger. . . ."

Lillah McCarthy was convinced that Granville Barker still loved her and was under a spell which would break and that he would return to her; but six months later she received another letter from Shaw:

My dear Lillah,

A new accusation! . . . I had hardly sent off my inquiry to you—my last one—when the subject of it turned up in person, very worried and impatient, and rapidly coming to your conclusion that it is all my fault, except that you blame me because he wants a divorce and he blames me because he hasnt got it. . . . However I know it is no use my talking. Go on tormenting one another, just as the rest are killing one another in France; it is the nature of the human animal. I will go on with my play and leave you all to your devilments.

Twenty years before this he had written to Janet Achurch admitting that "as an Irishman, an irregular artistic person, an anarchist in conduct, he was a creator of an atmosphere subtly disintegrative of households", and this had been working at full pressure all these years. Often it worked without his knowledge and he would become aware of the effect he had on happily married people years afterwards. He did not succeed with the Webbs and almost succeeded with the Charringtons. He had worked hard on the Charringtons with letters to Janet about her husband and vice versa and now hardly had he heard that Harley Granville Barker and Lillah McCarthy had divorced, news came to him that Janet Achurch was dead and he seized upon this to vent his sorrow. He had not seen her for a long time and suddenly her presence came back to him, young and beautiful:

"It is curious" (he wrote) "to see now how in the perspective of history, which forgets the jerry buildings and remembers only the cathedrals they hid, Janet detaches herself from all the rest and stands memorable and prominent in the void. . . . In fifty years she will be famous as the only woman who saw and took the really great chances of her time."

The third incident, and Bernard Shaw considered it only an incident very much like Bloody Sunday, was the Russian Revolution. Shaw expected it to be beaten down by the military and the police, but day-to-day news seemed to suggest that there was something more in it than a defiant gesture. The more successful the Revolution proved the more convinced Shaw was that it confirmed Sidney Webb's belief

in the 'inevitability of gradualness', and that the long years of propaganda by the intellectual minority had at last borne fruit. He feared
that there were no men of the right calibre in Russia for they were all
tutored in fortresses and prisons, in salt mines and in dungeons, tutored
in vengeance and not in practical statesmanship. They needed, in his
opinion, a host of Fabians to give them a long-term policy, but he
feared that this would not be because one of their leaders had denounced the Fabians as 'bombastics and ranting poltroons' and described
the writings of the Webbs as 'the most boring form of verbal
creation. . . .'

With his English friends, Shaw took up a bumptious attitude. He
wrote to G. K. Chesterton giving his opinion about European events:

"Nobody can differ with me: you might as well differ from the
Almighty about the orbit of the sun."

But when he met Russians he flattered them by saying that he was
going to write a play in the Tchekhov manner, that Stanislavsky inspired Granville Barker, that Tolstoi was greater than Shakespeare and
that the Russian ballet was the supreme form of art.

The fact that the Junkers imposed harsh terms on the new Russian
Government who were suing for peace, did not surprise Shaw. In his
opinion, a square inch of territory remaining in the hands of Lenin and
Trotsky would have enough incandescence to set the whole world
alight. The measure of power was in the thought and not in the number
of square miles to be administered. He begged of the Russian leaders
through Maxim Litvinov who was a friend of his, to keep their objec-
tives in mind and never to be deterred by capitalist conspiracies,
Prussian arrogancies and mutual misunderstandings. Their objective
was equality of income, and to get it, it would be necessary 'to send
their idle rich to England, the degenerate intellectuals to France and
their defectives to America'. Only those willing to work twenty-five
hours a day should be permitted to stay and build up the country. In
his opinion the problems were not insuperable if only they could build
up a large responsible managerial class able to take orders.

Meanwhile he tried to get himself nominated to the Irish Convention, but unanimity (negative) on that subject was achieved at once.
He noted down:

"I remain one of the very few who see a way through. I go up
to Dublin to stay for a few days with Sir Horace Plunkett, it may
be proposed that I should remain in Ireland to help in the propaganda of the as yet totally unpropagated solution: the federation of

L

the Disunited Kingdom of G.B. and I. If nothing comes of it, I'll
have to leave Ireland to stew in her own juice."

Nothing whatever came of it. He felt a lonely and neglected figure
in Dublin, and he was glad to return to England again to work at
*Peace Conference Hints* in case any of the countries in a moment of
sudden sanity asked him for guidance.

His most important suggestion was that Lloyd George and
Clemenceau and the Kaiser should be sent to Switzerland, high on the
Alps, to recuperate and cool their minds, while two or three people
who experience the actual fighting sat down and worked out a sensible
peace. In his opinion the people who did the fighting were rarely
revengeful.

The Life Force, not satisfied with the senseless slaughter of thirty
million lives and the hideous mutilation of many more, brought down
on the enfeebled people an appalling plague, a particularly virulent
form of influenza, and again millions died. Among those attacked were
the Shaws; Charlotte had 'a devil of a time', in fact Shaw despaired of
her recovery. He was certain she would have gone under if he had
permitted the doses of quinine which the doctors tried on their patients.
Fortunately the Shaws were wealthy enough to purchase fruits like
oranges and grapes which were priced so high that only war profiteers
could think of purchasing them.

The Shaws found no difficulty in getting all the food they required
from their own gardens and neighbouring farms. G.B.S. boasted to
everyone that the Great War to end war had come just in the nick
of time for he was looking in vain for five per cent on his spare money
which was lying unused in his bank, and when the war broke out he
lent the Government £20,000 at five per cent for which he would have
been lucky had he obtained three per cent before the war had started.
Added to that, in spite of his *Commonsense about the War*, his profitable
investment was applauded by the Press as a great patriotic gesture. This
was the second time that Providence had come to his aid, for in the
Boer War he had also invested £20,000 from which he obtained
£1,000 a year.

When it seemed to him that Charlotte might die, he wrote:

"The loss of one's wife after ten years is only the end of an
adventure. After twenty it is the end of an epoch and becomes
more and more the end of everything."

It was now he realized that he had been married for twenty years.
As he grew older, he knew that he was becoming more and more like

his father, both in appearance and in his attitude to life. His father had always chuckled at the thought that 'everything was a pack of lies'; in the play G.B.S. was now writing, old Carr Shaw acted as the model for a tipsy old man perpetually railing against the world like a prophet in the Old Testament. Like Carr Shaw, Captain Shotover always pretended to be busy when as a matter of fact he was making off to drink in his secret corner, coming out when there were people to listen, throwing out pregnant remarks and not waiting for an answer.

"It confuses me to be answered," the old Captain explained, "it discourages me. I cannot bear men and women. I have to run away. I must run away now."

Captain Shotover expressed Shaw's attitude to the young:

"I see my daughters and their men living foolish lives of romance and sentiment and snobbery. I see you, the younger generation, turning from their romance and sentiment and snobbery to money and comfort and hard commonsense. I was ten times happier on the bridge in the typhoon, or frozen into Arctic ice for months in darkness than you have ever been. You are looking for a rich husband. At your age I looked for hardship, danger, horror, death, that I might feel the life in me more intensely. I did not let the fear of death govern my life, and my reward was, I had my life. You are going to let the fear of poverty govern your life and the reward will be that you will eat but you will not live."

Shaw had gone far since he had written *Major Barbara* with its gospel according to St. Andrew Undershaft, where poverty was the greatest crime and the utmost dread.

Charlotte was the first to read it after her recovery from the war plague. She had a hatred of tipsy people and therefore had a physical aversion to the old man, but she loved every word he uttered.

A letter arrived which cheered the Shaws. It was from Czechoslovakian soldiers:

"Your work has always been the philosophical basement of our life, day by day, endeavouring to follow our great Irish teacher...."

He could never make himself feel that the play with Captain Shotover was finished. Nothing could be finished that ended on a note of despair. It was the duty, in his opinion, of the author-artist to transmute all experience into encouragement or not to write at all. Shaw would have considered himself merely a mental contortionist without, what the Prague soldiers called, the philosophic basement of life. He held that life was a thing of which it was necessary to have a theory; yet most people took it for granted and went on living for no better reason than that they found themselves alive. If the theory led to a nihilistic conclusion then it was false.

He heard that Kate Salt had died and he wrote to Henry:

"We would never have invented marriage if we had not found it in the world. Kate's death ends for me an intention that always haunted me. If haunting is the right word for an entirely pleasant obsession. My old visits to Oxted were quite unlike any other experience of the sort, and occupied a place of their own in my life. It was not solely because Kate spoilt me and pampered me most outrageously that I found them so harmonious. There was a congeniality so complete that the word seems ridiculous, as suitable only for states imperfect enough to make one conscious of them. Well, I never could think of that as a thing of the past, I took it for granted that some day I should escape from anything but a simple life, and spend another fortnight with you in the old way. I never did escape; and now I never shall."

In answer, Henry Salt had to remind him that the last time they had met was eight years ago, when Shaw had left the Executive of the Fabian Society to "become an executive of the Life Force or perhaps the Life Force itself!" while Kate and he went to join Edward Carpenter at Holmesfield, Derbyshire.

"What a forcing house of religious leaders the old atheists proved: Annie Besant is now the leader of the Theosophists and looks, in her white robes, as though she sits on the right hand of God; you, who insist on sitting on the right hand of the Devil to give him moral support and as for Dr. Aveling, you have transmuted him into Louis Dubedat and placed him with the gods of art."

It was Henry Salt who suggested the title for his new play: he wrote that he must leave his heartbreak house, quoting the last line of Wilfrid Gibson's splendid poem "Lament":

"Nor feel the heart-break in the heart of things?"

But the people were not ready for his play *Heartbreak House*. They were tired of hardship, danger, horror and death. They wanted, not an intenser life, but to laugh and be merry, to take everything lightly and not give heed to the sonorous warnings of a Shotover. "And who was Shaw to preach to us?" the young people, the tired people, asked. They had come back from the trenches in the spirit of *Arms and the Man*, prepared to laugh at heroics, to debunk the great, and to avoid highbrow stuff like poison. Shaw had only to meet a young man to hear that he had bombed cities, perhaps spent his young years behind barbed wire, or as the sons of his Fabian colleagues had done, spent years in the chill cells of English prisons.

G.B.S. was not deceived by this attitude for he knew that every tide turned and even admired the work of one of the young men who was debunking fast and furiously, Lytton Strachey, and looked upon him in an avuncular spirit.

This was the pause he needed: he would write a play which would take at least twelve hours to act, a play in which he would set out clearly the religion of the twentieth century newly arisen from the ashes of scepticism and nihilism. *Candida* and *Man and Superman* and *Heartbreak House* all had to be written to lead up to this new play. This was to be his immortal play which would give him immortal life, which would "Exploit the eternal interest of the philosopher's stone which enables men to live for ever".

As was his custom he read portions of his play to friends and he invited Granville Barker and his new wife, Helen, to a reading of *Back to Methuselah*. Shaw was conscious throughout the reading that the new Mrs. Barker looked upon him with intense dislike. He had never met a person who had so completely overcome him with her hatred.

She knew that she could only retain her hold on her husband by keeping him from this 'wicked man'.

## Chapter Twelve

Is sister Lucy died on March 27th, 1920, at Denmark Hill, South London and she was the last of his 'physical liabilities', as he termed her. He rarely visited her and he explained his neglect of her as due to "property, property, property, the real secret of my withdrawal from all human intercourse except with people I have actually to work with".

On March 27th, however, he happened to call on her, "guided by the Life Force". She was very ill and when she saw him she informed him at once that she was dying.

"No, no," he said conventionally, "you will be all right presently," and was rather disgusted with the situation in which he found himself. He took her hand in his and suddenly he discovered that he was holding the hand of a dead person and he sat there wondering what to do. There was silence in the house and he heard through the open window a piano badly played in another house. The doctor who came, in spite of Shaw's protestations, insisted on certifying the cause of death as starvation.

Lucy had made it clear during her lifetime that she was not to have any form of service at her cremation but when he arrived at the Crematorium he found it crowded with all her friends, none of whom seemed to recognize or know him. This audience seemed to call for some sort of ceremony and so he mounted the pulpit and recited Shakespeare's dirge from *Cymbeline*:

> "Fear no more the lightning-flash,
> Nor the all-dreaded thunder-stone."

He had looked forward to the burning and was disappointed that owing to the scarcity of coal, she burnt with "a steady white light like that of a wax candle!"

With *Back to Methuselah* completed he applied for membership of the Cremation Society because my 'creative days are over and I am as good as dead'.

He was approached, to his intense amazement, by a professional manager of whom he had never heard about the performance of this long impossible play and he assured Shaw that he was doing it solely to gratify his dramatic appetite and could afford any loss. Mr. Barry Jackson, the enthusiast, was asked to go ahead and produce the whole cycle at the Birmingham Repertory Theatre. Shaw was deeply impressed by the rendering of the play and declared it to be the crown and climax of his career as a dramatic poet.

"I have had five magnificent performances in four days, and what is more extraordinary, this has been done in Birmingham."

Hardly had he decided that his career as an imaginative writer had finished and that *Back to Methuselah* would rank as the longest swan-song on record than his faculties revived tempestuously and once more he was engaged on a new play. Charlotte had suggested the theme of *Saint Joan*. He wondered how it was that he had not thought of it before, for was she not a female personification of himself? She stood up in the minority of one against authority, she was above sex, she had discarded the conventional clothes for a rational dress and she had belief in her Voices, the intimations of the Evolutionary Appetite.

This play *Saint Joan* was first put on in New York by the Theatre Guild on December 28th, 1923, with Winifred Lenihan in the title part and the first London performance with Sybil Thorndike in the title part took place at the New Theatre, March 26th, 1924, with settings and costumes by Charles Ricketts. It was an instantaneous success with 244 performances, almost doubling the number of performances of his other success, *Pygmalion*.

From now on he was known everywhere as the author of *Saint Joan*. When he was asked why he went all out for the Maid he replied that he did not go all out for anybody or anything, that he was a poet and not a soot and whitewash merchant; that he gave Joan her own point of view and the others their point of view. At last, he thought, he had restored the theatre to its original religious function.

His reputation had stabilized and settled into a definite image of the dramatist. George Bernard Shaw was now the Sage, white bearded and with twinkling blue eyes and an upright athletic form, a young man within an aged body. Voltaire had said, that Sages, once acclaimed, retired into solitude to become sapless with ennui; G.B.S. was certainly the exception: he was expected to give a pronouncement on every conceivable subject and nothing but the most extreme and unexpected opinions were acceptable from him.

He received a letter from The British Broadcasting Company as follows:

10th March, 1924.

Dear Sir,

The British Broadcasting Company, which from its earliest days has included at least one informative talk in its nightly programme, is advised from many quarters that these talks are amongst the most popular features. The Company accordingly believes that the time is ripe to strengthen its programmes in this direction by arranging to broadcast simultaneously from London through all Stations, a steady series of addresses (of an entertaining though informative character) by the most eminent and best-known persons.

We would welcome your assistance in this development. The talk we have in mind should be one of about twenty minutes duration; it should be free from highly controversial matter, including politics and religion. The manuscript should be approximately 1,200 words in length. . . .

Shaw read this letter and came to the conclusion that it was a practical joke. To invite him, of all people, to give an address free from highly controversial matter! Surely this official had invited him because he was the very personification of controversy; wherever there was a verbal scrap he was bound to be in it. And how history repeated itself: the injunction to keep off religion and politics recalled his office days when he was made to promise never to discuss these subjects; the humiliation of his consent still rankled. What did they expect him to discuss? The talk was to be entertaining but his one way of entertaining an audience was to provoke it to fierce antagonism by telling the obvious truth.

Not until October 1924 could the Director of Programmes report that Shaw had agreed to broadcast. G.B.S. looked upon the affair, a reading by him of his playlet, *O'Flaherty, V.C.*, as "rather a lark". He sang Tipperary and assumed all the voices with such perfection that the listeners thought it uncanny. He enjoyed himself, because through a work of art he had put forward the most highly controversial matter. It was a soldier talking his mind and with the usual digs at the English, at domestic life, at heroics, at war:

> SIR PEARCE: "Strictly between ourselves, O'Flaherty, and as one soldier to another, do you think we should have got an army without conscription if domestic life had been as happy as people say it is?"

Just the right sentiment to end on, thought Shaw, as he visualized father, mother, sons and daughters sitting round the wireless.

George Bernard Shaw was awarded the Nobel Prize in Literature for 1925 and Dr. Per Hallström, the Chairman of the Nobel Committee for the Swedish Academy, spoke to the following effect:

"George Bernard Shaw showed in the novels of his youth the same conception of the world and the same attitude to social problems that he has ever since maintained. This provides a better defence for him than anything else against the long-current accusation of lack of honesty and of acting as a professional buffoon at the court of democracy. . . . What puzzled people most was his rollicking gaiety: they were ready to believe that the whole thing was a game and a desire to startle. This was so far from being true that Shaw himself has been able to declare with a greater degree of justice that his careless attitude was a mere stratagem: he had to fool people into laughing in order that they should not hit upon the idea of hanging him. . . ."

On the 26th of July, 1926, his seventieth birthday, he received the following letter from the German Ambassador in England: Herr Stahmer:

Dear Mr. Shaw,

I have been instructed by the German Minister for Foreign Affairs, Herr Dr. Stresemann, to convey to you his sincerest congratulations on the completion of your seventieth year and to express to you all his good wishes for your future welfare and happiness. . . . I think I am justified in adding that the interest taken by Herr Stresemann in the celebration of your birthday is shared by untold members of my compatriots, for whom, as you know better than I do myself, you are one of the most popular writers whose works have always been taken up most eagerly and continue to be highly appreciated and admired. . . .

With the expression of my highest consideration,

I am,

Very sincerely yours,

Shaw replied as follows:

My dear Stahmer,

The public honour done me by the message of the German Minister of Foreign Affairs is enhanced by its coming through your hands. It is the sort of thing that would never occur to a British Foreign Secretary, because as you well know, we are a barbarous nation in matters of culture. We have a genuine dread of intellect in any form and a conviction that Art, though highly enjoyable clandestinely, is essentially immoral. Therefore the sole notice taken of my birthday by the British Government was its deliberate official prohibition of the broadcasting of any words spoken by me on that occasion.

The contrast between this attitude and that of the German Government would be a painful one for a nation with cultural traditions; but our governing classes are rather proud of it. To them I owe my reputation as a dangerous and disreputable person: to Germany I owe my recognition in Europe as a thinker and dramatic poet. What is more important, Europe owes to Germany such sense as exists of the importance of thought and dramatic poetry and the value of lives devoted to them. Therefore a tribute from Germany confers on me a distinction that no other nation in the world could give me.

If I were a German I should be justifiably proud of this. As I am, if not an Englishman, (as you know I am an Irishman) at least a life-long and faithful servant of the English people, I am sorry that it should be so. But it is so; and I am none the less grateful to Germany.

These however are merely national considerations. There is a supernational republic of Thought and Art to the great German members and masters of which my debt is incalculable; and that their countrymen should admit my claim to be a member of it is a triumph which enables me to face without blushing all the eulogies and congratulations showered on me on the first birthday I have ever celebrated, and the last I intend to celebrate. . . .

Your faithfully,

It was a petulant letter from a person spoilt by fulsome adulation in England, which somehow did not fit in with his conception of the country.

Harley Granville Barker's place in the affection of the Shaws was taken by another young man, T. E. Lawrence, famous for his exploits in Arabia. T. E. Lawrence knew how to flatter Charlotte for he would tell her that there were only two women in his life and she was one of them. To others he wrote that she was "a plain old stick and very useful to Shaw because she was so ordinary", but Charlotte would not have worried in the least had she known this because she knew herself only as "the guardian of the world's grandest genius". With this T. E.

Lawrence certainly agreed and admired her for the way she kept herself in the background and the way she refused to exploit or dramatize her position. He confided all his difficulties to her, why he had cancelled his book *The Mint*, why he had given up everything to become an anonymous airman and why he had changed his name to Ross, and these confidences went to her heart.

Charlotte was extremely encouraging and overcame his habit of self-depreciation by persuading him to complete and publish *Seven Pillars of Wisdom* which her husband had corrected beyond recognition. When Lawrence modestly suggested that not a soul would be interested in the book, Charlotte pointed to *The Worst Journey in the World*, written by their neighbour, Mr. Cherry Garrard, who had accompanied Scott on the Antarctic Expedition, for this book had also had their help and proved a great success.

"Why should not sand have the same appeal as snow?" Shaw asked.

Dramatically this was a fallow period for Shaw but he refused to let the grass grow under his feet. Work was a habit with him and leisure something to be despised. When he first came over from Ireland he settled down to *A Practical System of Moral Education for Females*, now, fifty years after that, he felt an urge to complete it, for this female was certainly old enough to understand the subtleties of the social system in which she lived. He settled down therefore to write *The Intelligent Woman's Guide to Socialism and Capitalism*. It was at this period that he moved from Adelphi Terrace to Whitehall Court, because No. 10 was to be demolished, and they chose Whitehall Court because it was a symbolic dream of wealth and splendour to him. Years ago he had been invited to a dinner at Whitehall Court by Richard Burdon Haldane (later to become Lord Chancellor) and for the first time he donned a double-breasted black suit bought for the occasion and which he thought would be the correct dress, but when he arrived he was met by a display of lavish evening dress the like of which he had never seen. From that moment this place took on in his imagination a desirable place for a wealthy important person.

It seemed comic that he, who had a rich flat in London, an expensive country house, two cars, six servants and socialite friends hopping in and out of Windsor, should advocate the equality of income. In the book he was writing he explained carefully that:

> "Should you become a convert to Socialism, you will not be committed to any change in your private life, nor indeed will you find yourself able to make any change that would be the smallest use in that direction."

Small wonder it was said that Shaw not only made Socialism respectable but made it a fashion so that instead of its being the mark of a rebel, it became the done thing. Indeed Shaw had to warn the uninitiated that Socialists were a mixed lot:

"If joining them meant inviting them indiscriminatingly to tea I should strongly advise you not to do it, as they are just like other people, which means that some of them steal spoons when they get the chance. The nice ones are very nice, the general run are no worse than their neighbours; and the undesirable ones include some of the most thoroughpaced rascals you could meet anywhere."

G.B.S. was obviously growing tired of his doting admirers and was inclined to believe that all people who approached him were thoroughpaced rascals. One man actually defended his vices before a court of law on the ground that he was one of Shaw's disciples. When young people asked for advice he had one reply: "Never take advice. If I had taken the advice given to me when I was young I would now have been a decrepit unemployed clerk." He warned them, however, not to do what he did because it was only the accident of a lucrative talent which lifted him out of the poor house and perhaps the jail. Even now he still did not know where he might land before he died, for the very crowds which came to cheer and laugh might yet come to scoff and see him hanged. A great change had come over him when *The Intelligent Woman's Guide* was at last published in 1928: the headaches from which he had suffered for the last fifty years went from him miraculously because as he put it, "I transferred them to my readers."

The whole world was in a terrible state for a great depression in trade had started, at its worst in the United States of America, and it was leaving a large residuum of what appeared to be permanent unemployment. Even the Webbs lost faith in the inevitability of gradualness or in any form of modified Capitalism. Shaw felt that a consolatory message was called for:

"It may drive us mad if we begin to think of public evils as millionfold evils. They are nothing of the kind. What you yourself can suffer is the utmost that can be suffered on earth. If you starve to death you experience all the starvation that ever has been or ever can be. If ten thousand other women starve with you, their suffering is not increased by a single pang. . . . Therefore do not be oppressed by the frightful sum of human suffering. . . . Do not let your mind be disabled by excessive sympathy."

John Galsworthy was one of the first people to take up this point. Seventeen years back, in 1911, he had tried to interest G.B.S. in a public appeal against the use of aircraft in war, and the answer was, "It is all pious piffle." Now Galsworthy was deeply oppressed by the frightful sum of human suffering and appealed to G.B.S. to use his immense influence, his unprecedented popularity to help the miners. Galsworthy had visited a mining village and found two collieries closed and a third on the brink of closing. What appalled him was that about a quarter of a million of them regarded themselves as permanently unemployed. His suggestion to G.B.S. was that he might make a broadcast appeal which would go straight to the hearths and hearts of the people. The answer from Bernard Shaw was that it would be a pleasure to have the whole world listening to him, but he had no doubt that the world would go on just the same.

"You sentimentalists always wait until the cruel thing reaches its maximum fury before you act and then immediately you do the wrong things."

He was against helping privately when it was clearly the work of the State to do something constructive and permanent. His proposals were that comprehensive schemes of electrification and road construction should be put in hand at once. He even extracted amusement out of the world's predicament: a friend endeavoured to bring home to him the plight of the workers by pointing out that thousands had not tasted meat for months. Shaw answered quite truthfully:

"I have not tasted meat for over forty years. Vegetarians claim to be immune from most diseases but they have been known to die from time to time. I suggest as a slogan: Meat less Shaw."

He received this letter from an old flame:

July 3rd. 1928

My dear Bernard Shaw,
How kind of you to send me your book on Socialism. But do you consider me an intelligent or an unintelligent woman? Whichever I may be, I keep a corner for an old friend, I am ever a fighting Home Ruler and Socialist,

Annie Besant.

# Chapter Thirteen

IDOL worship called for a centre and a ritual, and Sir Barry Jackson, the founder of the Birmingham Repertory Theatre, thought of Malvern as a good centre and Shaw's plays as an appropriate ritual. He had already impressed Shaw by his rendering of *Back to Methuselah* and found no difficulty whatever in persuading him because the dramatist liked Malvern and felt that Festival might recapture something of the magic which music and art had for him in his childhood, and which it seemed so utterly impossible to preserve under the pressure of the profit motive.

The Malvern Festival was to strike a new note, for Shaw was already seventy-three years of age and he would be expected to provide a new play every year or so for the next twenty years. It was a tribute, not only to his genius but also to the vitality of old age. There was no doubt that those who would attend the intellectual shrine would expect the same raillery, the same jovial patter, the far-reaching vision, the contemporary comment, the grasp of life, the preaching and the castigation associated with his early years. The world had become familiar with his ideas and this familiarity only excited the appetite for more.

G.B.S. had a double intention in his first Festival play: first of all he wanted to make a laughing stock of popular government because he was ashamed of it as a political institution, thinking that it brought out all that was worst in the people and the politicians; the second was the impish mischievousness of putting an end to the gossip that was being circulated about him and was giving Charlotte so much unhappiness and shame, by giving the audience an overdose of it. The central character was the distinctive Shavian type. King Magnus was a wise and tactful king who

> "stood for the great abstractions; for conscience and virtue for the eternal against the expedient; for the evolutionary appetite against the day's gluttony; for intellectual integrity for humanity, for the rescue of industry from commercialism and of science from professionalism."

The king had a wife, a lady of high principle, and yet he was at the same time violently attracted to another fascinating creature who appealed only to his 'lower centres'. Shaw could hear the stalls remarking: Charlotte and Mrs. Patrick Campbell! So he makes his king say:

> KING MAGNUS: . . . "Every king is supposed to be a libertine; and as, oddly enough, he owes a great part of his popularity to this belief, he cannot deny without deeply disappointing his subjects."

When the play was produced at Malvern both Charlotte and Mrs. Patrick Campbell were deeply hurt and the former was heard to remark: "Fools who came to pray remained to scoff."

Mrs. Patrick Campbell had already pleaded with Shaw to be allowed to read the play before it was produced because she had heard from Edith Evans who was going to play Orinthia, the king's mistress, that she was 'going to be made fun of'. Shaw answered that he was too old now to read it to her and also that he had no copy to spare:

> "We must not be handed down to history by ignoble gossip and venomous slander. The world may very well laugh at us; but it had better have splendid fun than dirty fun. Our parts are fine parts; and if you really prefer Lady Patricia to Orinthia you deserve to be whipped at the cart's tail from Sloane Square to Drury Lane."

Mrs. Patrick Campbell received the play at last and she was scandalized by the 'mischievous vulgarity and untruthfulness'. She begged of him to tear it up and rewrite it:

> "With every scrap of the mischievous vulgarian omitted and all suburban backchat against Charlotte and suggested harlotry against me, and the inference of your own superiority wiped out. People will only say that old age and superhuman vanity have robbed you of your commonsense."

But as he had argued once before with Tolstoi and pained him deeply by the argument that if life was a jest it was better to make it a good jest rather than a bad one, so now he pained his friend Mrs. Patrick Campbell by insisting that it was better to have splendid fun than dirty fun. But neither of the women saw any fun in it, for it was unworthy of a Superman.

When it was produced at the Malvern Festival the critics brought out all their adulatory baggage: high farce, fantastic wisdom, high discourse. The sage was always being rediscovered.

The immediate effect of introducing the Orinthia scene was that his private life had become of greater interest to the public than his social views: reporters followed him everywhere seeking gossip at his backdoor. He was fully conscious of all this and enjoyed and encouraged it. There were photographs of G.B.S. bathing, sunbathing, posing in the nude, consorting with boxers and film stars, learning the tango and in every conceivable attire; he found himself inventing a sex life, a youth life and a child life and when Frank Harris informed him that he was engaged on a biography of him, he did not hesitate "to reveal everything". G.B.S. boasted to Frank Harris that the five novels he had written in his early years in London showed more knowledge of sex than most people acquired after bringing up a family of fifteen, that he had tried every experiment and learnt all there was to be learnt about sex; that from the moment he had earned enough money to dress presentably he was pursued by women in all walks of life, from members of the aristocracy down to mere actresses.

The climax of this intimate revelation came when he agreed to the publication of his correspondence with Ellen Terry. G.B.S. had given one of his numerous interviews, in this case to the *Daily Express*, in which he made it clear that he would never give permission and that he had also refused to publish the letters which Ellen Terry had written to him. But, in fact, he had agreed to their publication in spite of the objection of Ellen Terry's son, Gordon Craig. To G.B.S. literature was something that belonged to the Super-republic of Art, a region unconcerned with inhibitions and courtesies. It was only natural that other actresses wished to follow suit, for they had equally ardent letters, but he had to tell them that the bottom had fallen out of the Shaw market.

Beneath the din of loud approval he heard the still small voice of the Life Force exclaiming: "Fiddlesticks! What a frightful bag of stage tricks!" This came to him with great force while he was reading his works in connection with the Standard Edition of his collected works to be brought out in 1930 by Constable. He felt, as he read his early works, that he had not grown up at all, that superman Lee had given him all his themes, and his father the comedic sense.

An opportunity came to him to place his position four square before millions of listeners. He was not asked this time to be non-controversial or to avoid religion or politics in the invitation to broadcast in the series 'Points of View'. He felt like a schoolmistress addressing a huge kindergarten class as he began his broadcast:

"Your Majesties, Your Royal Highnesses, your Graces, and Reverences, my Lords, Ladies and Gentlemen, fellow citizens of all degrees . . ."

Rehearsing *Buoyant Billions* for the Malvern Festival
(in the garden of his biographer, Stephen Winsten)

His daily exercise until he took to
the pruning of the trees in his garden

At Whitehall Court, his town flat

Nearing his end

St. Joan
(sculpture by Clare Winsten)
where his ashes are scattered

He concerned himself with leadership, with how to convert the electoral system from the inefficient thing it was to a foolproof system. His suggestion was a graded series of panels of capable persons for all employments, public or private, with no person permitted to undertake the employment of governing us unless he or she were on the appropriate panel.

At first sight this suggestion smacked of a conversion to the need for competitive examinations but G.B.S. was no believer in such methods; he preferred a more scientific test and hoped that a process would soon be discovered by which the appropriate panel could be ascertained on the delivery of a drop of blood and a lock of hair because he had been convinced by Dr. Abraham that every part of a human being conveyed the personality and potentialities of the individual.

This was a physically impossible period for G.B.S. for he suffered acutely from insomnia. In spite of his playacting as a wonderful example of old age he had to say to his friends "that the wreck of a G.B.S. was at least more interesting than an average coaling schooner in full sail". To make up for his loss of sleep he would sometimes stay in bed for three days on end, refusing always the use of drugs or sleeping powders. He described his condition in the greatest detail to his friends and asked what they did to cure themselves. The advice he obtained from Sir Horace Plunkett was original and completely up to date:

18th July, 1929.

My dear G.B.S.,
    I thought you might like to know of my cure for insomnia. I am learning to fly. So far I have been only one and three quarter hours in the air. Yesterday I handled the controls for fifteen consecutive minutes in which I covered fifteen miles in a triangular course 2000 feet up. . . . I suggest that you take a lesson or two with the safest of pilots and see whether, as I should expect, you very quickly learn to fly. The world would not let you fly alone and the dual control costs no more than a single. It is most exhilarating and not at all fatiguing after two or three lessons. If you care to add this experience to your life I could arrange to have it kept out of the press. Of course Charlotte will have to be consulted; but I think she would be easily persuaded that, given a really first-rate pilot, you would be safer in the air than in your car in London.
                With love to Herself, I am
                                Yours ever,
                                Horace Plunkett.

M

Sir Horace Plunkett was seventy-five years of age and Shaw was his junior by one year.

Others came forward with suggestions. T. E. Lawrence told Charlotte that he had regained his power of sleep after the Arabian fiasco which almost drove him mad by changing his identity.

"What would you have me do," G.B.S. asked, "shave off my beard and get a job as a road sweeper for which I am not qualified?"

Professor Albert Einstein suggested that there should be long intervals when G.B.S. did no thinking whatever, because thinking, like the upright posture, was obviously unnatural to man and that was why man resisted it. He suggested strenuous physical exercises, like the sawing of wood or the scrubbing of floors, in other words to change places with the gardener. When thinking about this, G.B.S. wondered whether Professor Einstein's suggestion had not something in it, but he had not taken into consideration that the gardener and his maid would take serious objection to his meddling with their duties. That was why employers of maids and gardeners had to take to sport and games.

Albert Einstein was to be given a banquet at the Savoy Hotel on October 28th, 1930, and George Bernard Shaw was asked to propose his health. Shaw was glad to accept because it would be an artist philosopher greeting an artist mathematician, for he claimed that poets and artists were always ahead of the laboratory workers in science, that religion was always right and science could always be proved wrong. He wondered how Einstein had taken his statement in *Back to Methuselah*:

> "When a man is mentally incapable of abstract thought he takes to metaphysics; and they make him a professor. When he is incapable of conceiving quantity in the abstract he takes to mathematics; and they make him a professor."

Lord Rothschild, who presided, put this innocent question to G.B.S.:

"So you believe, Mr. Shaw, that if you and I gave all we have to the poor, life would become more tolerable to the masses?"

"What I object to," G.B.S. answered, "is the poor giving practically all they possess to the rich. What is bad economics is also bad religion."

"What exactly is your religion, Mr. Shaw?"

"Exactly the same as yours. I was brought up on the Bible to await the coming of the Superman."

"According to you, he has already come," Lord Rothschild's eye twinkled.

Shaw turned his attention to the guest of honour: "Tell me, Professor Einstein, this is a question I have asked many a scientist, if you find that the facts do not fit your theory, what do you do?" Shaw immediately proceeded to give the answer himself: "If the facts haven't the decency to accommodate themselves, eliminate them. I'd like to write a play one day which consists entirely of an argument between a religious person, an artist and a scientist."

"Unfortunately, my friend," Einstein explained, "your religious person, your scientist and your artist, would never find time to argue, and besides they may be one and the same person."

"Then *I* must find time for them, not only time but words, for most of them are inarticulate. I have taken upon myself the thankless task of making people conscious of their thoughts."

"And you do it remarkably well," Einstein responded, "they all talk as the greatest talker in the world."

The play G.B.S. was working on at this moment incorporated a portrait of T. E. Lawrence, for no friend could have a private life or come out of the crucible of Shaw's mind unembellished or undistorted. But the completion of this play was interrupted by a visit to Russia, undertaken by Lord Lothian and the Astors, who invited Shaw because they knew only too well that that country would smile benignly on Bernard Shaw, who was to the Russians an incarnation of Karl Marx and Shakespeare rolled into one. Thus his associates could glean some of the radiance and be received by Stalin himself. Charlotte did not accompany them but advised Bernard Shaw on no account to miss meeting Lenin's widow, Krupskaya. The Astors loaded themselves with tinned foods of every description, fearing that they were going to enter a land of famine, but Bernard Shaw took nothing but his clothes, having met many Russians in England and shared their taste for kasha and borst and he loved their black bread almost as much as he loved the Irish brown bread of his childhood. To the amazement of his companions their hotel in Moscow was filled with Americans and the food was not only super abundant but the kind that they were accustomed to find in the hotels of Europe and America. Before their arrival, Shaw alone was mentioned in the Russian Press and was built up as a 'human dynamo', the highest praise that could be conferred on any person in a country intent on production and more production. Shaw certainly looked the part when he arrived. They were given a magnificent reception in the Hall of Nobles which was as large as the Albert Hall and entertained to opera and ballets and speeches and banquets. Litvinoff whom he knew well accompanied him everywhere and acted as interpreter.

The great moment was his private meeting with Stalin who, as he put it, "had attained his position through the survival of the fittest, and had held it through years of the most appalling vicissitudes that ever attended the birth pangs of a new civilization". Stalin proved an appreciative listener and took in Shaw's flattery with a twinkle and a smile.

"I am pleased with everything I have seen," Shaw said meekly. "I especially agree with compulsory labour and the compulsory indoctrination of your creed. These things cannot be left to chance."

"Why *my* creed?" Stalin laughed. "Is it not *your* creed as well?"

"My creed doesn't matter. I'm an author, not the creator of a new civilization. I am a rickety figure in a worn-out waxworks," Shaw answered.

"Karl Marx was a mere author," Stalin twitted him. "And without him we might have blundered into chaos. We need authors to spread our view of life. Perhaps we are not ready for your laughter but one day we'll learn to laugh again."

"In my country we laugh when we do not want to face up to things. Here the people are facing up to things and so they do not need to laugh. My friend, Thomas Hardy, the poet and novelist, had a painting destroyed because it depicted him laughing."

"The three greatest authors are Leo Tolstoi, Charles Dickens and Bernard Shaw. Tolstoi succumbed to religion, Dickens to sentimentality, and as to you: well, you are too young for me to say what you will succumb to!"

Stalin was like the schoolboy who meets his old headmaster whom he had idealized to find him human. Shaw's attitude to Russia was of course sympathetic in advance and he could see nothing but good in it wherever he went: the factories, the shops, the cordiality of the people and the apparent equality and frankness. Instead of being the critic who castigated by ridicule he had to find a new vocabulary of acquiescence and praise.

When it came to visiting Lenin's widow, he found that difficulties were put in the way because she had heard that he had become a vain and ill-mannered reactionary, from "A good man fallen among Fabians", as her husband had once described him, he had become, according to reports, a bad man fallen among Tories, and this opinion was strengthened by the fact that he was accompanied by enemies of

Socialism. When, however, Krupskaya agreed to have them to tea at her chalet, Shaw was pleasantly surprised that, instead of the ugly woman he had expected to find, she turned out to be a fascinatingly lovable person. She told him that she could not understand how he retained his good spirits after such a long exile in a humourless country.

On his return to England he assured everyone that the people were extremely alive and open to ideas, especially to Fabian ideas. This enthusiasm sent the two Webbs to Russia to see things for themselves and to compose their book: *Soviet Communism, A New Civilization.*

To Charlotte his return presented new difficulties for in a letter to T. E. Lawrence she expressed her feeling of futility. T. E. L. could only answer:

> "September 25th, 1931.
> . . . You are very fortunate in your guard. The Services have made me pass so many days doing sentry-go over petrol pumps or guardroom or what-nots; never anything worthwhile alas. In saying which I feel only too keenly the wearisome duty it always must be for you. Only after we die it will appear that our petty lives could not be better spent. In one world I would put the creatures that create (and G.B.S. crowned amongst them) while in another world, working for them would be the cooks and shoe-makers and boatmen and soldiers, who might swell a chest only for the hour after they had been of use to them. At Ayot you are like the maker of a beautiful garden: whenever I enter it I find it lovely. Believe me Ayot is a very good work."

When Charlotte told her husband what she had heard from T.E.L. he expressed the opinion that Lawrence was right.

Henri Barbusse, the French author, was attempting to create a world organization of writers, scientists, artists, musicians and inventors to stand against the menace of war. This organization was to exclude all politicians. A letter from him came to Ayot at the same time as that from T. E. Lawrence and it gave G.B.S. the awaited opportunity to express his private contempt for authors in general. He told Barbusse that he had always found the so-called creative people entirely lacking in political sagacity, that it took him years to undo the mischief Wells had done in the Fabian Society and that in his debates with Belloc and Chesterton, two English authors, he had found no difficulty whatever in shattering their stupid beliefs.

In reply, Barbusse informed him that he had already obtained the active co-operation of Albert Einstein, Thomas Mann, Upton Sinclair, Maxim Gorky and Romain Rolland and he pleaded with Shaw to give his name if only for prestige value to save the peace of the world. Shaw's reply to this plea was in the manner of Eliza Doolittle.

A month later, Mahatma Gandhi was in London in connection with the Round Table Conference and Bernard Shaw was permitted a ten minutes' interview with him at Knightsbridge. Both sat on the floor and while Gandhi went on with his spinning Shaw reminded him that they had met before.

"You wanted to know where you could have dancing lessons."

"I wanted to become an English gentleman," Gandhi informed him. "I had come over to qualify as a barrister and meant to master at the same time the graces of civilization. Was it you I asked for the name of a good English tailor and whether it was possible to perfect one's accent with the help of an elocution teacher?"

"Fortunately for both of us, we both escaped the graces of civilization."

The ten minutes went all too quickly.

Both Charlotte and Bernard Shaw set sail on December 29th for Cape Town and though they had intended to avoid all public speaking he stretched a point by consenting to talk on the Russian experiment when they arrived. On the way to Port Elizabeth both almost lost their lives. G.B.S. had always boasted how wonderfully he could drive a car, and on the veldt, miles from anywhere, he insisted on driving himself. He was going along at full speed when suddenly, wanting to stop, he put his foot on the accelerator instead of the brake, a habit he had in all his activities, and it was by a sheer miracle that all the occupants survived this trial by error. They returned to a place aptly named Wilderness, where they were forced to stay for a whole month so that Charlotte, who was seriously hurt, could be patched up for subsequent removal.

G.B.S. thought this an intervention by the Life Force for here he could bathe every day and spend a great deal of time in writing. He started on a short story which he called *The Adventures of a Black Girl in her Search for God*. He declared that it was divinely inspired and that he himself could not say what the story signified except that the greatest need of the day was the simplification, clarification and unification of religious views. He chose a black girl for this adventure because she was more open to "an unbiassed contemplation of the Bible with its series of gods marking stages in the development of the conception of God from the monster Bogey-man, the Everlasting Father to the Prince of Peace".

"A mile further on she met an ancient fisherman carrying an enormous cathedral on his shoulders.

'Take care: it will break your poor old back,' she cried, running to help him.

'Not it,' he replied cheerfully. 'I am the rock on which the Church is built.'

'But you are not a rock; and it is too heavy for you,' she said, expecting every moment to see him crushed by its weight.

'No fear,' he said, grinning pleasantly at her. 'It is made entirely of paper.' And he danced past her, making all the bells in the cathedral tinkle merrily."

Shaw enjoyed these private little jokes, for 'paper' was the stuff of which his own loves and religion were made. The Black Girl naturally found her peace and satisfaction at last on the Platonic lap of an Irishman who had all the appearance and beliefs of Bernard Shaw. This Irishman was taught manners and cleanliness and she got accustomed to 'his dreadful jokes'. The ending was extremely happy, for he became an unconscious habit of hers, as if he were part of herself.

It was part three of the *Practical System of Moral Education for Females*.

In his new play for the Malvern Festival *Too True To Be Good*, he wanted to show that the Superman if thrown in any surroundings would soon begin to assert authority. Like T. E. Lawrence, he could be in the lowest rank and stay there but the high-ups would still be guided by him. He had met such people among the dockers, miners, railway men, clerks and navvies and they did not remain there because they were humble or modest or self-sacrificing, but it happened for them to be the point from which they could radiate power and it would therefore have been a greater sacrifice for them to have been placed at the top.

The Heartbreak House had become a heartbreak world and G.B.S. felt the need for a revival of hope:

"I must have affirmations to preach. Without them the young will not listen to me; for even the young grow tired of denials."

After much argument and renewed heart searching, Shaw worked out the fundamental conditions of human society:

(1) Government is necessary wherever two or three are gathered together, or two or three billions for keeps.

(2) Government is neither automatic nor abstract; it must be performed by human rulers and agents as best they can.

(3) The individual citizen has to be compelled to work productively.

(4) People who think they can be honestly free all the time are idiots; people who seek wholetime freedom by putting their share of productive work on others are thieves.

(5) The use of the word slavery to denote subjection to Government has grown up among idiots and thieves.

*Too True To Be Good* was produced at Malvern in 1932 and Sir Barry Jackson provided an aeroplane to carry the critics from London, and when they arrived at the theatre, were handed a printed letter from G.B.S. explaining the purpose of the play. He wrote, "The moral of my play is simple enough," but it was not as simple as all that, for he put his great speech, the speech that gave the state of his mind when in his seventy-fifth year, in the mouth of the Burglar:

"I have lost my nerve and am intimidated: all I know is that I must find the way of life, for myself and all of us, or we shall surely perish. And meanwhile my gift has possession of me; I must preach and preach no matter how late the hour and how short the day, no matter whether I have nothing to say or whether in some Pentecostal flame of revelation the Spirit will descend on me and inspire me with a message the sound whereof shall go out unto all lands and realize for us at last the Kingdom and the Power and the Glory for ever and ever. Amen."

Old age had taken a frightening form with G.B.S. for he felt that as the years moved on he would live to see his reputation dwindle into insignificance and that he would be left with nothing but a feeble body. He began to boast more than ever of the ideas that he had originated: he claimed responsibility for Bergson's *Elan Vital*, Einstein's Relativity, Sidney Webb's Inevitability of Gradualness and Stalin's Communism.

With his wife old age showed itself in a mania for travelling. No sooner had she returned from one place she was making plans for another trip and always as far away as possible. It seemed that she was running away from a danger. In December 1932, after Shaw had stopped Mrs. Patrick Campbell from publishing their mutual correspondence in fear of Charlotte's displeasure, they set sail on a world tour. The two outstanding impressions that remained with him were visions of heaven and of hell. He had been invited by a Chinese millionaire to visit his home and there he was ushered into a Chinese Temple to await the host. Here, as he sat, he felt all his thoughts "emptying from my mind and I was overcome by an ineffable peace such as I had never known before and probably will never know again".

The second was an experience he had in America: a nightmarish vision of standing on a platform, surrounded by ghouls.

Against Charlotte's advice, he had agreed to lecture to the American Academy of Political Science. He began with a warning that they must guard themselves against old people like himself, people who tried to foist on them the decay of their intellects and all the rest of their senile shortcomings.

> "I can look back with first-hand experience on generations of people whom you've never met. I can remember the sort of person an American was, say, in the year 1861 because I was already old enough at five to read the newspapers and see in them every day the heading: *The Civil War in America*."

Having thus staged himself as Methuselah, his lovely Irish voice and upright posture giving the impression of vitality and authority, he warned his audience against Democracy:

> "I have never spoken, nor listened at an election meeting without being ashamed of the whole sham democratic routine. The older I grow the more I feel such exhibition to be, as part of the serious business of the government of the nation, entirely intolerable and disgraceful to human nature and civic decency."

He diagnosed the shocking state of the world as due to the fact that it had no intellectual bearings, no general modern theory of society, and this was especially applicable to America where "all talk splendidly and have nothing to say, where they are always in a state of vociferous excitement about entirely trivial things and where they are always quoting me to give point to piffle".

This lecture exhausted him completely and it was then that he had his nightmarish vision of himself standing in the centre of a great auditorium of financiers and all talking Shaw. When he returned he found a childish delight in boasting of the thousands that they had spent on the journey, as for the other travellers on the same tour, he could only conclude that they must have saved money all their lives for this and they seemed more interested in him than in the Great Wall or the Himalayas. He was impressed with the Chinese alone, feeling that they were native to this world, while the white people were something crude and frightening: "I caught the Chinese looking at us with horror, that we should be human beings."

In 1933 there was no play at the Malvern Festival from Bernard Shaw, but instead there was one from James Bridie. Sir Barry Jackson had a good scent for talent and had dragged this young doctor from the obscurity of a hospital to the dangerous role of understudying George Bernard Shaw. His play was *A Sleeping Clergyman*, which proved an immediate success. It was not that Shaw had not completed a play, but he had given it for performance at the Winter Garden Theatre in London.

In this play, *On The Rocks*, he went all out to smash democracy out of existence. In it the Prime Minister, Sir Arthur Chavender, resigned his post because he was not ruthless enough to play the part of saviour of society.

In the Preface to this play, G.B.S. made it perfectly clear that he was serious when he advocated extermination as a political expedient. While in Russia he had heard of a Commissar, a poet, who, as Minister of Transport, had with his own hand shot those station masters who had ignored his orders. This 'strong man' attitude filled Shaw with admiration.

"If we desire a certain type of civilization and culture we must exterminate the sort of people who do not fit into it."

It was as well for the world and the theatre that Shaw himself had not been exterminated when he was castigating the civilization and culture of the day. One can imagine the result of the application of Shaw's political expedient: the Tories in this country eliminating all the Socialists, the Russian Communists eliminating all the British Tories, the Americans eliminating all the Russians, the Chinese eliminating the Americans *ad infinitum*, with Shaw, the Sage Methuselah, left to devise a new creation.

The other playlet he had thrown off on the long sea journey was a diminutive *Man and Superman* and it proved what a dulling effect a world cruise could have, for in *Village Wooing*, the fountain of irrational gaiety had completely dried up and the result was a slow-moving conversation between two uninteresting people who were called upon to revive old Shavian platitudes.

Within a short while they were off again, this time to New Zealand, for Charlotte saw that he was acting once more the role of disintegrator, this time with a friend of hers, and she had to arrange another long journey. This trip did neither of them much good, although Charlotte enjoyed the heat much more than G.B.S. He was toying with a play called *The Millionairess*, an analytical study of a great friend, but he was too ill to make much of it.

In the year 1935 his next play, *The Simpleton of the Unexpected Isles*, was completed. He was back again on eugenic problems: if we had equality of income and complete intermarriageability, what would be the resultant breed? Now, after his travels in the East he had come back with a new synthesis for the Superman, a blend of East and West. While his old friend, Annie Besant, had blended the two theologies into a theosophy, he was going one step further, he was going to be the Michelangelo of a new being.

In an island, a British possession, there are two Oriental Sages, man and wife, who had found the fullest satisfaction in contemplation. They realize that the world needs new beings and are therefore willing to experiment. Conscious of their sex attraction, they take advantage of the infatuation they inspire in two British inhabitants, one a male and the other a female. Twenty years later it is discovered that the four completely handsome children, two male and two female, lack one quality only, the sense of right and wrong. As in *Misalliance*, an unexpected stranger comes upon the scene, this time deposited by pirates, and it is found that he is a Curate, a man of conscience, the very man the Sages desired and they insist that he mate with both the girls to inject a little conscience into the stock. When therefore we have equality of income and all people who oppose it are exterminated, breeding will become a purely eugenic affair.

It was produced by the Theatre Guild in New York as well as at the Malvern Festival. In America it was far from a success. G.B.S. complained that when he was not on the spot to control the production, "the harder they tried, the wronger they went". The young Indian deities, instead of being full of mystery and enchantment, looked more like a native cabaret troupe in the latest Parisian undress, and the critics were unanimous in the opinion that 'the dramatist-sage had grown into a dignified monkey throwing coconuts at the public'. In Malvern, however, where the audience assembled to pay homage to every new quip and idea of George Bernard Shaw, the play was accepted as the last word in symbolism and sagacity.

If, at the age of eighty, G.B.S. was sometimes at a loss for ideas, there were always topical dramas ready at hand to exploit; there was, for example, the constitutional crisis in England, when the new king, Edward VIII, was forced to abdicate because he wished to marry not only a commoner but a divorcee. It gave G.B.S. the opportunity to write a fictitious conversation piece for the *Evening Standard*. It was a most witty bit of writing and had no relevance whatever to the actual characters involved. He was all on the side of the King whom he portrayed as a King Magnus outwitting Prime Minister and Archbishop. It gave G.B.S. a chance to have a chuckle all to himself:

"As she was an American, she had been married twice before and was therefore likely to make an excellent wife for a king who had never been married before."

"The Government would let whole districts fall into ruin and destitution without turning a hair, and then declare that the end of the world is at hand because some foreign dictator had said bluntly that there are milestones on the Dover Road."

"His wit had no influence whatever on the course of events for he had misjudged the issues entirely."

His answer to Henri Barbusse, when invited to co-operate in the International Association of Intellectuals to prevent war, had been haunting him. He felt called upon to give the Dictators a measure of fair play, for he considered himself one of the few sane men left in an insane world. In his play *Geneva* he brings together politicians of all schools, including the Dictators themselves, before The Court of International Justice. In view of the world situation, Shaw must have been the only man in the world who had the strength of mind to make laughter out of its predicament. Strength of mind was all he could muster for he had lost all sense of sympathy and charity for the human race, all sense of justice even. All that was left was a formula:

"What you call God's work, His hardest work, His political work, cannot be done by everybody; they have neither the time, nor the brain, nor the divine call for it. God has sent certain persons to His call. They are not chosen by the people: they must choose themselves; that is part of their inspiration."

Old friends of his asked themselves whether they had mistaken him, and even G.B.S. himself when he went to see the play said:

"It made me quite ill. It is a horrible play. Splendid for the actors though."

He began to apologize for it with the usual plea that the disaster which was fast coming upon the world could only be staved off by laughter. He quoted his *Cymbeline Refinished*, his suggested last act for Shakespeare's play:

IMOGEN: "Oh, do not make me laugh.
    Laughter dissolves too many just resentments,
    Pardons too many sins."
IACHIMO: "And saves the world
    A many thousand murders."

The play did not have the desired effect on either of the Dictators but he managed to complete it before the onset of an illness which was diagnosed by the doctors as 'Pernicious Anaemia'. He wrote, "I am not dead but keeping me alive is pure officiousness."

Dean Inge was one of the few who felt impelled to thank Shaw for the amusement he obtained from the play:

October 17, 1938.

My dear Mr. Shaw,
    Many thanks for *Geneva*. I read it aloud to my wife and we were as much amused as it is possible to be in this ghastly time. People used to call me a pessimist, but I never dreamt that I should see such diabolism and insanity as now prevails over most of Europe. Marsilius of Padua and the Jesuits maintained that to kill a tyrant is no murder; or as my friend Bishop Henson remarked: 'It is strange that in a country so rich in assassins as Italy no one is found to do the obvious thing.' I am told that our Foreign Office think that Hitler's position is insecure; in fact they give him about eighteen months more. I doubt whether they are right; the old and the middleaged hate Nazism and Fascism but the young are enthusiastic; and the poor in both countries are much smarter and more alive than they were. I am devoutly thankful that we are not going to war. We have not dug pits on our tennis lawns and ordered gas masks. The silliest scare that ever was.
    We love living in the country. Twenty-three years of Canons

and Minor Canons are enough for anybody and (here you will not agree) the long musical services make me feel that the prospect of having to listen to the instruments of the cherubim for all eternity is almost enough to deter me from the practice of virtue.

We both send our affectionate greetings to Mrs. Shaw,

Very sincerely,

W. R. Inge.

Desmond McCarthy, always extremely sympathetic to Shaw's work, rebuked him for this play:

"The snare of old age" (he wrote in his criticism of the play) "is mistaking indifference for wisdom; that is why the young discount so heavily and properly, the advice of the old; the old have forgotten what they are talking about. When Mr. Shaw began to be conscious of this inevitable tendency in himself, instead of being on guard against it, he wrote *Methuselah* in which complete detachment from the passions was glorified as the one qualification for controlling the world. The books of the old are apt to be ramshackle, garrulous and repetitive."

Shaw could have given the critic better arguments against old age and he had to remind Desmond McCarthy that it was the young who were following the Dictators and 'heiling' like mad. Shaw modestly claimed that he was not responsible for the make-up of the world or of human nature. He could only say:

"Old age is not enough; youth is not enough; patriotism is not enough; wisdom is not enough; what is enough? Faith to go through life without losing one's faith."

All the failures of humanity were, in his opinion, the outcome of our undeveloped minds and only faith could stimulate the mind to maturity. War, therefore, was not natural but an artificial event created by humanity's low state of development.

It was difficult for G.B.S. to keep up with all the money that was coming in, but the cries for help from stricken refugees, political and religious, only hardened him. He found it necessary to explain that this apparent callousness sprang from the fact that relieving people financially always resulted in mutual hate. It was an unnatural attitude, he admitted, but he had to be firm in order to preserve mutual regard.

# Chapter Fourteen

Out of the blue came another way of increasing publicity as well as wealth with very little effort on his part. A complete stranger, trekking across Europe, appeared one day at Whitehall Court without an introduction, without a penny in his pocket and without an address. By sheer good fortune he found Shaw in an affable mood. Both the Shaws were bewitched by this Hungarian visitor whose passionate avowals convinced them both that they had found a devoted slave; he seemed to them a character out of an oriental legend paying homage to a sage. Shaw was in need of this kind of discipleship. Gabriel Pascal had come to ask for permission to film the 'Master's' plays, and in his excited, incomprehensible speech argued that the plays would by his 'magic' reach the remotest corners of the world. "You, Master, will now speak to the villages, to the cotton pickers, to the miners, there wont be a soul in the world who will not hear every precious word of yours. You will see."

Gabriel Pascal would not leave them alone and they did not show any objection to his persistence. On each occasion his stories grew more fantastic: he sprang from a love marriage between a gipsy and a prince, he rode invisibly through the ranks of the enemy in the Great War and he alone survived in a cavalry charge; when in China with an important film contract he was called by a voice to go straight to Bernard Shaw! Here he was. But all this time G.B.S. would give no reply and Gabriel Pascal would return every night to a little room in Hammersmith behind a fish and chip shop to help serve and thus earn his keep.

The day came when he could wait no longer and he warned G.B.S. that if he did not hear within the next five days, he would have to return to Tibet. "I am ready to wait until Friday the 13th of December, four o'clock!"

Exactly to the minute, when Big Ben struck the hour, a messenger boy arrived with the contract of *Pygmalion* and a signed photograph of G.B.S.

All the finance had to be found by Gabriel Pascal himself and with the stipulation that not a word was to be altered.

G.B.S. described this new association thus:

"Until Gabriel Pascal descended on me out of the clouds, could find nobody who wanted to do anything with my plays on the screen but mutilate them, murder them, give their cadavers to the nearest scrivener.

When Gabriel appeared out of the blue, I just looked at him and handed him *Pygmalion* to experiment with. His studio was immediately infested with script writers, and he thought that everything they did was wrong and everything I did was right. Naturally I quite agreed with him."

With a contract in his pocket, Pascal told everybody triumphantly:

"You English, you do not understand Shaw. You do not realize he is, yes, he is the great heart. He is the highest spirit in the world. I vibrate with his vibration in every word."

Although he was penniless and inexperienced in the financial and film worlds, Pascal managed to obtain the large sum necessary in an equally miraculous way. With the contract in his hand, he had only to wave this magic wand and banks emptied their tills, peers were ready to help and financiers to speculate. It was not long before production commenced at Pinewood with Leslie Howard and Wendy Hiller in the chief parts. Since Leslie Howard was to direct as well as play, Anthony Asquith was appointed co-director.

All the still photographs had to be submitted to G.B.S. for examination and the Master visited the studio and advised on every move. Nothing was permitted without the full consent of the playwright. G.B.S. was as excited as when *Widowers' Houses* was first staged and he agreed to almost all Pascal's suggestions even to the point of interpolating a bathroom scene in which Eliza Doolittle floated in foam.

The film was a great success, especially in America. It was acclaimed there as a revolution in films. Gabriel Pascal declared:

"British producers must go for the great writers. America does not want little monkey stories, because they have plenty little monkies there themselves. Everyone there is crazy for Bernard Shaw. His are not little monkey stories, you see? Understand me?"

G.B.S., with his defence mechanism in full action, announced that the huge fortune that came from the film had almost ruined him through the heavy taxation involved. One of the first to congratulate G.B.S. on the success of the film was the first Eliza, Mrs. Patrick Campbell.

9 Dec. 1938.

Dear Joey,

    . . . I was overjoyed to hear of your miraculous cure. . . .
I know a poor lady who had to eat a quarter of a pound of par-
boiled bleeding liver twice daily, and she never touched meat!
It was nice too, to hear of you and Charlotte at the Book Fair
'shown round like Royalty' and why not, and 'both looking so
well.' Also from a friend I heard of the huge success of *Pygmalion*
at the Odeon Theatre, Chesterfield, with a population of twenty-
three thousand, and there were twenty-one thousand seats sold in
the week. And I hear that the miners came in their rough clothes
straight from the mine and enjoyed every word of your wit. And
you on a percentage! You must be making more money than you
know what to do with. I wonder if you remember all the trouble
I took, how I took the play to Tree and begged him to ask you to
come and read it to him, and said I would play Eliza. How I stood
your insults at rehearsals, how I worked day and night over the
accent, how loyal I was to you when Tree came to me just before
the curtain went up and begged me to cut the bloody (I would
have liked to have heard the miners' laughter). How I spilt my
heart trying to make Eliza common and beautiful, something about
her to fit into dreams, of course you have forgotten all. . . . I am in
one little room here, but I have an open wood fire and a lovely view
over the Tuilleries Gardens, and the sun all day. The covered colon-
nades go all down the street so I can go out wet or fine. The
Duke and Duchess of Windsor live three doors down on my right.
He looks tranquil, she looks calm. . . .

Stella.

His answer conveyed that her letter was "a dismal string of lies
and not worth twopence".
Immediately came her reply:

    "What do you mean 'a string of lies', even if your memory is
failing you you cannot have forgotten that I speak the truth. In the
House of Life there are many windows, and from each a different
view. And so in the Home of the spirit where imagination dwells.
Only villains and weak women tell lies. So far as I am concerned the
story of *Pygmalion* is rather a dismal one to me, and not worth
twopence to anyone else. . . . I am going to tell you a tragedy that
came upon the world of Art through that cocksure critical attitude
of yours. It's no use for you to be indignant and deny it, for it is

pathetically true. Ambrose McEvoy was painting my portrait and so far as he had gone it was most rarely beautiful. Then I made the mistake of taking you to see it. I say mistake because you did not know the man and had no idea of his sensitiveness. You showed no reverence or recognition of what was on the canvas, but called in critical tones for what was *not* there. The next day I went for my sitting, he had blackened the portrait completely out. . . ."

For his new play, G.B.S. chose a group of men living in the reign of Charles II and who were, like himself, seeking the philosopher's stone. In *Good King Charles' Golden Days* he could introduce George Fox, the founder of the Quakers, Isaac Newton, the mathematician, and Kneller, the artist, all three impelled by the Life Force to push forward human development.

It was while writing this play that Shaw hit upon what he considered was his unique contribution to human consciousness: the discovery that God made the world as an artist. G.B.S. thus endowed God with the gift of Art, like a parent who hoped that his child might have the ability that he himself lacked.

With the performance of *Good King Charles' Golden Days* at Malvern it was calculated that of the sixty-five plays performed in the eleven seasons of the Festival, 1929–1939, no fewer than nineteen had been by Bernard Shaw, ranging from his very first, *Widowers' Houses* written in 1885, to the last play in 1939. This last play he felt was the coping stone of all his thinking and like his earliest thoughts seemed to run counter to the tide. Just as Europe was rolling into chaos, he came to the conclusion that there was form, significance, pattern in Creation.

Neither G.B.S. nor Charlotte were able to be at the Malvern Festival for both were ill and Charlotte was crippled with pain. Fortunately the coming of Gabriel Pascal and the filming of *Major Barbara* kept them from dwelling on the state of their health and the universe. The film was a new mechanical toy which yielded in his old age the delight he had always found in photography. The dramatic potentialities of this new medium made him wish that he was at the beginning of his career rather than at the end, for when he wrote for the stage he had always borne in mind the utmost economy of production, but now he could let his imagination run to elaborate scenes. *Major Barbara* itself struck him as shockingly out of date, wealth from death and destruction was cynicism magnified a thousandfold in view of the present state of Europe. Gabriel Pascal, however, smothered the theme with the latest styles in furnishings, twentieth-century architecture and the Albert Hall itself was put into use for the great Salvation Army gathering, and whole orchestras and brass bands made real what the author could only suggest by mere words.

Shaw became so enthusiastic that he invested in this film part of his royalty payment of *Pygmalion*, knowing that it was bound to bring in a large return. It was not difficult for Pascal to persuade him to write sixteen new sequences, for now he had attained a great hold on G.B.S., because he was in the true succession of legendary characters woven into his life, from Vandeleur Lee to Richard Deck, from J. L. Joynes to Dr. Aveling, from Annie Besant to Eleanor Marx, from Frank Harris to Cunninghame Graham and from Granville Barker to T. E. Lawrence. Pascal could beat every one in flattery. To him Shaw's eyes were as blue as the sky reflected in the two lakes in his home in Hungary, his beard as soft and white as the snow on the mountain peaks of his native land. The dark, short, stocky man, swarthy-faced, bloodshot eyes, with a mop of coarse black hair over his low brow, looked up with voluptuous delight at the tall, thin, white-haired Sage; everything Shaw said, did, looked was wonderful:

"You, Master, are the only man who could put Hitler on your lap and give him the smacking on his bottom he deserves. You are the only man who could exert authority. If I had my way I would make him meet you and the war would stop dead at once."

Shaw's eyes sparkled with mischievous pleasure. At that moment Hitler had already overrun most of Europe and it seemed to Pascal that there was only one person to stop him.

"The great ones of the world have already acclaimed you as the Master mind. Churchill has called *Major Barbara* a masterpiece. Now every servant girl and every peasant will vibrate to you. Already a quarter of a million pounds has been spent in the production."

Dean Inge had been far too optimistic when he had referred to the 'silliest scare that ever was!' When Britain came into the war thousands of school children were evacuated and hundreds of cars took adults to safe country places, but Charlotte and G.B.S. stayed in their top flat at Whitehall Court. In the evening, both sat, their windows blacked out, he playing his beloved Mozart and bursting into song, she consoling herself with Eastern philosophy. He constituted himself:

Defender of the Faith, Protector of the Arts, Father Confessor of Youth.

When the bombing became really serious and continuous both left London for Ayot St. Lawrence, and at the same time those who had been evacuated returned to London because they felt alien in the villages and provincial towns. In his spacious garden and the quiet of the shelter the war seemed a distant thing; when petrol became difficult Ayot St. Lawrence might have been in the Antarctic as far as visitors were concerned. Shaw declared that it was a good thing for it gave him more time for his writing. He worked out the course of the war, came forward with military suggestions and prophesied the early defeat of Hitler because there was no doubt that all who attacked the Jews suffered for it. The two old servants found the strain of running the house with only one maid to help them intolerable, and when the secretary also joined them, they both became ill, the man going up to London for special spinal treatment and his wife cook-housekeeper feeling all the time that she could not bear it for long. It was for Charlotte's sake that she stayed on and bathed and dressed her and carried her into bed, for her mistress was bowed with ostitis deformans.

To keep himself occupied G.B.S. started on his last effort to clarify the confusion of the world by setting out in the simplest language 'for all to misunderstand' the cure for civilization. It would be addressed to the abstraction called Everyman, the lowest common intelligence as opposed to the Intelligent Woman for whom he had written a previous guide.

Anatole France once complained to him that the monstrous orgy of words was leading the world into a mental paralysis but Shaw could not help himself: writing had become a habit with him, and the very sight and feel of paper excited his nerves and made him pick up his pen even if he had nothing whatever to say.

Charlotte wished that he could devote his last years to a religious book in the manner of Saint Bernard. She was tired of politics and blamed the politicians for all that was happening. She was brave in her illness and when she suffered most she would say: "What have I done to deserve this? I must have done something." She urged him to keep up with his literary acquaintances, and so he sent a gift to Virginia Woolf to 'propitiate the Bloomsbury crowd'. This was a painting by Roger Fry which they had found in a chest and he could not say how it had come to him, for he had never purchased works of art.

The letter he received from Virginia Woolf pleased them both, for it was Roger Fry whom G.B.S. once advised not to take up art.

13th June 1940.

Dear Mr. Shaw,

It was only last week I was in London and saw the Roger Fry picture that you sent me. It is one of his best I think, and to have it from you adds to its beauty. One day I hope you will come and see it hanging in my room. And if ever you have time, and a half a sheet of paper, and would write upon it that it was your picture and that you gave it me, my debt of gratitude to you would mount, if possible, higher. But I am not going to bother you any more.

This is only to thank you for sending it, and to assert the affection which, though suppressed, is always alive in the heart of yours gratefully,

Virginia Woolf.

The time had come for the showing of *Major Barbara* and G.B.S. was extremely nervous about its reception. A letter from H. G. Wells reassured him:

16th April 1941.

My dear G.B.S.,

I was going to write to you to-day, our minds move in sympathy. I saw *Major Barbara* on Monday and I found it delightful. You have given it fresh definition. Andrew Undershaft might have been better cast with a more subtle face. As it is he seems to be astonished at himself throughout. The house was packed. Moura and I got the last two seats and you could not have had a more responsive audience. They laughed at all the right places. Mostly young people in uniform they were.

That old Fabian audience is scattered for ever more. I firmly believe that we are getting the young; we shall rise again sooner than Marx did and for better reasons.

This getting old is getting tiresome. I dont feel old in my wits but my heart seems to falter and I have phases of brain anaemia when I forget names and all that small print stuff. I've written a guide to the New World Order and I am writing a novel. So get on with your play.

Whatever happens now we've had a pretty good time.

Yours as ever,

H.G.

In spite of their squabbles, their mutual accusations, their bally-ragging, they were, as Wells put it, moving in sympathy.

Hearing that Wells was staying in London during the heavy raids the Shaws invited him to stay with them, but there was no reply. Again Shaw wrote to him suggesting that he would not mind the destruction of London as long as Wells and Westminster Abbey remained standing, but again there was no reply. Wells was obviously out to die bravely.

Though there had been a Shelley Society and a Browning Society, no Englishman had thought of forming a Shaw Society, and it was left to a German refugee to start such an organization in England. This German had known of a Goethe Society in his native country and he considered Shaw a contemporary incarnation of Goethe. At first there was the usual opposition from G.B.S. who remembered how, in his early days, he had shocked the Shelley Society by declaring himself a socialist, an atheist and a vegetarian, the very principles for which Shelley stood; and how he had attended the meeting of the Browning Society and found it made up of a few pious old ladies. But as in the case of Herr Trebitsch and Gabriel Pascal, Charlotte at once saw value in it and so on Shaw's eighty-fifth birthday the Shaw Society was formed, and it was not long before it was engulfed in internal bickering and trivial curiosity about their Master's private habits. The membership was small and Shaw put it down to the fact that old people are repulsive to the young. It was not so, of course, as the following letter from Osbert Sitwell proved:

18–2–42.

My dear Master,
    I cannot refrain writing to you because you are the only prophet who has never misled me. You were right about Russia, but, of course, no one could foresee the endless blundering to which our amateur set of dictators in this country commit us. And the boasting too, of what we are going to do! I wonder if we always boasted like that, or if it is a new development of the British character? It is like the blowing of trumpets outside the Walls of Jericho: only the Walls dont seem to fall down so easily as they did in Biblical times.
    With many greetings to yourself and Mrs. Shaw.
                                                    Yours ever,
                                                    Osbert Sitwell.

G.B.S. was engaged in controversy about Art with Sir William Rothenstein, about Music with Sir Henry Wood and about Culture with Sir Almroth Wright, the eminent doctor who had once thrilled him with the statement that sanitation was aesthetic. Sir Almroth enjoyed deflating G.B.S.'s pride:

March 5th, 1942.

My dear G.B.S.,

You say you are a highly educated man, and confident in this, you say things no really highly educated person would say, for such a person is able to admire intellectual merit everywhere.

I know quite well that we poor scientists have not your aesthetic education, not your creative endowments, but I would not have you exaggerate your aesthetic education. You know all about music and Shakespeare and Bunyan, but Greek and German, and for aught I know, French and Italian are to you all of them *terra incognita*. You cannot get at them through translation. I have thousands of poetical tunes in these languages in my head which come up daily in my memory, as music for its part comes up into yours. Now no passages in translations ever lodge in the memory. There are in your writing two wonderfully worded passages which would never bear translation: one is the passage where you speak about Shakespeare 'who never understood virtue or courage' and you contrast him with Bunyan's hero 'who leaves his sword to him who shall succeed him in his pilgrimage, and his courage and skill to him who can get it'.

The other passage of yours which is constantly in my mind is: 'To dream that the world is like that, is to lead the heavenly *life*.' These couldn't be put into German or into French.

Affectionately yours,

Almroth Wright.

The book Shaw was writing, *Everybody's Political What's What*, the last of his *Moral Guides*, was plumful of heresies, but the heresies were all remarkably familiar and read like quotations from that shocking young author, G. Bernard Shaw. He did not know what public he was writing for, as it was obvious that the people who might survive the war were altogether different in kind to those who survived the 1914–18 war. The present soldiers were carrying pamphlets in their holsters and strange thoughts in their heads and he was hurrying to get in his truths before the others got in with their lies.

"When you consider" (he said) "who the people were who set out to reverse the whole basis of society which seemed, in those far-off days impregnable: a few refugees working in the British

Museum, a few spouters, one or two saints, a number of cracked writers and artists who spoilt their chances of ever making a livelihood, it is amazing what we have achieved."

Until now Shaw had behaved as a young man with long years before him; now he wrote as an old man with long years behind him. Once more he gave the arguments which gently led up to the well-known climax of longevity and equality of income but the novelty in this book was the subtle analysis of different types: the political man, the military man, the educated man, the corruptly educated man, the medical man, the aesthetic man and his new pet, the statistician. In his long-sustained argument two postulates stood out: one, that there was a force in Nature which threw up sufficient rulers as it threw up sufficient rebels, and two: that the Life Force also threw up artists, mathematicians and religious people, unswayed by any other passion but the passion for truth, who acted as the phagocytes in the social structure and were the mainstay of human progress. Wise rulers realized this but the not so wise, by ignoring this important fact, led the world to disaster.

On the 13th April, 1943, Bernard Shaw heard that Beatrice Webb had died and his first reaction was one of dread, for he knew that she had kept a diary in which she had jotted down her personal impressions of all the people she had worked with. He knew that in spite of their long association in the Fabian Movement she had never cared for him and had despised him as a playwright. He meant to go to London immediately to suppress, if possible, any objectionable references to him.

He did not tell Charlotte of her death because she had always liked Beatrice and the death would have come as a great shock to her, and as her own life was hanging on a thread it did not seem wise to recall the hazy past.

## Chapter Fifteen

IN the summer of 1943 the Shaws left Ayot for their London flat because the old housekeeper, Mrs. Higgs, had at last broken down and had to go into a hospital for a serious operation. Although it might have been possible for G.B.S. to have obtained nurses and temporary help, as Charlotte had obtained for him when he had been ill, there was no effort made to do so. Charlotte was now helpless and acquiescent.

At Whitehall Court G.B.S. received visitors, and mainly spent his time walking about London, visiting his old haunts, and examining the war damage which seemed to fascinate him. The substantial buildings which he had known for many years and had stood as solid as rocks had crumbled into rubble, while he had remained vertical.

One day, Charlotte woke up looking young and beautiful as he had never seen her before and he felt that the journey to London had not been harmful after all. In the evening he led her to her room earlier than usual and went for a walk. The next day the maid found her lying at the foot of her bed, clutching her clock in her hand and her face bleeding. She was put back into bed and a nurse was called but she died within a day on the 12th of September, 1943, five months after the death of Beatrice.

Her cremation at Golder's Green sadly disappointed G.B.S. because he was not permitted to see the burning. On September the 20th the following notice appeared in *The Times*:

"Mr. Bernard Shaw has received such a prodigious mass of letters on the occasion of his wife's death that, though he has read and values them all, any attempt to acknowledge them individually is beyond his power. He therefore begs his friends and hers to be content with this omnibus reply, and to assure them that a very happy ending to a very long life has left him awaiting his own turn in perfect serenity."

He felt that it would not be very long when his own ashes would be joined with hers, for he had promised her this in her last days. He did not know what part to play after this experience. To some he boasted of his new-found freedom and how enjoyable it was; to others, he was lonely and bereft of all guidance; and again to others that nothing mattered because he lagged superfluous and was only here on this earth for a few more days.

Offers of help came to him from everywhere and he preferred to call them offers of marriage as he now considered himself the most eligible man in the world. A cable from America summarily announced that an old flame of his was actually embarking and would be with him within a week or so. This frightened him, for he saw himself abandoned by his servants and made the laughing stock of the village. He sent by return a long cable threatening his old friend with expulsion by the police and worked out his schemes to the last detail. She did not appear. Another day, an elderly woman arrived on foot to take charge of his household. She was tired, and it was a relief to her to have reached her Temple at last. But within ten minutes he had stormed at her and bullied her out of the village to walk another six miles along the winding Hertfordshire lanes back to the station.

All the worry in the world could not prevent him being himself. He wrote to Sir Henry Wood suggesting the introduction of his favourite ophicleide and bass saxophone into the orchestra and impressed upon him the obvious fact that conditions had changed since the days of Bach and Handel. He received a letter from Sir Henry reminiscent of Sir Osbert Sitwell:

October 28th. 1943

Dear Mr. Shaw,

I have only just got back from concerts in Bedford, Oxford and Bradford, late last night. Of course I absolutely agree with all you say about Handel's *Messiah* and they apply to a great many other works written about this period. You know how "Klenovsky" for many years past, has been accused of tampering with the great masters' scores, but conditions and the quality of our instruments, *has entirely changed* since the days of Bach and Handel and in my opinion *you* are the only person who has the right conception of what has occupied my thought for many years in the public performance of the old masterpieces, in the changed conditions of the present time. . . .

The Ophicleide idea of yours is excellent, but our modern orchestral musicians would kick at studying it, and Concert Managers would kick still more at the demand of the player for an extra three guineas. . . .

A Bass Saxophone would I think be better, for doubling the

lower strings, more flexible and many more players could tackle it, but we conductors are always up against the Concert givers, *one* extra instrument calls forth a storm of protest, at the last Norwich Festival Committee Meeting, the Chairman observed: "Why does Sir Henry want three flutes, we are giving him two."

If I suggest a Bass Saxophone for a Beethoven Concert, the Concert would certainly be postponed and probably never take place,

Sincerely yours,

Henry J. Wood.

Household responsibilities assumed giant dimensions. Mrs. Higgs, now out of hospital, informed him that she and her husband wished to retire before they were dead, and the problem of retaining a new housekeeper loomed so large that it shut out his obsessive interests, his Will and the phonetic alphabet.

Everyone he knew had to listen to his tale of woe:

"I want a person who would know her place and would not be interested in my ideas and books. This is a lonely place and it would be fatal to me to have to entertain her; no servant is a heroine to her own master."

Gabriel Pascal interested himself in this calamity and could do nothing, for he, himself, used hopeful actresses and young actors to staff his household.

The problem solved itself for their London maid was out of work and was willing to come to Ayot. All was well again. However, in spite of his upright carriage, the swinging stick, the grandiose talk of high finance, the plaint of being overwhelmed with correspondence, he was lonely, and would not admit it even to himself. He had to remind himself continually of his unique position in the world of literature, of what he meant to the theatre and to politics, and that he was a man of wealth and property. There were moments when he would forget these things and then his body would droop into the shape of a question mark and he would look the oldest man in creation, but it was only for a moment, for he would regain his self-conscious posture, stretch to his utmost and be a superman once more.

When his *Everybody's Political What's What* was at last completed he had to think of the paper, the binding and dust cover, none of which he left to the publishers. It was a large book and war restrictions prevented him from making it as impressive as he wanted it to be.

How was he to gauge the demand for it? The cost of production was covered by him entirely and at first he thought of a modest thousand or so, but he ventured on a hundred thousand as a daring gesture and they were not enough. For the second edition he used a dust cover chosen by Charlotte and a further fifty thousand were printed. They went as rapidly, although the Press was unfavourable.

He received this letter from his Tormentor, H. G. Wells:

September 5th, 1944

My dear Shaw,

In the interest of artistic photography, you must never die. Your wicked old face in the frontispiece is the best piece of camera work you have ever inspired. I am glad I provoked the book (*The Political What's What*) and later on I will send you a comment on it. . . .

In the meanwhile bless you,
Yours ever,
H. G.

All that was left for him to do, he felt, was to revise his Will and make it lawyer-proof in every respect, for he meant to leave his fortune to the founding of a phonetic alphabet to be used universally in the English-speaking countries, and he particularly liked the position of being in the minority of one. As his personal popularity grew he took on these hopeless causes, for a saint had to be in a minority of one at all costs. The Evolutionary appetite demanded it.

Meanwhile the filming of *Caesar and Cleopatra* went ahead in spite of protests of many experts who pointed out to Mr. Rank, who was financing it, that the play had never been a box-office success and that it was most untimely to show a film lauding a dictator. But Rank had the American market in mind and felt that the film would increase the prestige of the British film. The beginning of the shooting of the film coincided with the landing of the Allied troops in Normandy, and Gabriel Pascal, who was a superstitious man, thought it a happy augury for both events.

The film needed intense sunshine as it was placed in Egypt, but instead there was perpetual cloud and dismal rain and the whole schedule went wrong. The filming took much longer than was expected and was swallowing up hundreds of thousands. Shaw was not pleased with the way it was going and if he had had his way he would have had it scrapped completely, for it seemed to him that Pascal had turned it into a dull, prosaic, illustrated history. G.B.S. would not have minded illustrations because he himself had learnt much from illustrated Shakespeares and Bunyans and Chaucers; but this film gave the wrong approach entirely to his play and it was doomed from the start. He was sorry for Gabriel Pascal, who had lost his way in this film. This view was not held by Pascal, who was forced to make up for the lack of love interest by elaborating on the incidental scenes, padding with crowds fleeing in panic, stately banquets and immense crowd scenes. Gabriel Pascal sensed the lack of enthusiasm in his Master but felt confident that the public response to the film would soon change Shaw's mind.

Poor Pascal was having troubles all round and called the film his Cross. There was trouble with his stars, with whom he was often not on speaking terms, there was trouble with his mechanics and his health was consequently deteriorating. He tried to persuade Shaw to appear in person in the film but G.B.S. was adamant:

"There is enough talk already in the film without me. One Sphinx is enough."

The defeat of Germany was not unexpected by him for the moment Russia was attacked by Germany he foretold the collapse of the Hitler regime. All he feared now was the coming of visitors again because he was afraid of giving more work to his staff. There were few young people whom he knew personally. To him the Army was a composite impersonal image. So that when he heard that a very young friend of his was going to Germany on relief work among the miners and the prisoners he wrote as though to the whole of youth:

"Do not stay too long in contact with a world which, never forget this for a moment, is not the natural world but an artificial world created by a catastrophic convulsion called war. You have to see children dying of starvation and not share your food because you can only add to the general misery if you disable yourself. That is not human nature; it is utterly repugnant to it. You have to see morality reversed by hunger. Nothing could be less natural. You can learn nothing from it except that it happens when war happens just as drowning happens in floods and scorching in fires. Keep a grip of this and dont let it overwork or starve you and you will come through without losing *your faith*."

Without losing your faith. He had not lost his faith. Wars and revolutions, financial blizzards and famines, had not diverted or blurred his vision, for he had foretold these very things and had tried to explain their causes so that people should know that they are the outcome of their own mistakes.

He had lived to see a Labour Government again, this time with a huge majority over all parties, and overwhelmingly Fabian in its training, and he felt that it was the fruition of the efforts of Sidney Webb and himself, now two hopeless dodderers who would never meet again.

Besides the phonetic alphabet there was one other thing which he wished to see fulfilled in his own lifetime. This was the 'coupled vote', suggested to him by an artist neighbour. The idea at once caught his imagination. After seventeen years of woman suffrage in a nation of men and women virtually equal in numbers, it appeared unbalanced that there should be twenty-four women Members of Parliament in a House of six hundred and forty. To remedy this, it was suggested that the representative unit should be, not a man or a woman, but a man *and* a woman, with the result that the elected body would consist of men and women in equal numbers. It was argued by him that it would be a safety measure for men because women were accustomed to think of the welfare of men.

> "I leave it to our old Parliamentary hands," he stated, "to devise a plan by which our electorate can be side-tracked, humbugged, cheated, lied to or frightened into accepting the coupled vote."

He was honoured by a request from the War Office to select his three best plays for circulation among the troops. He went through all his plays most critically again and could not make up his mind which he considered his best, "because," as he put it, "I am not a schoolmaster accustomed to give examination marks". He liked different bits in different plays and had strange sentimental attachments to some; to *Mrs. Warren's Profession* and *The Showing Up of Blanco Posnet* because they had been banned; to *Candida* and *Man and Superman* because of Granville Barker's superb acting in them; to *Arms and the Man* because he had guyed his best friends in it, and above all to *Back to Methuselah* because he had emptied his whole thought in it; how could he choose three? He wished that the War Office had invited him to write a new play, for that would have been unique in the history of the drama and there was no one in the world more able than he to do unique things.

Ultimately he chose *Androcles and the Lion*, *Pygmalion* and *Saint Joan*, for the strange reason that there was real pathos in them and in a time of so much suffering they may be cathartic in their effect. He made one stipulation only, and that was that the Prefaces should be included. The first page read:

"I am ready to admit that after contemplating the world and human nature for nearly sixty years, I see no way out of the world's misery but the way which would have been found by Christ's will if He had undertaken the work of a modern practical states man."

And the last words in the book ended in a prayer uttered by Saint Joan:

"O God that madest this beautiful earth, when will it be ready to receive Thy saints? How long, O Lord, how long?"

Young men who had proved brave beyond compare, who had endured pain and torture, now came all the way to Ayot to see him but fled at his approach. To one who had come out of the war a nervous wreck and desiring to put himself and his children to death, G.B.S. answered:

5th January 1946.

Dear Sir,
 Killing yourself is a matter for your own judgment. Nobody can prevent you. If you are convinced that you are not worth your salt, and an intolerable nuisance to yourself and everyone else, it is a solution to be considered. But you can always put it off to to-morrow on the chance of something interesting turning up that evening.

As to killing the children, it would be the act of a madman or a murderer. They may have the happiest dispositions; they may even be born to greatness: the children of good-for-nothings (Beethoven and Isaac Newton for instance) have grown up to be geniuses. My father was a failure: only his latest years (he was long-lived) could be called happy. I am conceited enough to believe that it is just as well that he did not kill me in a fit of low spirits. Instead he relieved himself by drinking occasionally, though it only made him worse.

Have you consulted a psychologist? Soul torment is not a philosophy: it is a disease, and usually cures itself after a time. A quick medicine for it may be discovered to-morrow. Read the autobiography of John Stuart Mill, who gives a graphic description of a long fit of depression which passed away completely and was the prelude to an illustrious future.

In short, dear sir, dont be a damned fool. Get interested in something.

G.B.S.

He decided that after his death his house would be given over to the National Trust and to make it more attractive he wanted a sculpture of Saint Joan in bronze and larger than natural size to stand in the garden, high on a hillock overlooking the English fields and hills which he saw every day from his bedroom window. He invited the artist who had recently painted his portrait to do this sculpture. When the statue was finished he wrote:

> "Europe is crowded with images of Joan of Arc, but this is by far the best statue of the Maid I have ever seen, and the only one I would let into my garden to live with."

On his ninetieth birthday he picked up his writing pad and went off in his Rolls-Royce to London. To the world at large he had announced that he would ignore his birthday, but, with characteristic unpredictability, he decided in the end to attend the special exhibition opened in his honour by the Very Rev. Dr. W. R. Inge, K.C.V.O., who said:

> "We have come here to do honour to one of the most eminent of our fellow-countrymen. I suppose most people would put Winston Churchill first. I think a great many of us would put George Bernard Shaw second. He has given enormous pleasure to millions of people all over the world, and has not been content to give pleasure, he has made a very serious attempt to show the English people what an absurd nation they are. We are the most downtrodden nation in Europe. We cant govern ourselves and are nearly always governed by Scotsmen, and occasionally by Irishmen. It is rather humiliating, but still the Scripture says: 'Blessed are the meek.'"

Besides the exhibition of Shaviana at the National Book League Gallery, a memorial volume entitled *G.B.S. 90* was published in which his work was examined by experts in each field of knowledge. There were articles on G.B.S. as philosopher, G.B.S. as a dramatist, as a scientist, as a theologian, as an economist, as a critic, as an educationist and as a music critic; and he came out of this exacting scrutiny extremely well. In an age of specialism, the existence of such a comprehensive mind was felt to be unique and irreplaceable.

The letters he received on July 26th, 1946, outnumbered even those he had received after he had published his *Commonsense about the War* in 1914, but thirty-two years ago all had been abusive and even his friends had condemned him, but now all vied in adulation. It was for Aldous Huxley to express the necessary warning to the applauding world:

> "If, instead of just applauding Mr. Shaw's plays and chuckling over his prefaces, we had also paid some serious attention to his teaching, what remains of our civilization might not now be lying under sentence of death."

The desire to write yet another play came upon him: the characters were to be completely uninhibited. Shaw knew, of course, that even in their wildest extremeties his characters could not possibly shock the tenderest susceptibilities of the present generation. The time had gone by when the mere utterance of the word 'bloody' could create roars of shocked laughter. This new play would be completely static and would be a discussion about the old old themes, about love and religion, wealth and old age, education and taxation; it would be a summing up and an *envoi*. Roy Limbert was anxious to start the Malvern Festival again and was pressing him for a new play. Shaw let him know in advance that not a penny would be forthcoming from his own pocket, for he was strangled by the unjust taxation which took "thirty shillings for every pound I earned". Roy Limbert, however, was too enthusiastic an admirer of Shaw to be put off by such a statement. He asked Shaw to endow the annual performance so that it could fly the Shavian flag forever. George Bernard Shaw answered as the hard-headed business man:

> "I havent a half penny to my name. Neither will I be present at the performance because I would set a bad example to the audience by falling asleep and waking up the others with my snoring. It is enough that I have to pay for my funeral, why must I pay for my posthumous fame?"

He was extremely worried about his posthumous fame. H. G. Wells had died on August 13th, 1946, and as in the case of Beatrice Webb, Shaw was anxious to prevent the publication of a spiteful parody of himself written by H.G., as merciless as the one of Henry James and of the Webbs. Shaw had asked to see Wells when he heard that he was very ill but had been refused entrance to the house. Now that Wells had predeceased him he meant to build up strong defences against posthumous calumny. As a precaution he made it clear in an obituary notice that Wells was not the kind of person whose word could be relied on. Shaw hated literary caricatures of himself as much as Charlotte had hated the caricatures of her husband by Max Beerbohm, which she was known to have bought in order to destroy.

In order to prevent busybody biographers from gleaning harmful material from any of his records, he revised his notebooks and diaries and burnt hundreds of letters and created fictitious matter to put people off the scent. When news came to him that old acquaintances like Lord Alfred Douglas and Erica Cotterill had died, he made every effort to get hold of any letters they had left; and to complete his scheme of self-projection he sent out through various people information about himself knowing that it would infiltrate into the public consciousness. His formula was: "I may tell a lie about a person and the whole world will believe me, but I will arrange that if the truth is told about me, nobody will believe it."

Why had he this dread? The whole world was at his feet and as far as he knew not a soul was uttering malicious nonsense about him. It was because, he explained to a friend, he had lived long enough to know that a depression always sets on a reputation, however great, after the person's death. He had seen it happen to Thomas Hardy, to George Meredith, to John Galsworthy, to Anatole France, to Rodin, and it would happen to himself unless he took precautionary measures. He knew that in such a depression every little weakness was magnified. It was happening to John Ruskin at that very moment and to G. F. Watts and to William Morris.

A few weeks after the death of Wells, he heard on the wireless that Granville Barker had died on the 31st of August, 1946, in Paris. Shaw had not seen him for years, had often longed to see him, but had been denied this pleasure. G.B.S. wrote a pathetic letter to *The Times Literary Supplement*:

"The shock the news of his death gave me made me realize how I had cherished the hope that our old intimate relation might revive. But

Marriage and death and division
Make barren our lives

and the elderly professor could have little use for a nonagenarian ex-playwright."

Even in this case the reaction to Granville Barker took a new turn, for he began to tell visitors that Barker never understood his plays and was only "playing *himsef* in whatever part he was doing".

When Sidney Webb died, on the 15th October, 1947, G.B.S. adopted an entirely different attitude. He launched at once a campaign for the burial of the Webbs in Westminster Abbey and succeeded, thus making way for himself and the other pioneers of the Fabian Movement.

This death was followed in January 1948 by the assassination of Mahatma Gandhi by a Hindu fanatic. The telephone at Ayot St. Lawrence rang frequently, for the whole world was battering at G.B.S. for a word on the saint's death. Only a few months before, G.B.S. had talked of Gandhi prospering in health by his self-inflicted fasts and prophesied that the Indian would live up to two hundred years by prayer and fasting. At last the phrase he was waiting for came to him and it spread across the world:

"I always said that it was dangerous to be good," he shouted into the telephone.

G.B.S.'s grief was mixed with curiosity as to what would happen to the murderer. Would they forgive him as Gandhi had already done?

Now that all these people had gone there was only one thing left for an old and healthy man to do and that was to take his own life by writing his autobiography. While therefore the King and Queen were enjoying the presentation of *Good King Charles' Golden Days* at the People's Palace in the East End of London, and the Malvern Festival was preparing to put on the play he was just completing, he sat unconcerned in his hut at the foot of his garden, putting together scraps and pieces of his life. He had to confess:

"I am not at all interesting biographically. I have never killed anybody, and nothing very unusual has happened to me."

If he had not killed a person he had seen one institution after another reel before his mockery. In *G.B.S. 90*, Laurence Housman had written of him:

"I cannot think of anybody whose non-existence would have made a more profound intellectual difference to this transitional age of ours. Had God, in mistaken mercy, decided not to inflict on us the gibes and ruthless commonsense of this brilliant Irishman we would have been, if not a different people, a very different upper middle class and a very different intelligentsia."

It was in this autobiography, entitled *Sixteen Self Sketches*, that G.B.S. finally settled on how the future was to regard him. He arranged to have, as the frontispiece to this book, a composite engraving of G.B.S. The Legend. It was done by a Russian who had never seen him and could reveal nothing of the irrational gaiety with which Shaw had conquered the world, nothing of the dramatist, nothing of the idealist but the cold calculating dictator, ruthless, inhuman and humourless. In his dedicatory verse he stated:

> "Not from the life did Pikov draw me,
> (To tell the truth he never saw me)
> Yet shewed what I would have you see
> Of my brief immortality."
>
> G.B.S.

This book was prompted by great urgency; old articles reeking of mothballs were put together to form a protective covering for the *Persona*. Biographical blunders were corrected, parents and relatives resurrected and the Superman firmly established.

In the postscript, G.B.S. refuses to say hail and farewell: "for I have still enough kick left to make fresh outbursts possible". Most of these outbursts were made in the correspondence columns of *The Times*:

"Sir,

I am now a political nobody, subject to nameless penalties if I attend the Meetings of the Parish Council of the village where I have resided and paid taxes for forty years. Of my ninety-three years, seventy have been spent in England. My many political activities have been occupied with English questions, never with specifically Irish ones. I am a Freeman of the City of London. But I am also an Irishman, honorary Freeman of the City of Dublin, and registered as a citizen of the former Irish Free State. Net result as aforesaid, I am a political nobody.

May I suggest that aliens residing permanently within the Commonwealth shall, under a new category of Guest Citizens, enjoy all the rights and privileges, and bear all the responsibilities, of natives? This could be extended to any international combination; but its application to Ireland (and perhaps India) is urgent.

G. Bernard Shaw.

April 24th, 1949."

He could not and did not appear at the production of *Buoyant Billions* at the Malvern Festival, but heard how his play drew huge crowds and was enthusiastically received at each performance. One could forget as one listened to the witty conversation on the stage that the author was in his ninety-third year, and was probably sitting at the moment amending his Will for the tenth time. The Princes Theatre, London, was taken but it proved too large for such an intimate play.

The play exudes the joy of age and the passion of youth. The old man is full of wisdom, sympathy and understanding. The secret of his perpetual vitality is contemplation, the ability to empty his mind and let the Life Force take possession.

The young man is a world-betterer:

SON: "As a world betterer I shall spend most of my life hiding from their police. And I may finish on the scaffold."

FATHER: "Romantic nonsense, boy. You are in a free country, and can advocate any sort of politics you please as long as you do not break the law."

SON: "But I want to break the law."

And the son gently explains to his father that the cause of his unhappiness springs from the fact that there are poor people in the world and that to him, living in a world of poor and unhappy men and women, is like living in hell. His father understands and bestows a kiss of love and blessing on his son, a gesture unknown in any other of Shaw's plays.

In *Buoyant Billions*, G.B.S. answered at last the question put to him by Aldous Huxley in *G.B.S. 90*.

"Like patriotism intelligence is evidently not enough. Then what is enough?"

Shaw's answer was:

"Love is not enough: the appetite for more truth, more knowledge, for measurement and precision is far more universal: even the dullest fools have some glimmer of it. Mathematical passion alone has no reaction: our pleasure in it promises a development in which life will be an intellectual ecstasy surpassing the ecstasy of saints."

This belief in the mathematical passion which came to him late in life was inspired by a book lent to him by a young Cambridge mathematician. G.B.S. read G. H. Hardy's *A Mathematician's Apology* and felt as Keats did when he read Chapman's *Homer*:

"Then felt I like some watcher of the skies
When a new planet swims into his ken."

Within a short while G.B.S. was occupied with another play. A Russian lady had learnt to live on air. G.B.S., convinced that he was fast falling into penury, welcomed this as an economic way of living and introduced it into a play which he called *The Far Fetched Fables*. While writing this play he was suddenly faced with the demand for £140,000 by the Inland Revenue, and this convinced him that he would have to live on air if he was to live much longer. On going over his accounts, however, he found that he was able to render unto Caesar that which was Caesar's and he sent the huge sum with his compliments to 'Homo Rapiens'.

He boasted to his friends that he was helping to pay for the Crimean War, the Boer War, the War to end War and the War after that one; and he was especially happy to support the schools, prisons and medical services which he had always condemned and still thought damnable.

He was visited by an ex-Cabinet Minister who, before the War, had been one of the richest country gentlemen but now, because of taxation, had just enough to live on and meet his engagements, with a car thirty years old and not a penny to spare. This was the equality of income both had fought for all their lives.

An opportunity came to him to make a speech once more, and in the open air too. The village gathered on the Green in front of the demolished Abbey on the occasion of a presentation of a gate by neighbours of Shaw as a thanks offering to the village. It was on Palm Sunday and G.B.S. was there as one of the inhabitants. Suddenly he felt the call to speak and in a voice as clear as a bell he expressed his faith:

"Forty years ago when I came to this village it was still back in the 14th century, the modern world had passed it by. My coming did not interfere with it in the least.

The people in the 14th century knew God and being domestically minded had to give God a home and a habitation.

And so they built a church on this spot. This Abbey was built by loving hands, by masons, to the glory of God, and therefore to the glory of man.

While on this point I must ask you not to call this House of God a ruined church. It is a demolished Abbey. What happened was this: centuries later, the lord of the manor, a widely travelled man had seen churches built in the modern style and like a lady faced with a new fashion, at once proceeded to demolish the old. He had seen churches built by Sir Christopher Wren and so wanted one built in this manner. The act of demolition therefore was an act of piety, or, as we would say nowadays, an aesthetic gesture. So he demolished this and proceeded to put up in the meadow yonder a classic church in the style of Sir Christopher Wren. Fortunately for us, the Bishop had an eye for beauty as well as for property and he prevented the complete destruction of the Abbey.

It is in my eyes, and I hope in your eyes, still the House of God. There are no stained glass windows, in fact there are no windows; there is no vaulted roof, in fact there is no roof. It is exposed to wind and rain but it is my House of God and it is your House of God. It is most fitting therefore that this beautiful gate should be erected here which will open on to the Abbey, not as a deterrent but as an invitation to all of us. To-day, on Palm Sunday, I awoke singing:

> Lift up your heads, O ye gates,
> And be ye lift up, ye everlasting doors
> And the King of Glory shall come in.

This is His way, That is His house, and here is His Gate. I invite you all to pass through the Gate with me."

In the wonderful hush of the twilight all walked through the Gate and into the grounds of the demolished Abbey. This was one other added to his very few happy moments.

If he had been given the right to choose the moment of dying, he would, without a shadow of doubt, have chosen this moment. Like Moses he would have liked to have disappeared.

.  .  .  .  .

One evening, after a short walk he felt a strong desire to do a little pruning, for this exercise had been his delight for the last few years. He went along the path, camera still slung over his shoulder, tool basket in hand and the eternal whistle in his coat pocket in case he needed assistance. Within a short while the maid heard her name being called. She rushed out and saw her master crawling towards the house, obviously in great pain. It seemed to her that he had broken his back and was dying.

His attitude when he found himself at the Luton and Dunstable Hospital was one of amused curiosity. He had always expected a ghastly anti-climax to his life, but this seemed to be even worse than he had ever imagined. There he lay with all these people fussing about him; to be incapable and inactive was hell, especially when he had no faith in doctors. Even then, knowing that millions were watching and were expecting a few quips to amuse them, he gave them what they wanted.

The one thing he himself wanted was to get back home, away from this hell; away from continuous washing, making of beds, being awakened and being told to sleep; at no point would he accept this roll of passive parasite. The doctors were permitted to deal with him because it meant getting away earlier. His broken thigh healed quickly but the shock of the fall had affected his whole system and especially the prostate gland, which failed completely. He was taken home and a bath chair was prepared for him so that he could be wheeled round the garden. After a short while he refused all food, drank only a little water and the passing from life into death was slow and deliberate. A document had to have his signature and for this purpose a pen was put into his hand and guided: his name was the last word ever written by him.

On November 2nd, 1950, his death was announced and his own sense of comedic anti-climax persisted in the way in which certain people took possession of his body, in the strange unrepresentative gathering at the burning of it, the huge crowds that came flocking into the village and destroying the very peace and beauty he had loved; and finally in the publication of the Will which proved him the wealthiest author that had ever lived, for he left a gross estate of £367,233 13s., excluding the value of his copyrights worth another £430,000. The Public Trustee was named as the sole executor and the house went over to the National Trust. After annuities totalling £2,915, he left the residue of his estate on trust to institute and finance inquiries into the use of an alphabet containing at least forty letters. The ultimate residue was to be divided between the British Museum, the National Gallery of Ireland, and the Royal Academy of Dramatic Art.

The Will when published caused a howl of disgust among a large number of people because he had been refusing donations and help to needy causes on the plea of penury. But it was his money and his right to dispose of it as he wished. He wanted to be in a minority of one and he believed in the phonetic alphabet, and it may well be that in this as in many another cause in which he was in a minority he may well prove a benefactor to humanity. Every day Wills are published in the Press and they are more or less ignored except by those directly concerned, but the fact that the whole world was interested in the Will of G.B.S. proved how well he had entered the consciousness of the people. He had become a personal intimate of everybody.

There was an abortive effort to get him buried in Westminster Abbey, but instead his ashes, mingled with Charlotte's, lie scattered at the feet of Saint Joan in his garden.

# Notes

## Chapter One

Dalkey played an enormous part in Shaw's life. He described it as follows: "For brilliancy of colour, making rocks raining pools and herbage look like terrestrial jewellery, I have seen nothing like the heights above Sligo Bay. . . . Whoever has not stood in the graveyards at the summit of that cliff among those beehive dwellings and their beehive oratory does not know Ireland through and through. It is the beauty of Ireland that has made us what we are. I am a product of Dalkey's outlook."

## Chapter Two

Shaw received the following testimonial from his employers: "Mr. George Shaw left at his own desire, having attained the position of cashier. He is a young man of great business capacity, strict accuracy, and thoroughly reliable and trustworthy. Anything given to him to do was always accurately and well done. We shall always be glad to hear of his welfare."

G.B.S. tells this story: "I left Ireland and escaped from clerking in 1876 when I was twenty. More than thirty years passed before I again set foot in my native town. A fancy took me to walk past the old office without being obliged to go into it. It happened that I had in my pocket a document which I had to attest before a Commissioner of Oaths. And as I passed the old door, I saw that there was on the first floor the office of such a commissioner. So I went in and mounted to the first floor. There I was received with distinguished consideration by the commissioner's clerk: a frock-coated gentleman of the utmost respectability and dignity. He regretted that his principal was out at the moment. We then had a friendly chat, in the course of which I said, 'Thirty years ago I was a clerk in the Estate Office downstairs.' Instantly his manner changed. With undisguised contempt and incredulity he said, 'I don't remember you.' I gasped. This man had been coming to the office every day during the thirty years in which I had wandered over the globe and changed from a nobody on an office stool to a celebrity with half a dozen reputations. And he seemed the happier man. Certainly he left me nowhere in point of self-esteem."

In his essay entitled "Exhausted Arts", written soon after he arrived in London, he declares: "There are not as many paths in art for creative genius that we can look with complacency on the successive blocking of one after another of them by the hands of the great artists in the past and present, or easily imagine how our posterity will entertain themselves when they are satiated with their great inheritance. . . . What will they read? What will they listen to? What will they look at?"

He decided that there was one field of creative art which had been neglected and that was the 'Art of Living' and so he concentrated on "A Practical System of Moral Education".

As Mr. Bradlaugh stated that he would move for a writ of error, they were both liberated. This was granted, proved successful and the verdict was quashed.

CHAPTER THREE

One of the articles Shaw completed but could not get published was "Open Air Meetings": "How many parks are there in London? One, you reply, if you are a man of fashion. On reflection, you believe that you were wrong in saying that there was only one park: there is one called Battersea Park across the river. Did you ever hear of Victoria Park, Southwark Park or Finsbury Park? Ever been there? Certainly not. You regard it distinctly as an outrage. On being asked further whether you walk in Hyde Park in September, you set down the catechist as a man lost to society, and inform him compassionately that no one walks in Hyde Park now as the season is over. Like most Londoners on the subject of London, you are wrong in every particular. Walk from Knightsbridge Barracks to the Marble Arch next Sunday afternoon, or through the avenue in Regent's Park, and you will find at its height a season of intellectual activity evinced by clusters of public meetings. . . ."

G.B.S. haunted the parks and knew his London very intimately. The description of the all-night walk is as given to me by him.

CHAPTER FOUR

Kate and Henry Salt played an important part in the life of G.B.S. So did Kate's brother, J. L. Joynes. In his Introduction to my *Salt and his Circle*, G.B.S. wrote: "I was always happy at the Salts. We never talked politics but gossiped endlessly. The bond between us was that we were Shelleyans and Humanitarians. . . . Kate loved me as far as she could love any male creature."

It was through the influence of her Socialistic son, that Mrs. Carr Shaw obtained the important teaching post of music mistress at the North London Collegiate School. Mrs. Sophie Bryant was a member of the Fabian Society.

William Archer did not get on too well with G.B.S.; they were temperamentally incompatible. But W.A. ten days before his death (17th December, 1924) sent a pathetic post card to G.B.S.: "Though I have sometimes played the part of the all-too-candid mentor, I have never wavered in my admiration for you or ceased to feel that the Fates had treated me kindly in making me your contemporary and friend."

CHAPTER FIVE

When G.B.S. saw May Morris for the first time he noted down: "I was immediately conscious that a Mystic Betrothal was registered in heaven, to be fulfilled when all the material obstacles should melt away, and my own position rescued from the squalors of my poverty and unsuccess." May Morris in a letter to G.B.S. (23rd April, 1936), replied: "As to our harmless personal relations, I should have been inclined to let them lie 'unsung' on the grounds that no one cares a hang about me."

Bertha Newcombe, who hoped to marry G.B.S., found him unsatisfying because "he refused to give more than amusement. Love-making would have been very delightful doubtless, but I wanted, besides, a wider companionship. Shaw, was, I should imagine, by preference a passionless man. He had passed through experiences and he seemed to have no wish for and even to fear passion though he admitted its power and pleasure. The sight of a woman deeply in love with him annoyed him."

CHAPTER SIX

The pen-name of Corno di Bassetto appealed to Shaw's inherent snobbery. As a 'downstart' he could by taking on an aristocratic name assume his rightful inheritance. His editor always referred to him as 'His Ladyship'.

In his Preface to the Fabian Essays he stated that the Essayists "make no claim to be more than communicative learners. In *Buoyant Billions*, the last of his plays to be performed at the Malvern Festival, he made exactly the same point: "The future is with the learners."
He loved the Webbs not because they were omniscient but because they were learners. His advice to people who had lost heart was: "Get interested in something. Become a learner."

Oscar Wilde's reference to roadmakers was, of course, to the appointment of John Ruskin as Slade Professor at Oxford in 1870 which led to him making his students build roads in 1874 for the sake of their souls. The ode-maker, Oscar Wilde, was one of these undergraduates.

CHAPTER SEVEN

What would have happened if Henry Irving had agreed to put on the *Man of Destiny*? Would it have transformed his bitter opponent into a docile admirer? Would G.B.S. have specialized in writing plays for Sir Henry? Ellen Terry did her very best for G.B.S., as later on Mrs. Patrick Campbell did her utmost for him with Beerbohm Tree. G.B.S. was too comprehensive an intellect to permit himself to become "a narrow dramatist like Shakespeare". He was able to say, "My reputation as a dramatist grows with every play that is *not* performed."

CHAPTER EIGHT

Dr. Max Nordau called on my wife and myself and confessed his con-version by G.B.S. We explained that Bernard Shaw enjoyed writing the *Sanity of Art* because Lucy had always taunted him with being a degenerate like his father. He therefore set out to prove that artists (and he regarded himself as one) were a *"regenerative force"*.

CHAPTER NINE

Shaw's confession that he always failed in his attempts at managing people sounds strange from the pen of an arch-schemer. But it is true all the same. The quarrel with Wells was very much to his liking, for he enjoyed ragging authors and artists, refusing to believe that any other author had the least understanding of politics or economics.

CHAPTER TEN

Rainer Maria Rilke in an unpublished letter (16th April, 1906), describes Shaw as a 'sitter': "I doubt if a portrait was ever given a better chance of succeeding by the sitter, than this bust of Bernard Shaw. It isn't merely that Shaw poses admirably with a combination of steadiness and energy and with unconditional obedience to the sculptor's directing hands; he also understands how to concentrate and collecting himself in that portion of his body which will have to represent the complete Shaw within the limits of a bust in such a way that the essence of the man leaps into the clay feature by feature, with an incredible heightened intensity."

I watched G.B.S. sitting for his portrait to Clare Winsten forty years later and the description still applied.

CHAPTER ELEVEN

G.B.S. felt that he had a way with animals and loved them much more than he loved people. Sir Desmond MacCarthy in *A Personal Memoir*, tells this story: "Two impressions of my visit to Shaw remain with me. Granville Barker must have said that he and I were going to visit Meredith for I re-member saying to Shaw, after describing Meredith, that it must be a terrible humiliation for a man who gloried in physical excellence to suffer from such a disease as *Locomotor ataxy*, that terrible jerking stammer of the hands and feet. Shaw assented briefly. Soon after, happening to look out of the window and catching sight of a large building with big windows, obviously not a block of flats, I asked him what it was. His face contracted with intense and painful sympathy and he said: 'It is a place where they torture animals. I can hardly bear the sight of it.'"

CHAPTER TWELVE

The meeting to which Shaw refers in his letter to the German Am-bassador was of the Labour Leaders who had come to pay homage to the sage on his seventieth birthday. It was, of course, a mean act to prohibit the broadcast and it did no good.

It is interesting to note that when Ramsay MacDonald was the first Labour Prime Minister he read the *Intelligent Woman's Guide* and declared, "After the Bible this is in my eyes the most important book that humanity possesses."

## CHAPTER THIRTEEN

Professor Einstein had the greatest affection for Bernard Shaw in spite of the latter's contempt for professors which he considered "an unnatural profession which addled the brain". "What profession doesn't?" Einstein would ask. Both agreed that God made the world as an artist but Shaw was convinced that God learnt by trial and error, while Einstein maintained that the more one learnt, the more one realized that God was a consummate artist. Comparing Shaw with God, Einstein said, "God created people of flesh and blood, but you, my friend, can only create elfin creatures of wit, humour and grace."

Virginia Woolf met Bernard Shaw in Hyde Park after his world tour and noted this down: "G.B.S. said: 'Of course this tour cost thousands; yet to see us, you'd think that we hadn't the price of the fare to Hampton Court. . . . I found myself on a platform with the whole university round me. They began shouting, 'We want Bernard Shaw.' So I told them that every man of twenty-one must be a revolutionary. After that of course the police imprisoned them by dozens. . . .'"

The speech referred to was at the Hong Kong University and this is how one of the professors reported it: "You made a mistake by asking me to speak in this place because I don't believe in universities. If I had my way I would burn every one of them down and sow the ground with salt. They stereotype the mind."

## CHAPTER FOURTEEN

When Gabriel Pascal tried to raise money in Ireland to film *Saint Joan*, he failed miserably. He reported it to G.B.S. as follows: "Not a penny will your people give. I tell them that St. Joan is a Catholic play but they look at me as if I invented her. Perhaps if I tell America that it is a Protestant play, money will come."

## CHAPTER FIFTEEN

On the assumption that Stalin was always right, Shaw had to reconcile Lysenko's Materialism with his own Vitalism. He wrote (January 1949): "After a careful observation of my own acquired habits I pointed out, in the course of a lecture on Darwin to the Fabian Society, that evolution means that all habits are inherited. I cited the fact that as breathing is an inborn habit, and speaking, like skating and bicycling, one which every generation has to acquire, proves that habits are acquired by imperceptible increments at each generation, the inborn habits being those already fully acquired, and the rest only in process of acquirement. I was followed by Bergson. . . . After Bergson . . . Lysenko broke away from Fatalism, not polemically, but by simply ignoring it. Lysenko has to pretend that he is a Materialist when he is in fact a Vitalist, and thus muddles us ludicrously. . . ."

By this time most thinking people were muddled 'ludicrously' by what was going on in the spheres of literature, art and science in the Stalin regime.

The story of the last ten years of Shaw's life is told in the greatest detail in *Days with Bernard Shaw* and *Shaw's Corner*.

The lull in Shaw's popularity after his death has surprised nobody. It must be taken as a natural phenomenon and does not reflect on his genius. It gives the young saplings, at least, a chance to grow. When, on his death-bed, a friend of his pleaded with him to make an effort to survive, he smiled and replied, "There are plenty of fish in the water without a whale." It was a good pun, for his whole life had been a wail against acquiescence and defeat, a wail against the immaturity which robbed the human race of its rightful inheritance. Maturity, to G.B.S. was an aesthetic development, a delight in life and living. His, therefore, was a lover's quarrel with life. This explains why, in the words of Professor Auden, "his writing has an effect nearer to that of music than the work of the so-called pure writers."

# INDEX

Printed in Great Britain by *The Anchor Press, Ltd., Tiptree, Essex*